THE FACE ON THE CUTTING ROOM FLOOR

The Story of Movie and Television Censorship

Murray Schumach

A DA CAPO PAPERBACK

Library of Congress Cataloging in Publication Data

Schumach, Murray, 1913-
   The face on the cutting room floor.

   (A Da Capo paperback)
   Reprint of the ed. published by Morrow, New York.
   1. Moving-pictures—Censorship. 2. Moving-pictures
—Moral and religious aspects. I. Title.
[PN1994.A2S3   1975]   363.3'1   74-23937
ISBN 0-306-80009-8

First Paperback Printing 1975
ISBN: 0-306-80009-8

*Grateful acknowledgment is made for permission to quote (on
pages 223 and 224) from the lyric of* West Side Story, *copyright
© 1957, 1959 by Leonard Bernstein and Stephen Sondheim. Reprinted by permission of G. Schirmer, Inc., and Beta Productions.*

This Da Capo Press edition of *The Face on the Cutting Room Floor* is an unabridged
republication of the first edition published in New York in 1964.

Copyright ©1964 by Murray Schumach. Reprinted by permission of William Morrow
and Company, Inc.

Published by Da Capo Press, Inc.
A Subsidiary of Plenum Publishing Corporation
227 West 17th Street, New York, N.Y. 10011

TO IRMA

"You would not believe how, from the very commencement of my activity, that horrible Censor question has tormented me! I wanted to write what I felt; but all the time it occurred to me that what I wrote would not be permitted, and involuntarily I had to abandon the work. I abandoned, and went on abandoning, and meanwhile the years passed away."

Tolstoy

Contents

Illustrations

Freud
Gone With The Wind

Following page 180

The Defiant Ones
The Nun's Story
The Longest Day
Francis Goes to West Point
Exodus
Bridge on the River Kwai
Can-Can
Tea and Sympathy
Sanctuary
Sweet Bird of Youth
A Place in the Sun
Gulliver

Following page 212

Romeo and Juliet
Cleopatra
Elmer Gantry
Town Without Pity
Samson and Delilah
Mae West
Rita Hayworth
Betty Grable
Lana Turner
Ava Gardner
Notorious
The Blackboard Jungle
I Am a Fugitive from a Chain Gang
West Side Story
Ben Hur
Spartacus

Following page 244

1 | The law and the profits

The first law of censorship—and probably the only important one not inscribed on the statute books—is this: in a democracy, the more popular the art form, the greater the demands for censorship of it. This theorem has two corollaries. First, the quality of the art has little to do with the matter. Second, those who arrogate to themselves the privilege of exercising censorship may or may not be cultured, unbiased and/or sincere. These are the lessons that emerge from the first thirty-odd years of this century. It was during those decades that the nation's fabulous movie industry underwent its first censorship troubles. Harrassing scandals led to early compromises and finally the industry worked out a method of self-censorship that is unique in the world. In this first third of the twentieth century, as the country's movie business grew from peep shows in musty stores to a billion-dollar industry supporting the most lavish theaters ever seen, the censorship issue grew with it, causing first sporadic municipal squabbles and later arousing national fury. In its turbulence, complexity, scandals and the eventual development of a censorship code, the story of this first major phase of movie censorship is drama on a national scale and offers a vast panorama of the country's changing morals and mores that is more exciting than any film. But before reviewing it we should examine the latest film conflict. The specific issue is new, but all "the rules" of censorship that have developed since the first foot of film was shown to the first paying customers can be discerned in the present battle about nudity.

1. *Censorship in the Nude*

Hollywood, while mass-producing generations of amour and glamour, has generated the most intense censorship wars in the nation. Millions of otherwise placid men and women, the most reserved religious and civic organizations, fervent money-grubbers and fanatic idealists have all clashed swords on these battlegrounds. Speeches, petitions, demonstrations have split the people into verbal armies. Cops have blundered in where Supreme Court justices stepped with greatest delicacy. Local ordinances, state laws, the federal Constitution have become excuses for political oratory. The fever of a movie censorship war is almost as intense as that of a patriotic rally. A full-fledged movie censorship battle in the United States is a national phenomenon; a sociological convulsion.

This sort of conflagration is being ignited by Hollywood right now as it drifts into the mid-sixties. This time the issue is nudity, a subject that contains the most potent censorship dynamite. Nudity on the screen rouses a basic conflict with the moral standards professed by the nation. Whenever the gap between movies and public morality is wide it becomes filled with the whirlpool rush and turmoil of censorship.

Samuel Goldwyn, Hollywood pioneer, who in more than half a century of movie-making has lived through and studied all major censorship wars, thinks the issue of nudity is one of the most dangerous he has known.

"I feel very strongly," he says, "that motion pictures should never embarrass a man when he brings his family to the theatre. Public morality is a very important factor on the screen. A picture can be dramatic, effective and have a great love story without any nudity or excess of sex. I seriously object to seeing on the screen what belongs in the bedroom."

Why should a naked human body, in a Hollywood movie, create so much more furor than the same subject in a picture frame? To say that the painting is more artistic than the film is an evasion. For even if the movie were artistic and the painting the work of a sloppy dauber, the reactions would still be the same. The answer is that the American movie is the original mass medium of the arts. To survive, it needs a vast audience. The price of mass appeal is conformity to mass morality. Hollywood has always been aware of this even when it has not said so. The movie industry could engrave, as its motto, the advice of Saki: "Never be a pioneer. It's the early Christian who gets the fattest lion." In the jungle of censorship, nudity is as healthy a lion as can be found. That is why the vast majority in Hollywood huddles fearfully on the sidelines as nudity takes shape as a censorship issue.

Never again may there be such an opportunity to study a censorship hurricane in formation. One can trace here the elements that make it; the forces that churn it up. See each gust as it descends on the community. To examine movie nudity in its Hollywood infancy is to gain an insight into all film censorship since the beginning of the century, to discover the strong affinity between movies and morals.

Bare flesh in American movies has been a sort of barometer of national mores. The strongest puritanical streaks show up in this area. One can, by studying the exposure of the female anatomy in films of different periods, almost calibrate the attitudes of the average man and woman in the United States toward sex, obscenity, vulgarity, pornography. In this aspect of censorship hypocrisy slips perfectly into Samuel Butler's definition—the homage that vice pays to virtue. From the first coy cinematic views of ankle and calf, to the scantiest of Bikinis, one can follow American social behavior in transition in the twentieth century.

For decades, American movies, like the American public, have been shortening and discarding clothes. Bedroom photography, like American conversation, has become increasingly uninhibited. Not only normal sex, but also homosexuality, have gone from literature, to theater, to newspaper, to public discussion, to movie.

Language in the films has trudged behind the public along the path of casual profanity.

In the late fifties, nudity in films moved closer to legal acceptability through a ruling by the New York State Court of Appeals. A film about a nudist colony, *Garden of Eden,* had been banned. In reversing the censors, the court asserted that "nudity in itself, and without lewdness or dirtiness, is not obscenity in law or in common sense." This picture, however, was more in the nature of a documentary than a subject of drama or entertainment.

With the sixties came the most favorable climate for the injection of nudity into American commercial pictures. In European films, nudity was already an old story. In this country, film executives saw the chance for large profits in the sensationalism of an unclothed woman, particularly a star. Adding to the impetus was an articulate, but small, minority that looked upon nudity as a step toward artistic liberation.

The unwilling alliance of greed and idealism is one of the most fascinating ironies of the movie censorship story. No two groups could dislike one another more than these. The creative men, in particular, find it embarrassing and irritating to be advocating the same cause as the money men. They feel their own honorable motives will be subject to suspicion. No political issue has ever made stranger bedfellows than has the issue of movie censorship.

The first serious challenger to the censorship code's stand on nudity began on a balmy summer evening in 1961, when a few dozen movie addicts entered the Warner Brothers studio in Burbank, California. As they strolled along the grass-bordered walks, they could see the sound stages, those movie factories that loom like giant crates, their concrete sides ghostly in the night. Somewhere a sound track was being raced in reverse, shattering the silence like some monstrous, maniac Donald Duck. In the distance a red light flashed, indicating a sound stage in which a movie was being shot. To the visitors, many of whom were in the business, none of this was new or even particularly interesting. Such sights and sounds were a normal part of studio life. Of greater interest that night was a much smaller building situated to the left of the walk before the sound stages. On the upper floor of this two-story structure was a small theater, with some 200 comfortable seats and a screen wide enough for a much larger theater. In this screening room Warner Brothers planned to reveal a movie it considered the best of 1961.

The script was the first original screenplay by William Inge, the Pulitzer Prize-winning playwright. One of the stars, Natalie Wood, was certain this was her finest performance. But the main reason for audience interest was the director, Elia Kazan. With Kazan one never knew what would happen. It might be another Oscar-reaping masterpiece such as *A Streetcar Named Desire* and *On the Waterfront*. Or it might be a dud, like *A Face in the Crowd* and *Wild River*. Of one thing the spectators were sure, as they settled back to watch *Splendor in the Grass*, something unusual would turn up in this film about hyprocrisy and frustration in midwestern life during the 1920's and '30's.

The select audience had quite a surprise. It came fast. In one sequence Miss Wood was in the bathtub, in bitter argument with her mother. The girl became hysterical. Cornered by her mother, she had only one way to escape and that was to flee the tub. The next scene was the one the audience never expected. It showed Miss Wood from the rear. She was naked, running down a short hallway. The camera showed her nakedness from head to heels. Her buttocks were unmistakably bare. Her rush down the foyer lasted seconds. The next shot showed her bare legs kicking on the bed, indicating she was on the edge of nervous collapse.

What this audience witnessed may some day be marked as the beginning of a new era in movie censorship: the first time the star in a feature-length American movie was naked. Here was something that made a joke of all earlier censorship controversies about hem lengths, bathing suits, transparent chemises, suggestive silhouettes, low décolletages, tight sweaters, clinging gowns. The powerful taboo on nudity was deliberately defied.

The ban on nudity is more than just Hollywood folklore, or an understanding that has grown up, like the English common law. Nudity is forbidden in writing in the movie industry's voluntary censorship code, to which all major movie companies subscribe. This code says, in one section: "Complete nudity, in fact, or in silhouette, is never permitted, nor shall there be any licentious notice by characters in the film of suggested nudity. Indecent or undue exposure is forbidden." An exception is made for documentaries that deal with primitive peoples in native habitats.

The official Hollywood censors, paid by the movie industry to interpret and enforce provisions of the code, saw no alternative but to order the nudity deleted. Kazan thought he might be able to persuade the censors to allow it in the interests of art. But then he received from the Warner Brothers studio suggestions said to reflect the thoughts of the Legion of Decency, which speaks for Catholics on movie morality. High on the list was the nude scene. Kazan met with representatives of the legion. He found the legion as unyielding on nudity as the Hollywood censors. He cut the scene. The public never saw Miss Wood in the hall. The camera picked her up on the bed, bare legs thrashing.

"I did the nude scene," Kazan said two years later, in 1963, "because I thought it was the honest way. I still think so. It was not done for sensational reasons or as a promotion stunt. If I had wanted to be sensational I would have used a close-up instead of the long shot down the hall. I was trying to stress the hysteria. A girl in her state would not stop to dry herself and put on clothes. She would just run. Natalie knew it was honest. She wanted very much to do it that way."

Word of the outcome of Kazan's fight spread faster than scandal among the studio executives and then filtered down among producers and directors. Judgment was quick. This proved that nudity was still out. Hollywood would have to be content to deliver its sex kicks by playing games with camera and costume. Peer a little bit deeper into the cleavage. Display a little more of bust and buttock. But no nudity. The code was impregnable there.

This opinion was premature. Even before Kazan had cut Natalie Wood's nakedness from *Splendor in the Grass*, naked women became epidemic in Hollywood films. Free-lance producers, often cameramen, began grinding out cheap movies that featured little else but bare bodies. Some were mixed with broad comedy. These pictures were not submitted to Hollywood censors because the producers were not members of the Motion Picture Association. The movies were shown in only a limited number of theaters. They became known as "nudies," and they were, for the most part, profitable. The pioneer of this art form, Russ Meyers, a camera-man, made *The Immoral Mr. Teas* in four days at a cost of $24,000. Meyers estimated it would eventually gross $1,000,000. It had no professional actors. No script. No dialogue. Meyers just improvised with the camera as he went along. At first, only thea-ters in the Skid Row sections of large cities would show his movie. Eventually, however, some "art" houses that had formerly spe-cialized in foreign films switched to "nudies."

As these pictures increased in number and in theater outlets, they touched off the first symptoms of a widespread censorship controversy over nudity in the movies. In many communities, the complaints of civic organizations prompted local authorities to ban such films. Then came the international ramifications. In Great Britain, where nudity had been permitted in a number of serious movies, the censors turned down the nudies. John Trevelyan, secre-tary of the British Board of Censors, explained they were barred because they had no dramatic justification and could hardly be considered educational in the documentary sense. Incidentally, *Garden of Eden* had been shown in England after a good deal of controversy.

Nevertheless, in spite of all their vulgarity, there was a degree of honesty about the American nudies. They did not pretend to be art or realism. The audience knew what it would see. There was nothing surreptitious about the nudity either. A woman working in this sort of movie accepted the job as a professional commit-ment, no different from that of a model posing for a painter. One of the most successful producers of nudies used his wife as the naked star. Everyone knew the score with the nudies. They were filmed for the buck. And they made it.

This profit from "nudies" tantalized Hollywood producers who figured the code was keeping them out of a lush market. Also moving into this territory, they felt, were foreign movie makers who outdid them in the sex field by making what were generally called quality movies. To many of these frustrated Hollywood producers *Les Liaisons Dangereuses*, *Hiroshima Mon Amour*, *La Dolce Vita*, and *Boccaccio 70* were just excuses to show larger areas of lush females and more concentrated sex than anything the censors would approve in Hollywood.

This double pressure was too much for some Hollywood movie-makers. They devised methods of outwitting the code. One scheme—and this was done with the knowledge of the studios financing the pictures—was to shoot a movie one way for the American market and then, with fewer clothes and greater sensuality, for export to Europe. The next step was to use professional strippers in nude sequences intended only for the foreign market. Finally, professional actresses, generally of considerably less than star level, were told by producers that they could have small roles in movies if they agreed to be filmed in the nude or wearing very little clothing.

Perhaps the most ingenious device came with *Irma La Douce,* the comedy about Parisian prostitution. Shirley MacLaine was filmed nude in a bathtub. In this scene her co-star, Jack Lemmon, looks in her direction through a hand telescope. But he peers through the wrong end. The image on the screen was deliberately made tiny. The audience never knew if Shirley was naked or not. Actually, the camera angle was such that if a spectator were to turn field glasses on the screen, he would see that her image stopped just above the nipples.

Suddenly, in 1962, the partisans of nudity received a setback from an unexpected source. George Chandler, veteran actor and, at that time, president of the Screen Actors Guild, spoke out angrily in an interview in *The New York Times.* He attacked producers and directors who took advantage of actresses in need of jobs and money by forcing them to go before cameras indecently attired or entirely nude. "These producers," he said furiously, "are not asking an actress to act when they do this, any more than if they asked her to jump from a high building." As head of the union of some 14,000 actors in movies and television, he insisted the conditions were vile. He made it clear he was not worrying about the fly-by-night makers of "nudies." His fear was the trend toward nudity that was winning acceptance with established producers and companies pledged to abide by the censorship code. Chandler's courageous attack slowed down the drive toward nudity in American films.

The position of the average actress on nudity went far beyond Chandler's terse comments. It touched a nerve that ran back into history and was as sensitive to disparagement as the ganglia of Negroes to burning crosses. For centuries, actresses had been regarded as the social equivalent of prostitutes. Even during the first two decades of this century a successful actress was supposed to feel honored if a man of great wealth acquired her as a mistress for a time. She was regarded as a symbol of instability. As late as 1963, in New York and even in Hollywood itself, many landlords refused to rent to them, and one of the most exclusive golf clubs in Los Angeles barred Jews, Negroes and actors.

Nevertheless, in most respects the actress had won social equality—at least in large cities—by the 1960's. She had attained it by getting a solid formal education and by adopting a highly professional attitude toward her craft that combined grueling training with talent. In fact, some old-line actors lampooned the studiousness of the new breed. It was suggested that actors and actresses of the newer generation were stifling talent with pedantry.

For such actresses the threat of nude exposure was a nightmare. If stars were willing to appear without clothes, how long would it be before other actresses lost their inhibitions? In no time at all, the work of generations would be undone and actresses would be classified once again as the morally maimed of society. They were terrified.

In the summer of 1963 there was an attempt to extend the use of nudity in full-length Hollywood movies. An example was a screen test held at Warner Brothers. Ursula Andress and Gia Scala, testing for an important feminine role in *Four for Texas*, wore transparent nightgowns beneath which were only brief panties. When the tests were made by Robert Aldrich, the director, their breasts were clearly visible.

About the same time came an even stronger challenge to the code's nudity clause. Joseph E. Levine purchased the movie rights to Harold Robbins' extremely lascivious novel, *The Carpetbaggers*. The previous owner, Eddie Fisher, at that time still happily married to Elizabeth Taylor, had decided the book was a little too much for him—or his wife. Levine, who brought *Boccaccio 70* to the United States, with its record-setting cleavage shots of Anita Ekberg, was not afraid of *The Carpetbaggers*. When asked one day by an acquaintance how he expected to make the movie without violating code provisions on sex, Levine laughed and replied: "I got enough in this book for six movies."

So it was that in the summer of 1963 *The Carpetbaggers* was being made into a film at the Paramount studio, with Carroll Baker as star and Edward Dmytryk directing. Those Hollywood reporters who make frequent trips to sets of movies in production became suspicious when told, on several occasions, that the stage was closed to the press. As a rule, the studio is eager to have as many reporters as possible visit a set to gather stories. The reason was that some nude scenes were being filmed. The naked actress was Miss Baker. Blandly, she said she thought there was nothing wrong with this because it was called for by dramatic developments. To show how proper her unclad performance was, she pointed out that her husband was present during the filming.

"The decision to do the scene in the nude was mine," Miss Baker explained. "I am an actress. As such I am called upon to interpret a part. There is no question that European film-makers have had considerable influence on me. The trend in the United States has been influenced by Europe. The trend now is toward showing human emotions in more depth. This involves sexual instincts. I want to show the emotions as realistically and truthfully as I can. Why should I give less than someone in another country can do in interpreting my art? I am against nudity for the sake of nudity. I am against sensationalism. But I am also against dishonesty and romanticism that shows human emotions in a false light."

The picture was finished. Hollywood waited tensely. Weeks passed. The movie censors were told nothing officially. They saw no film. All they knew was what they read in gossip columns or heard in conversation. Privately, however, they were resolved to be ruthless with this movie. If they permitted nudity, they said, they might as well throw out the code and quit.

Since an important studio was involved, those producers who were opposed to nudity remained discreet. Typical of their attitude was the behavior of one of the leaders of the movie industry, who confided to a reporter that nudity would bring about the "downfall" of Hollywood. When asked to say this publicly, he demurred. "I have to live here," he pleaded. "They would gang up and beat the daylights out of me." The tension about *The Car-*

petbaggers finally ended in the autumn of 1963, when Levine said he would not submit nude scenes to the Hollywood censors.

Of particular interest was the thinking of cameramen who filmed American movies with nude scenes for some of the major studios. One veteran cameraman, after completing one of these films, typified the attitude of American cinematographers. He said: "Nudity is something I don't go for at all. It leaves a bad taste in your mouth. I do what I can to make such shots as unoffensive and as artistic as possible. I make the shot diffused. I use dim lights. I try silhouette as much as possible. Frankly, I don't think that putting nudity into a picture tells the story any better. It's much better when the imagination is allowed to work. I think the main reason studios want nudity in movies is because of the sensationalism and the publicity. And I don't believe these comments I read in the papers where an actress says she does not mind working in the nude. My own experience has been that the actress was embarrassed and uncomfortable. I just can't believe that any real artist or any audience with good taste wants nudity in movies."

The eagerness with which Hollywood executives were trying to exploit the possibilities of nudity was shown by the secret discussions that surrounded *The Victors*. This movie, written, produced and directed by Carl Foreman, was about World War II, with the theme that war has no victors. In one brief sequence, an American soldier in Italy is leaving the Italian woman with whom he has gone to bed. Two versions were made of the scene in which she walks to the door with him as he departs. In the first, for Europe, the actress Elke Sommer was filmed nude. But since Foreman knew nudity was not for the United States, he filmed a second version, for the American market, in which the camera went below her shoulders just far enough to suggest she was naked.

The British censors had already allowed the nude scene in the film when Foreman arrived in Hollywood, in the autumn of 1963, to turn the film over to the movie industry's censors. Studio executives advised Foreman to include the nude sequence. They pointed out that even if it was deleted, this concession would give him bargaining power should any other objections be raised. They also talked of the publicity value of even a sham battle with the censors. Foreman refused to submit the nude scene. The movie was praised by the censors and a censorship battle was averted.

No one can say, now, when the nudity explosion will occur. But when it happens it will be bitter, noisy and exciting. It may be that eventually the sight of an uncovered adult in a movie will be no more disturbing than a cleavage. Conceivably, if nudity becomes commonplace, movie-makers may have to use clothes to heighten sexual appeal, as the Devil did in *Penguin Island* when he clad the ungainly lady penguin to prove that "modesty communicates an invincible attraction" that "arouses in the male love and its mad torments."

But the final decision on nudity will be made by the public, whether it is expressed in the words of Hollywood censors or Washington Supreme Court justices. So long as movies remain a mass medium they will have to reflect popular standards of morality. As long as Hollywood caters to the multimillions, nudity in the American film will be an ideal point of observation for students of movie censorship. For some, nudity may be a cinematic peak from which to scan the low grounds of hypocrisy. For others, it may be the bottom of a dirty pit from which to look up to the heavens of discreet purity. But all this is the ideal point from which to look back on the history of movie censorship; to consider the symptoms and cures of censorship in a mass medium of the arts—television as well as movies.

2. *Birth of an Unseen Star—The Censor*

Periodically the movie industry goes into a state of catalepsy unique even among the weird tales collected by Hollywood's most expensive psychoanalysts. The symptoms are unmistakable. Executives develop a sort of mental paralysis so numbing that they are, at first, unable to summon their publicity chiefs. They abandon the pretense that they are shrewd judges of public opinion. The chore of passing the buck between Hollywood and New York, a pastime made almost ritualistic by experience, suddenly assumes hysterical overtones. Reactions might, for once, be correctly called "colossal" by Hollywood word-mongers. It is impossible to confuse this cinematic catalepsy with the painful, but more localized, coma that descends on Hollywood when a studio goes bankrupt. Impossible to mistake it for the happy daze that accompanies the canonization of some new super-star. For with this truly deep shock there spreads over the movie business a curious air of disbelief, as though Santa Claus had just been found kicking his reindeer. When this condition cloys over Hollywood like chocolate syrup on ice cream, it means only one thing: another censorship crisis, from coast to coast.

The most amazing aspect of this phenomenon is that the movie industry is genuinely surprised each time a censorship war erupts, though the warnings are as blatant as a star's tantrums before a contract fight. It seems incredible that, after all these years, the industry still receives each new censorship wave as though it had never happened before; as though the entire Federal Bureau of Investigation had been unleashed to arrest a child for putting his hands in the cookie jar. From shock the industry moves to injured innocence, then to a combination of constitutional oratory, secret negotiations, semipublic pressures and coy tactfulness.

The story of movie censorship (followed by television censorship) is—because film was the first great mass medium—as much the story of changing American morality in the twentieth century as it is a tale of quick-buck chicanery, hypocrisy, bigotry, ignorance and the admirable struggle to raise movies to a great art form. The censorship laws for both films and the written word that are still on the books of some states and many cities are remnants and by-products of the conflicts that produced the Motion Picture Production Code. This code has been used as the basis of movie censorship by many other nations. The self-censorship of the television industry is, to a large extent, derived from the movie industry's production code.

At the turn of the century, when movies were literally a "peep show," there seemed to be no need to worry about the future repercussions of the movie industry on American society. In those days customers could peer through a magnified lens and see, on a moving film, enlarged images of what we might now call a segment of a primitive newsreel. By means of these devices one could see James J. (Gentleman Jim) Corbett, heavyweight champion of the world, give a demonstration of his jabs, hooks, uppercuts and fancy footwork. Or it might be Annie Oakley showing her prowess with a gun. Or perhaps some dancer committing her grace to film. There seemed to be no need for moralists to worry about this innocent pleasure.

The year 1903 may be the beginning of the era that led to censorship. In that year *The Great Train Robbery* was released, and, with it, movies began trying to tell stories in dramatic form. Within a few years the nickelodeon was a national epidemic. The nickelodeons—so called because a nickel was the price of admission—were places in which storytelling movies were shown. The demand was so great for this form of entertainment that by 1907 there were reported to be about 5,000 nickelodeons, varying in size from vaudeville houses to a room over a store. Sometimes they were open all night. Among the titles of the nickelodeon favorites were: *Cupid's Barometer, Old Man's Darling, Modern Brigandage, A Seaside Flirtation, Child Robbers, Beware My Husband Comes, The Unwritten Law, The Bigamist, Course of True Love, College Boy's First Love, The Female Highwayman, Gaieties of Divorce.*

These titles were contained in a letter to a Chicago newspaper from a judge who asserted that nickelodeons "cause, indirectly or directly, more juvenile crime coming into my court than all other causes combined." At that time, there were in Chicago 116 nickelodeons, 18 ten-cent vaudeville houses and 19 penny arcades. It was estimated that daily attendance at these "entertainments" was 100,000. By March of 1907 the *Chicago Tribune* was writing editorial attacks on "The Five Cent Theatre."

One editorial said of the nickelodeons that they ministered "to the lowest passions of childhood"; that they should be suppressed; that no one under eighteen should be allowed to enter these iniquitous places; that their influence was "wholly vicious"; that "there is no voice raised to defend the majority of five cent theatres because they can not be defended. They are hopelessly bad."

By May of 1907 New York City was in the act, with the Children's Society assailing penny arcades and nickelodeons. Some reformers, cognizant of the fact that there were such movies as

Cinderella, The Passion Play, and assorted travelogues, all of which were shown in schools and churches, thought there might be some good in movies. Thus Jane Addams, at her famous Hull House in Chicago, suggested regulation rather than suppression of these theaters.

In spite of the widespread criticism of movie houses, they continued to boom. This may have been the first evidence that "bad publicity" is sometimes the most profitable kind of movie publicity. Soon theaters were being built solely for movies, eliminating all vaudeville. The films became longer and popular acclaim for some actors produced movie stars. As the movie industry expanded, so did the serious censorship rumbles. In New York City, in 1909, Mayor George B. McClellan ordered all movie houses closed to appease the flood of complaints about the morality of their offerings. The ban was lifted when a group of prominent New Yorkers proposed to examine films before they were shown.

This was the introduction of the concept of prior restraint, a subject that was eventually to torment the United States Supreme Court. By prior restraint is meant the right of governmental officials to pass judgment on a movie before the public sees it. In 1911 Pennsylvania gave legal sanction to prior restraint when it established its censorship board. Other states followed. Congress entered the picture in 1915 when it held hearings on the financial activities of the industry as well as the morality of its films. As pressure mounted, the fledgling movie magnates established a self-censoring organization called the National Board of Review. Advocates of movie censorship considered this solution inadequate. In desperation, the movie men formed, in 1919, the National Association of the Motion Picture Industry. The association had two functions: first, placate critics; second, try to block censorship legislation.

The censorship regiments were still dissatisfied. With state censorship boards now a reality, the pressure began building for federal censorship of movies. The extent and tone of some of the ensuing censorship campaigns was indicated in a statement issued from Washington in 1920 by Dr. Craft, a Protestant clergyman who claimed to head an organization "to rescue the motion pictures from the hands of the Devil and 500 un-Christian Jews." Dr.

Craft asserted that the movie potentates had raised $40,000,000 to lobby against censorship in Washington.

This assault on the movie industry was appraised by Terry Ramsaye, in his delightful history of the silent screen, *A Million and One Nights*. "This dispatch," he wrote, "betrays several of Dr. Craft's major errors. In the first place he should have known that taking the movies away from the Devil would be a mere chore compared with taking them away from the able gentlemen who have them. He should also have realized that if the movie men of 1920 had surrounded $40,000,000 they would have gone to Albany and incorporated a new company, not to Washington to spend it."

Whatever the naïveté and bigotry of many advocates of governmental censorship, the inability of movie men to abide by their own agreement worked for censorship. Their suspicion of one another led them to violate the rules of their young association so flagrantly that the association became a mockery. The importance of this first step, however, was that it was the precursor of what was to become a voluntary code for the movie industry.

During the twenties movie attendance soon reached a weekly figure of about 50 million with nearly half a billion dollars taken in annually at some 14,000 theaters around the country. The cries for censorship became louder and more furious as pictures were released with such titles as *A Shocking Night, Lying Lips, Luring Lips, Red Hot Romance, Flame of Youth, Virgin Paradise, Scrambled Wives, The Truant Husband, The Fourteenth Lover, Her Purchase Price, Plaything of Broadway*. Skirts were shorter in the pictures. Make-up was heavier. Kisses were longer. Embraces were more clinging. Cinematic sin was well on the way to becoming a billion-dollar business.

By this time, another important pattern in the censorship conflict had become established. This was the technique of blaming the movie for undermining morals when, in fact, they merely—and generally belatedly—reflected them. For the Jazz Age had begun. The astonishing changes in American life that followed World War I were sweeping the nation. The movie industry became the scapegoat, a focal point for the fury of those who felt the entire national moral structure was crumbling.

By the end of 1921, thirty-six states were considering censorship legislation. In the United States Senate, Hollywood was labeled "a colony . . . where debauchery, riotous living, drunkenness, ribaldry, dissipation, free love seem to be conspicious." The fact that movie stars were making what were astronomical salaries of $5,000 a month was used as a weapon against the movie industry in the early twenties when the nation was suffering from a postwar recession and workers considered twenty dollars a good weekly wage. Each time an actor became involved in a scandal it became another argument for censorship of movies. The censors and their legislative supporters thus promulgated the strange doctrine that an actor's performance shall be judged by his private life—and even vice versa—a dogma that is still going strong.

In desperation, in 1921, the movie industry hired Will H. Hays, a professional Republican politician from Indiana, to try to create for the movie business what, in later years, would have been called "a new image." Hays resigned as Postmaster General under President Harding to head an organization called the Motion Picture Producers and Distributors Association of America, Inc. "The object for which the corporation is to be created is to foster the common interests of those engaged in the motion picture industry in the United States, by establishing and maintaining the highest possible moral and artistic standards in motion picture production."

As a man with many political friends in high places—and with a large fund from the affluent movie industry—Hays was able to stave off the most serious threats of governmental censorship. Men were hired to plead with civic groups, newspaper editors and legislators. Pressure was brought on stars to avoid public scandals. Titles of movies were made less sensational and the industry was exhorted to permit Hays and his assistants to see synopses of screenplays so that the Hays Office (as the association was known in his time) could give advice on what material might be offensive to some groups. In 1927, the Hays Office made a survey and suggested a list of eleven "Don'ts" and twenty-seven "Be Carefuls" to movie-makers.

The movie-makers were no more concerned with morals than with the constitutional right of free speech. Their concern was money. With the Hays Office pouring the oil—and cash—on troubled censorship waters, the film-makers did mainly what they wished. Intermittently someone would continue to rise in Congress and introduce a bill for federal censorship. Occasionally a state, or a brace of communities, would adopt censorship laws. But the profits were good and the industry did not worry too much about continuing complaints.

Another outbreak was unavoidable. It came after sound became prevalent in films during the late twenties and early thirties. To supply dialogue the movie producers hired playwrights, short story writers, novelists—men and women accustomed to writing with more freedom than the captions of the old silent films required. The pressure groups that had been irritated by the mere pantomime of what they considered sinfulness became infuriated when they heard the words to match the actions. When, on top of this, the stock market crashed in 1929, followed by the deep depression, the movie studios became terrified. Their reaction was summed up neatly by Raymond Moley, in his book *The Hays Office.* "And now," he wrote, "it was apparent that the competitive spirit among the companies would give greater impetus to the companies' tendency to seek short cuts to public patronage. And short cuts had always meant a drift to sensationalism and lower moral standards."

The industry found solace in the success of gangster and sex movies; in *Scarface* and *Public Enemy;* in the allure of Jean Harlow and Mae West. But, as a sop to its attackers, the movie industry gave leave to Martin Quigley, a Catholic publisher of a movie trade paper, and to the Reverend Daniel A. Lord, a Jesuit, to draft what has since become known as the Motion Picture Production Code.

It was adopted by the industry on March 31, 1930.

This code should have ended the industry's most serious censorship troubles. But there were too many producers who looked upon it—and to a large extent upon Hays himself, the ultimate arbiter of the code—with cynicism. To them the code and Hays were tidy bits of camouflage, behind which they could continue to do what they wished. The four years following the adoption of the production code became a farce. On the one hand, Hays went about making placatory speeches to clergy, civic groups and legislators. On the other hand, he met secretly with producers to plead with them to show some respect for the code they had ratified.

One of the most amusing aspects of the code was its machinery. It was like putting Jack the Ripper in charge of a beauty contest. Theoretically, scripts were judged by a group within the code set-up known as the studio relations committee. The trouble was that there was no one to enforce objections raised by this committee. On paper the committee would appeal to a group made up of officials of the top movie companies. But it was exactly at this point that the censorship dice were loaded. For this appellate group somehow saw things in favor of the producers. Theirs became so established a point of view that they became known as the Hollywood Jury. Eventually the chief enforcer of the code under Hays, Colonel Jason Joy, gave up the fight and resigned.

These devious attempts by the movie industry to ignore and evade its own vows finally enraged the Catholic clergy. Cardinal Dougherty of Philadelphia declared all movies in that city out of bounds to Catholics in 1933. In April of 1934, a committee of Catholic bishops announced the formation of the Legion of Decency. The purpose of the organization was to alert Catholics as to which movies to avoid. Though this drive on movie immorality was spearheaded by the Catholic clergy, it received considerable support from Protestants and Jews. The Federal Council of Churches, for instance, warned movie moguls that unless the code was enforced it would seek federal censorship. The original pressure widened and deepened. In Chicago alone nearly 500,000 Catholic women joined the campaign against objectionable films. Finally the movie industry heeded the warnings of Hays.

The Hollywood Jury was eliminated from the production code machinery. Then the code was given teeth. Joseph I. Breen, who had been put in charge of enforcing the code under Hays, was empowered to withhold a seal of approval from any picture that violated the code. The industry promised it would not distribute or exhibit any picture without a seal of approval.

With the seal of approval as a weapon, self-censorship in the American movie industry became a reality and the Motion Picture Production Code became the bible of the industry.

3. *Sodom by the Sea*

Scandal of the most lurid and violent sort was an important factor in forcing the movie industry to censor itself. It is quite possible that the scandals of the twenties and early thirties were more responsible for the adoption of the censorship code than complaints about the sex and violence in the movies themselves. Actually, the scandals were more offensive to the American public than the most tasteless scripts ever concocted. They featured orgies, dope addiction and murder. Marital infidelity was trifling in this pageant of crime that gave Hollywood the name of Sodom by the Sea and brought denunciation upon the movie colony from clergy of all faiths, and from legislators ranging from community councilors to Congressmen. The scandals were the sorts that are delectable to censors and would-be censors. Scandal ruined the careers of some of Hollywood's most famous stars and the public uproar terrified Hollywood's rulers. Entwined in the stories that acquired page-one priority in the nation's press was strong evidence that the movie industry often prevailed upon the authorities to do something less than their duty to solve crimes and convict criminals.

The first of the scandals were the three trials of Roscoe (Fatty) Arbuckle for the rape and death of a rather minor movie actress, Virginia Rappe. The circumstances of this case were better suited to the talents of William Faulkner or Krafft-Ebing than to those of the hordes of newspapermen who spread it around the world. So odious were details of this sensation that film leaders overcame their basic distrust of one another long enough to form a mutual defense association and hire Hays to stem the spread of statutory film censorship and try to rebuild public and legislative good will for Hollywood.

Arbuckle, one of the greatest stars in movie history, was second only to Chaplin in popularity in the silent film era. His girth, ill-fitting clothes, slapstick comic talents were symbols of innocent merriment. His comedies were particularly popular with youngsters. Until he was tarred by scandal his salary rose steadily until it had reached a contract sum of $3,000,000 for three years—in an era when taxes were low.

Arbuckle's tragedy came in 1921 in the wake of great hilarity in the St. Francis Hotel in San Francisco. A generous host and lover of liquor and ladies, he had organized a party at the hotel on September 5, to enjoy a Labor Day weekend between films. Among the guests at the suite was Miss Rappe. She had been a model, and her face was probably best known at that time for its appearance on the sheet music of "Let Me Call You Sweetheart." She had obtained work in movies and there was a chance she might get a leading role. Arbuckle could have helped her career.

The considerable consumption of liquor on this Sunday of the Prohibition era, combined with the casual arrivals and departures of uninhibited guests, created a natural confusion. But there was no doubt that Miss Rappe became ill and was in great pain. She was taken to another room and then transferred to a hospital. She died there four days later. The entire affair might have gone unnoticed by the press except that a woman employed at the hospital telephoned the deputy coroner to ask if he planned to perform an autopsy. The deputy coroner, Dr. Michael Brown, became curious. He examined the body at the morgue and saw that the bladder had been ruptured by violence. He notified the police. Their investigations revealed a wild party accompanying the death. Then came the headlines of the "Arbuckle Orgy," the "Orgy Death."

Before the first of the three trials it looked ominous for Arbuckle. A woman who had been at the party, Mrs. Maude Delmont, told the police that Arbuckle had gone into a room with Miss Rappe and locked it behind them. Then she heard the actress screaming. After kicking and pounding on the door Mrs. Delmont called the assistant manager on the phone. But before help arrived Arbuckle left the room, wearing pajamas and Miss Rappe's hat. Mrs. Delmont said she entered the room and found Miss Rappe sobbing on the bed in pain. She was almost naked and some of her clothes were torn and scattered on the floor. Another guest at the party quoted Arbuckle as saying he had forced a chunk of ice into her genitals. The coroner's jury decided Arbuckle was responsible for her death and demanded "steps to prevent a further occurrence

of such events, so that San Francisco will not be made the rendez-
vous of the debauchee and gangster." He was tried for raping and
killing the actress.

The chief witness for the prosecution, Mrs. Delmont, did not
testify. The defense discovered that she had committed bigamy
and the prosecution decided her testimony would be subject to
considerable doubt. Each side accused the other of suborning, perjury and bribing or trying to bribe witnesses. The defense pointed
out that Miss Rappe had died of peritonitis that followed the bursting of her bladder. They stressed that the bladder could have been
ruptured when women tried to ease Miss Rappe's pain—or revive
her—by putting her in a tub of ice water. The prosecution contended that the weight of the comedian—it was well in excess of
250 pounds—on Miss Rappe during intercourse might have ruptured her bladder, already distended from drinking.

The jury deliberated forty-one hours and could not agree.
When dismissed, the jury stood ten to two for acquittal. The second trial, early in 1922, also ended in a disagreement of ten to two
for acquittal, after forty-four hours' discussion. The third jury
acquitted the star in six minutes. And then it issued a most unusual
statement: "Acquittal is not good enough for Roscoe Arbuckle.
We feel a great injustice has been done him and there was not the
slightest proof to connect him in any way with the commission of
any crime."

The public's attitude was different. Three Arbuckle pictures
completed before his arrest were not released, despite his acquittal.
They were never shown. His earlier movies were withdrawn from
circulation as mayors and police officials ruled that his films were
not to be shown in their communities. As William H. A. Carr
pointed out in his study of the case in *Hollywood Tragedy:* "Who
cared if such orders were unfair, unconstitutional, and unlawful—
they were on the side of righteousness and morality."

As public resentment grew, making Arbuckle a symbol of Hollywood, the heads of the movie industry turned again to Hays, an
elder of the Presbyterian Church as well as former Postmaster General. On January 14, 1922, he had gone to work for the industry
for $100,000 a year. He retained the industry ban on Arbuckle's
movies. Then a few months after Arbuckle's acquittal, he de-

clared: "Every man in the right way and at the right time is entitled to his chance to make good. It is apparent that Roscoe Arbuckle's conduct since his trouble merits that chance. So far as I am concerned, there will be no suggestion now that he should not have his opportunity to go back to work in his own profession."

Hays had made a mistake. He was attacked by some of the most important religious and women's groups in the nation. Not until nearly a dozen years later, 1933, did Arbuckle finally have an opportunity to make some comedies for Warner Brothers. But then, before they were released, he died in his sleep at the age of fifty-two after a party celebrating the first anniversary of his second marriage.

On February 1, 1922, while Arbuckle was preparing for his second trial and Hays was trying to pacify the American public, a second Hollywood scandal broke. This time there was no question that it was a case of murder. This time two famous stars were ruined. This time, also, the police seemed a bit lethargic. The result was an unsolved murder and a second wave of public vilification of Hollywood.

The murdered man was a Hollywood director, William Desmond Taylor. He was handsome, affluent, influential, attractive to women, interested in books—and in places that catered to dope addicts and connoisseurs of sex. He was found dead on the floor of his home. Symptomatic of the investigation of this murder was the fact that the first doctor who examined him said he had died of a hemorrhaging ulcer. It was not until he was later turned over on his stomach that two bullet holes were noticed in his back.

Before the case was closed Mabel Normand, one of the most talented comediennes in movie history, was without a career. So was Mary Miles Minter, already an important star regarded by many as a second Mary Pickford because of the sweet and virginal impression she made on her vast movie following. In an appraisal of this fascinating murder case for *Esquire*, Morris Markey wrote: "The shot that changed that inordinately handsome and debonair creature into a ghost also saved Hollywood from its own debauchery."

During the tragic afternoon of February 1 Miss Normand arrived at the director's home. Whether she came there for cocktails or to pick up a script or books is still in dispute. Present for the serving of drinks was a butler, Henry Peavey, who had a talent for needlework and a soprano voice. First the butler was dismissed and was seen leaving the attractive home by neighbors. (In fact, considering the number of people who kept the Taylor home under intermittent surveillance it is surprising that the murder was never solved.) Witnesses also saw Miss Normand leave about half an hour later in her chauffeur-driven car. When the car left, Taylor, who had accompanied her to the auto, re-entered his house. Miss Normand said later that she had declined to stay for dinner.

About 8:15 P.M. neighbors heard what they declared, under subsequent police questioning, might have been a shot. Mrs. Faith Cole MacLean, whose home had a huge window overlooking the Taylor place, gave an intriguing account to the police. "I wasn't sure, then," she told detectives, "that it was a shot at all, but I distinctly heard an explosion. Then I glanced out of my window and I saw a man leaving the house and going down the walk. I suppose it was a man. It was dressed like a man, but you know, funny-looking. It was dressed in a heavy coat with a muffler around the chin and a cap pulled down over the eyes. But it walked like a woman—quick little steps and broad hips and short legs."

Late that same evening Edna Purviance, who was then Charlie Chaplin's leading lady, saw, from her window, that lights were still on at the Taylor home. She decided to drop in on him. Miss Purviance was a friend as well as neighbor. Taylor's doorbell was not answered and she returned to her own house. Considering the number of women known to visit the handsome director at night, there was no reason for her to have been suspicious of foul play.

About seven-thirty the following morning, when Taylor's butler, Henry Peavey, came to work he found his master dead on the living room floor near his desk. He was fully clothed and his jacket was buttoned. There was no evidence of a struggle or robbery. The butler rushed into the street screaming in his unusually high voice that his master was dead. A doctor who happened to be passing by was stopped by a neighbor. He took a quick look at the director and said death had been caused by a gastric hemorrhage. He called the coroner and left.

Quite a few persons must have wandered around Taylor's house before either the coroner or police arrived—enough, in any event, for the director's boss, Charles Eyton, general manager of Famous Players-Lasky, to arrange for immediate removal of a substantial supply of liquor, lest the dead man's reputation be soiled by his violation of the Prohibition Amendment. Taylor's assistant, another in the group, passed the time by foraging through the house collecting love letters. When an assistant coroner arrived and commented on the orderliness of everything, Eyton suggested it might be a good idea to turn the dead man over. That was when two bullet holes were found in his back.

In the room when gastric hemorrhage gave way to murder was Miss Purviance. She made two surreptitious phone calls. The first was to Miss Normand. The second to Miss Minter. That actress was not at home, so she left a message with Miss Minter's mother, Mrs. Charlotte Shelby. The older woman sought out her daughter and, in a stormy session, told her that Taylor had been murdered. Miss Minter hastened to Miss Normand's home where the two stars held a conference. At Miss Normand's admission that she feared eavesdroppers and "listening devices," the talk was held in her bathroom.

Miss Normand, apart from their profession, had at least one other interest in common with Miss Minter—the murdered man. Both of them had sent him love letters. The chivalrous detectives returned these notes to the beautiful actresses. One of Miss Minter's notes became known to reporters. It said: "Dearest. I love you—I love you—I love you. Yours always. Mary." Miss Normand's letters remained secret. But a critique of their style as well as content was made by the district attorney, Thomas Woolwine. He called them "the usual vaporings of a young woman in love."

How sincerely Taylor returned their love was a matter for conjecture in Hollywood. Some students of the case claim he preferred Miss Normand. They base this opinion on two facts. First, during an argument at a New Year's Eve party, he had been upset because the ebullient actress was being attentive to other men and drinking more than he thought proper. She told him he was too stuffy and being melodramatic. The other bit of evidence offered as proof of Taylor's affection was that he pleaded with her to raise her literary standards by discarding *The Police Gazette* in favor of Nietzsche and Freud. In fact, according to the butler, the last time he saw his employer with Miss Normand—the evening before he found the body—the director was lecturing her on literature. She was eating peanuts, dropping the shells on the floor.

In addition to Miss Normand and Miss Minter, the police found clues leading to another suspect. He was the valet Taylor said he had fired for forging checks, stealing his clothes and pawning his jewelry. He was known as "Edward F. Sands."

The investigation was almost comic at times. First, while the police were presumably keeping an attentive eye on the case, someone entered the Taylor home and searched it thoroughly. Second, a batch of letters from Miss Normand to the dead man were found by detectives in one of his boots. Since the police presumably had looked there for evidence when the crime was discovered, the letters must have been placed there after they took over. Interestingly, Charles Eyton was present when the letters were discovered.

Nevertheless, some interesting information was uncovered about the murdered man. It was learned that the dead man's real name was William Cunningham Deane-Tanner. Born in County Cork, Ireland, he was the son of a British army officer. As a young man, with his brother Denis, he had an antique shop in New York. He married one of the Floradora Girls. They had a daughter. He borrowed heavily from a wealthy uncle of his wife's. The uncle, from whom he had expected to inherit a large sum, left him nothing. He deserted his wife and his daughter. His wife divorced him. His brother subsequently deserted his own wife and two daughters.

The police realized now that there was something intriguing about the valet named "Sands." He had pawned his "employer's" possessions in the name of William Cunningham Deane-Tanner, the director's real name. He had mailed the pawn tickets to the wife Taylor's brother Denis had deserted. She was receiving fifty dollars a month from Taylor, before his murder. The police could never find "Sands." Nor could they locate Taylor's brother, Denis, to learn if the two were the same person.

Then there was Miss Minter's mother, for whom the actress had no great affection. The police learned that Mrs. Shelby had been practicing shooting with a .38 caliber gun. A .38 caliber gun had killed Taylor. Apparently the police did not think this unusual. They did not try to prevent her from leaving for Europe.

Finally, the police, after listening to scores of "confessions" to the murder by deranged persons, even looked into the possibility that Taylor had been killed because he had given narcotics men information about the dope traffic in Hollywood.

Though no evidence was ever produced that either Miss Normand or Miss Minter participated in the murder of Taylor, their careers were ruined by the scandal. Sensing that the same kind of public indignation that had destroyed Roscoe Arbuckle would end the careers of these two stars, Famous Players-Lasky, which had two unreleased movies with Miss Minter, hastened to distribute them. Mack Sennett rushed to release a picture he had completed with Miss Normand before the murder. All three pictures were virtually boycotted. Sennett, however, refused to give up. He starred Miss Normand in two more movies, but she was still taboo across the country. In 1926, four years after the murder, she tried to make a comeback in a Hal Roach movie, *Raggedy Ann*. It was a box-office disaster.

An epilogue to the sensational murder was unfolded two years after *Raggedy Ann* by Miss Minter in a statement in which she described her mother's attempt to destroy her romance with Taylor. Had this episode taken place twenty years later when psychoanalysis was a subject of popular interest, it might have won her considerable sympathy.

"Mother's actions over Mr. Taylor's attentions to me," she said, "were not inspired by a desire to protect me from him. She was really trying to shove me into the background so that she could try to monopolize his attentions and, if possible, his love."

It seemed that Hollywood was determined not to let a year pass without a first-class scandal that would amaze the rest of the nation—and the world. In 1923, a year after Taylor was murdered and two years after the Arbuckle scandal, came another Hollywood sensation. It was shorter lived, but attracted enormous attention. That was the year Wallace Reid, one of the most popular of silent movie idols, died while trying to cure himself of dope addiction. His death, while it created a wave of sympathy for him, and admiration for his courage, served to impress on the public mind more deeply than ever that Hollywood was one huge den of sin.

The Reid case had hardly been forgotten when Charlie Chaplin cut capers with the ladies that extended his fame beyond his performances on the screen. His most widely publicized scandal began in 1924, some four years after his divorce from Mildred Harris. Chaplin got top billing in the scandals competition through his sexy adventures with sixteen-year-old Lita Grey. The great comedian had planned to use her as his leading lady in *The Gold Rush*. About this time a relative of the adolescent actress pointed out very sharply to Chaplin that premarital sex with a female that young was considered statutory rape. Chaplin married her, rather quickly, in November of 1924. In substantially less than the usual nine months allowed for conception a son, Charles Jr., was born to them. The next year Sidney Chaplin was born, to be followed, a year later, by a juicy suit for divorce filed by Mrs. Chaplin.

She said, to the surprise of no one, that they had had intercourse before marriage. She added that during the marriage he had been involved with at least one other woman. Then there was the usual accusation of mental cruelty.

Chaplin's reply for the press probably saved his career. "I married Lita Grey because I loved her and, like many other foolish men, I loved her more when she wronged me and I am afraid I still love her. I was stunned and ready for suicide that day when she told me that she didn't love me but that we must marry. Lita's mother often suggested to me that I marry Lita and I said I would love to if only we could have children. I thought I was incapable of fatherhood. Her mother deliberately and continuously put Lita in my path. She encouraged our relations."

When the great comedian was not stirring up the bloodhounds of censorship Clara Bow took over the job—and did it very well. Miss Bow was the sex queen of Hollywood in the late twenties. She was known as the "It" Girl. Her love affairs ran a greater gamut than her acting roles. She became attached to stars, directors, producers, athletes, policemen. What hurt her most was a court fight with a former secretary who testified that the actress supported many of her lovers, thereby virtually reducing them to the status of gigolos.

But the troubles of Chaplin and Miss Bow were just preliminaries for the main bout, the last major Hollywood scandal before the movie industry finally agreed to give more than lip service to its own code of self-censorship. Appropriately, the big scandal involved Miss Bow's successor as the glittering sex symbol of Hollywood, Jean Harlow. Originally Harlean Carpenter, she arrived in Beverly Hills as the sixteen-year-old bride of a youthful playboy son of a wealthy family. Domesticity was not enough to keep her occupied so, under the name of Jean Harlow, she obtained work in movies as an extra, despite her husband's objections. Divorce followed and Howard Hughes, the aviation magnate who had decided to make movies, made her famous as the star of his film *Hell's Angels*. Her next partisan was Paul Bern, first lieutenant of Metro-Goldwyn-Mayer's top movie-maker Irving Thalberg. Bern, unlike the platinum blonde with the low-cut dresses, had no interest in the wild social life of Hollywood. He was known as an intellectual, with a tendency toward introspection. They were married in July of 1932. He was forty-two, about twenty years older than Miss Harlow. In September he was found dead in their home. A bullet fired into his temple had killed him. The .38 caliber revolver that had killed him was several feet away. He was naked. The case was eventually called a suicide. But, as in other Hollywood scandals, some of the circumstances surrounding the death were most unusual.

One of these was the virtual contempt with which the movie industry apparently regarded the police, indicative of its assumption that it could "fix" things. The butler who found the body first called the studio. Next the head of the studio police notified Louis B. Mayer, then the head of Metro. Not until about two hours later were the police notified. By then Mayer, Thalberg and the head of the Metro private police had spent a good deal of time at the home of the dead man. After the police came, Mayer started to leave with Howard Strickling, the studio's publicity boss. He told Strickling that he had swiped a suicide note by Bern. Strickling advised Mayer to return the note. Mayer did so, reluctantly. The note read:

> Dearest dear:
> Unfortunately, this is the only way to make good the frightful wrong I have done you and to wipe out my abject humiliation. I love you.
>
> Paul
>
> p.s. You understand that last night was only a comedy.

Subsequently, the police did not doubt the authenticity of this note. Mayer brought pressure to block the possibility of a murder indictment against Miss Harlow. There were rumors that the actress had conspired with Bern's former common-law wife. A few days after Bern's death, the common-law wife's coat and shoes were found on the deck of a boat in the Sacramento River. She was not among the passengers when the boat arrived in Sacramento. Her body was later found in the river.

She had used the name Mrs. Paul Bern and he had supported her as long as she lived. Their relationship had apparently remained cordial even after their separation many years before his marriage to Miss Harlow. There is little doubt that he had told Miss Harlow about her.

At the time of Bern's death Miss Harlow was at the home of her mother and stepfather. For some reason Miss Harlow was not called as a witness at the inquest. Two years later a grand jury investigating the district attorney who handled his case released interesting testimony given to the 1932 grand jury. The gardener had told the 1932 grand jury that he thought Bern was murdered and that the butler had lied when he said there had been no arguments in the house. He also contradicted the butler's claim that Bern had talked about committing suicide. Finally, the gardener claimed the so-called suicide note was not in Bern's hand-writing. A cook told the 1932 grand jury that a woman whose voice she did not recognize was with Bern the last night he was alive. She said she found a woman's wet bathing suit and two empty glasses beside the swimming pool. None of this information was investigated. Nor was anything done with information that Miss Harlow had gone to San Francisco a few days before her husband's death.

Bern's former common-law wife was in San Francisco about that time. In 1960, Ben Hecht, the novelist and screen writer, revived interest in the case by charging in a magazine article that the suicide note was a forgery. When the Los Angeles district attorney questioned Hecht, it developed that his information was based on a talk with a director, who in turn had heard it from someone else. So the case remains a mystery.

Scandals have continued to explode periodically in Hollywood and are still portrayed as typical of Hollywood life. The most recent examples were the suicide of Marilyn Monroe and the escapades of Elizabeth Taylor, particularly with her co-star Richard Burton during the filming of *Cleopatra*. But such happenings no longer are considered as arguments for or against movie censorship. Once the industry's production code became a serious factor in movie-making, the censors shifted their attention to the code and movies, not the private lives of Hollywood celebrities.

4. *That Old Code Magic*

With the increased importance of the code, it would seem logical that movie-makers should learn it thoroughly. But the movie business is not that rational. Hollywood probably knows more about the seating capacity of the movie houses of Borneo than it does about the code that governs the moral tone of its movies. Producers, after occasional skirmishes with the Code—official title of the industry's self-censorship regulations—are apt to speak as though they had been immersed in the Kabbala. They set off on trips to the chambers in which the meanings of the code are interpreted as though they were seeking the source of the Amazon. Writers and directors, in discussing the code, sometimes sound as though it were the property of the Delphic oracle. The truth is that American movie-makers have probably done more to surround the code with confusion than have any of its critics outside Hollywood.

For example, one of the movie world's top film-makers, a man with at least a quarter of a century of solid experience, is convinced that if a man and woman embrace on a bed or sofa, one foot of at least one of the two must be touching the floor. This, he says, holds true even if the couple is fully clothed. The fact is that this rule was followed many years ago. In the last decade, however, there have been many movies in which it has been ignored. This movie-maker, nevertheless, still rages against infractions of the long-dead bit of foolishness. His belief is shared by many producers, directors and writers in the movie business.

Another example, also concerning bedroom ritual. It is widely believed among reputable Hollywood producers and directors that a man and wife, when shown asleep, or lying in bed in the same room, must be assigned each to his or her own twin bed. This ancient custom has been the cause of many gibes at the movie code, ranging from the amusing to the lascivious. But it too is part of code mythology.

The origin of this particular erroneous belief is traceable to Great Britain. Until fairly recently, the English censors insisted on the twin-bed routine for married couples. Since Great Britain has always been a huge market for American movies, the Hollywood movie-makers acquired the habit, long ago, of treating the double bed of marriage as though it was vaguely connected with incest. And since it is almost axiomatic that Hollywood would rather complain about the code than learn it, the mistaken beliefs persist. It is extraordinary how producers, who can take pride in reproducing some fifteenth-century costume down to the least detail, know so little about the censorship code governing their films.

And yet, contrary to legend, the Motion Picture Production Code is a document that any reasonably intelligent high school student should be able to understand. It is certainly much simpler than the United States Constitution. The words of the code are simple. The sentences are short. The material is arranged in logical fashion. It is almost as though the men who wrote—and then revised—the code, realized they must overcome an antipathy to reading among movie-makers.

Though the code was revised in 1956—mainly to permit movies to deal more frankly with narcotics addiction—most of its provisions remain virtually the same as in 1930. Today, as then, the code is administered by the chief censor. The code is a twelve-page pamphlet, made up, for the most part, of generalities. Thus, Section III (Sex), says: "The sanctity of the institution of marriage and the home shall be upheld. No film shall infer that casual or promiscuous sex relationships are the common thing."

Under this general heading are subcategories covering adultery, illicit sex, scenes of passion, seduction, rape, abortion and perversion. None of these subheadings is difficult to understand. For instance, of seduction and rape the code says: "These should never be more than suggested, and then only when essential to the plot. They should never be shown explicitly. They are never acceptable subject matter for comedy. They should never be made to seem right and permissible." In recent years this clause has been interpreted leniently, particularly in comedy.

Or consider Section I (Crime). It says: "Crime shall never be presented in such a way as to throw sympathy with the crime as against law and justice, or to inspire others with a desire for imitation." There are nine classifications under crime. Thus, the subsection under murder declares that "brutal killings are not to be presented in detail"; that "revenge, in modern times, shall not be justified"; that "mercy killing shall never be made to seem right or permissible."

Under Section IV (Vulgarity), the code says that "vulgar expressions and double meanings having the same effect are forbidden." And in Section IX (Special Subjects), the code lists subjects that "must be treated with discretion and restraint within the careful limits of good taste." These include bedroom scenes, hangings and electrocutions, liquor and drinking, surgical operations and childbirth, third-degree methods. The code makes two declarations about obscenity (Section V). First: "Dances suggesting or representing sexual actions or emphasizing indecent movements are to be regarded as obscene." Second: "Obscenity in words, gesture, reference, song, joke or by suggestion, even when likely to be understood only by part of the audience, is forbidden." In the category of brutality (Section II), the code says: "Excessive and inhumane acts of cruelty and brutality shall not be presented. This includes all detailed and protracted presentation of physical violence, torture and abuse." Other sections of the code cover blasphemy and profanity, costumes, religion, national feelings, titles and cruelty to animals.

The code prefaces its twelve sections with three general principles. The first forbids pictures that "will lower the moral standards of those who see it. Hence the sympathy of the audience shall never be thrown on the side of crime, wrongdoing, evil or sin." The second calls for "correct standards of life, subject only to the requirements of drama and entertainment." The third principle says: "Law—divine, natural or human—shall not be ridiculed, nor shall sympathy be created for its violation."

Since the code is written so simply, why is there so much controversy over it? First, there are those who think the code should be changed. The most notable fight along this line was made by Otto Preminger, who produced and directed *The Man with the Golden Arm*. This movie was denied a seal of approval by the industry's censors. Mr. Preminger, backed by United Artists, which distributed the film in 1956, decided to show it in movie theaters without a seal. At the same time Mr. Preminger and United Artists fought to have the code changed to permit narcotics addiction in films. The code was altered in a series of moves and fascinating countermoves discussed in Chapter II.

Much more irritating causes of friction, however, are disagreements over interpretation of the code, which can make differences of opinion among constitutional lawyers seem naive. The most learned members of the United States Supreme Court might be tempted to give up law if they had to deal with the arguments— let alone the temperaments—of those who defend their scripts or films before the censors.

For example, under the section on sex, there is room for considerable disagreement about whether a movie does or does not "infer" that promiscuity is generally acceptable. And who shall say whether a rape in a picture is or is not "essential to the plot"? Consider the case of *One-Eyed Jacks*, directed by Marlon Brando, who also starred in it. In this picture a rape was permitted. The explanation was that it was essential to the plot. Yet when the movie was shown, this section was no longer there. The censors had not cut it. It had been deleted by Mr. Brando when it was found the film was too long. Its absence did not seem to undermine the plot. It is very unlikely that the audiences even vaguely suspected this stimulating sequence had ever been in the movie.

Who shall say whether a movie about crime will "inspire others with desire for imitation"? A classic example is on file at the offices of the movie censors. There one can find a clipping about a youth who murdered his teen-aged date while they were necking in a car shortly after seeing a movie. The film was Walt Disney's *Snow White and the Seven Dwarfs*. The censors shudder at what might have been the public reaction if the picture had been something like *Anatomy of a Murder*, in which both rape and murder figured so prominently.

Then there can be honest disagreement about what constitutes a "vulgar expression." Strong language that is obviously permissible during a battle scene in a war movie could be offensive if used by children in a quiet classroom. Or in considering the point at which cruelty becomes "inhumane" it is impossible to judge in a vacuum. Thus, the key to what is acceptable under the movie code very often is dependent upon the interpretation of code provisions.

Back in Hollywood's happy days before television, when the studios had a great deal of money, each studio used to have its own expert on the code. The studio expert would argue each controversial script before the code administrator and his assistants as though he were a lawyer pleading a case in court. It is likely that during these years studio executives, producers and directors became so dependent on these few experts that they did not bother to learn the code. But now that the censorship experts have been lopped off so many studio payrolls as an economy move—by 1964 only Metro-Goldwyn-Mayer still had one—a new business is getting under way in Hollywood. This is the free-lance consultant on censorship problems.

The most adroit of the independent censorship consultants was Bill Gordon, who died in 1962. He operated out of a small, file-cluttered office in Hollywood. Mr. Gordon, whose censorship tussles on behalf of producers went back to the thirties, was unusual in his field because he was held in high esteem by the movie censors. "Producers and studio executives," he said shortly before his death, "are almost one hundred per cent wrong about what will never be passed by the code. And what they think will pass easily is often stopped. They have a great ignorance of what will encounter opposition."

Robert Vogel, Metro's authority on censorship regulations, thinks that the most important change in movie censorship has been the growing tendency of the censors to judge a script or film by its overall content, rather than by an isolated word or sentence. Some directors, he concedes, may deliberately insert something into a film when it seems certain the code administration will demand its deletion.

Sometimes the solution to a censorship problem can be more effective than the original sequence. This happened as a result of an impasse on *Battleground*. In a section about the Battle of the Bulge, an American squad was isolated by Germans. The Germans flew over the area, dropping leaflets saying that if the Americans surrendered they would be well treated; otherwise they would be annihilated. In this sequence an American soldier put the leaflet in his pocket. His buddy asked him what he intended to do with the leaflet. He replied: "Guess." The industry's censors refused to allow this. They called it toilet humor. The solution was simple. In the new version he merely picked up the leaflet and, without saying a word, walked off. With effective camera work and acting, the new version left little doubt about what he intended to do with the leaflet. Nevertheless, the scene was approved in its new version.

Since censorship is usually taken with such intense—sometimes near-hysterical—seriousness by combatants, it is rare for either side to treat the matter lightly. But once in a long while one of the participants in a censorship row combines enormous talent with indestructible humor. John Huston, the writer who turned director, is that rare movie type. In making *Heaven Knows Mr. Allison*, he chose a subject that was, inevitably, censorship-prone. For this is the story of a nun (Deborah Kerr) and a marine (Robert Mitchum) stranded on a desert island, ostensibly for life. This subject was so ticklish that one of the movie censors, John Vizzard, was on location for filming of much of the movie. After much discussion it had been settled that the beautiful nun would repulse the advances of the handsome marine. The scene had been shot.

But one day Huston told Vizzard he would reshoot the scene. While Vizzard stared in horror the nun, in the reshot version, succumbed to the marine's passion. A heated argument followed between Vizzard and Huston. When Huston figured the censor had spent enough time in a rage, he revealed that the camera had no film for the "reshot" version.

Though censorship discussions are, of necessity, conducted in secrecy, the code's administration tries to follow judicial procedure in its operations. Thus, anyone who thinks the ruling of the Hollywood censors is unfair has the right of appeal. To do this the protestant notifies the secretary of the appeals board in New York of a desire to file an appeal. An appeals hearing is then set up in New York. The appeals board is made up of the heads of the major movie-distributing companies, plus four independent producers and six representatives of theater owners. The board sees the movie in question. Then it listens to the arguments of the appellant and reads the ruling of the Hollywood censors. All interested parties are then asked to leave while the appeal is considered and a vote taken.

It is rare for the board of appeals to reverse the Hollywood ruling. From 1954 until 1964 there were only six appeals and none in 1962 and 1963. Sometimes such reversals have been among the most ridiculous aspects of movie censorship. Such was the case of *Happy Anniversary*. This was a rather flimsy comedy in which a man, after fourteen years of successful marriage, confides to his in-laws that he had gone to bed with their daughter on one occasion before he married her. Because of this debonair attitude toward premarital sex, a seal of approval was denied the picture. The ruling was appealed to New York. After some haggling, a curious solution was reached. It was agreed that a couple of sentences would be spoken off camera for the film. In the added sentences the husband reflected: "I was wrong. I never should have taken Alice to that hotel room before we were married. What could I have been thinking of?" With this bit of repentance the movie received its seal.

Once the court of appeals has ruled, there is only one recourse for a producer who still disagrees with the ruling. He can release his picture without a seal. To do this he must first find a distribut-

ing company that agrees with him. This is very difficult. One reason is that many theaters will not handle any movie that does not
have a seal. Second, movies without a seal are banned from American military establishments. Finally, a movie without a seal is almost certain to encounter strong resistance from religious and
civic groups as well as from state and local censors.

Nevertheless, a picture can be successful without a seal. This is
often true of foreign films, many of which do not even bother to
seek a seal because they know it is hopeless. Among the most successful foreign movies shown in the United States in recent years
were *Room at the Top,* and *Never on Sunday*, neither of which
had a seal.

The most famous cases of American movies released without a
seal were *The Moon is Blue* and as already noted *The Man with the
Golden Arm.* Both were enormously successful. Some years afterward, in an unprecedented action, both pictures received seals of
approval.

Though the code can be changed, it is, like amending the Constitution, a difficult procedure. First, arguments for a change in the
code must be made before a subcommittee set up to hear such
cases. If it passes this hurdle the matter then goes before the full
code committee, headed by the president of the Motion Picture Association of America, and including the presidents of Paramount,
Universal and Columbia. If it wins approval, or tolerance, at this
hearing the case then is heard by the Motion Picture Association's board of governors. This is made up of the representatives of
the eight major movie companies now in the association—Metro-
Goldwyn-Mayer, Twentieth Century-Fox, Universal, Warner
Brothers, Paramount, Columbia, Allied Artists, United Artists.
Then comes the tedious job of doing the actual revisions.

From 1930, when the code was adopted, until 1961, there was
only one major change in the code. This was the one permitting
movies to show dope addiction. Other sections of the code were
rewritten at the time, but those changes were made mainly to
tighten, clarify and simplify the code. Then, in the fall of 1961,
the Motion Picture Association lessened the severity of the code
regulation governing homosexuality.

But no matter what changes are made in the code, the trend seems to be to allow greater artistic freedom to movie-makers. The code, in this respect, has the same sort of strength as the federal Constitution. It is difficult to change, but it is subject to generous tolerance in interpretation to suit changing times. It can bend a great deal without breaking. Its endurance in an industry that has undergone a virtual revolution since the introduction of television and been beset by economic furies is a testament to its strength. If anything is certain in Hollywood, it is this: no matter how often the code is criticized and revised, the industry will cling to the idea of a code as the most sensible way of cross-breeding art and business in good taste. Without a code the industry, long marked by cutthroat competition, would degenerate into anarchy.

5. *Hollywood Cato*

In the eye of the Hollywood censorship hurricane is a man who prefers obscurity. He is Geoffrey M. Shurlock, the administrator of the movie industry's code. As chief censor, he hands down the interpretations to studio heads, producers, directors and writers. A small, roundish, middle-aged man with staccato speech and a modest manner, he is the nation's chief performer on the movie censorship tightrope. Shurlock is a sort of human radarscope who must send out, in spoken and written opinions, warning blips to guide movie-makers on a course that permits maximum artistic maturity and a minimum of public friction. Since Shurlock bestows the industry's seal of approval on movies before they are shown to the American public—or to state and local censors—he is probably the most important nongovernmental censor in the world. Shurlock is Hollywood's equivalent of Cato, who, as consul and senator of ancient Rome, earned the title Cato the Censor by his vigorous attacks on immorality. He is also, by the same token, Hollywood's official whipping boy and shock absorber.

The convictions of Mr. Shurlock—or any other man who holds this office—are of considerable importance in determining the cultural level of American movies and, indirectly, in presenting the "image" of the United States abroad. His personality and his manner of running his office are not subjects of publicity releases —in fact, they are far removed from public attention—but they exert great, though subtle, influence on the censorship of American movies.

Though Shurlock is the conscience of Hollywood, he no more fits the Hollywood pattern as a person than the original Cato the Censor conformed to the Roman mold. In the Hollywood world, where anyone with a smattering of culture generally poses as an aesthetic giant, Shurlock, who is much better read than the majority of those whose movies he judges, speaks slightingly of his own attainments. Yet he is fluent in French and Spanish and competent in German. He is extremely knowledgeable about plays, from the ancient Greek to avant-garde French and American. His knowledge of music—symphonic, chamber and operatic—probably exceeds that of most newspaper music critics. A widower, he lives in a modest apartment, without benefit of swimming pool or barbecue pit.

In the American movie capital, where selective gregariousness can be very rewarding, Shurlock keeps pretty much to himself. When it is suggested to him that this ivory tower approach might narrow his horizon, he replies: "A greater danger than the ivory tower in movies is that you will be sucked into personal relationships with the people whose work you have to judge."

In his dealings with subordinates, Shurlock is a chronic violator of the Hollywood business code. Without affectation, he and his six assistant censors address one another by their first names. But, more important, Shurlock's assistants know they can disagree with him freely and that their dissenting opinions on a script or film will be judged by what they say, not by the dissenter's rank. At the same time, Shurlock speaks up to the head of a studio with just as much firmness as he does to a fledgling producer. Such indifference to hierarchy is exceptional to the point of treason in the movie industry.

Shurlock has an interesting theory that governs his relations with producers. "Whenever we reach an impasse in discussing a controversial point, one of our tricks is to make a suggestion. The producer immediately denounces our idea. He may even go into a tantrum, shouting: 'It won't work. It will ruin the story. I may as well give up the picture.' And so forth. Then the first thing you know, he has talked himself into the idea that alternatives are possible. From that he comes up with a suggestion that does work. The tactic is to make him offer the suggestion. Any suggestion. It gets him out of a state of shock. They start tearing you to pieces and by the time they have finished with you they have worked up an idea of their own."

It is not uncommon for Shurlock to make suggestions that are acceptable to a producer. In one gangster movie—*Capone*—the story was to have been developed in flashbacks as told by a reporter who had been on the gangster's payroll. Shurlock contended that such a script tended to glorify the gangster. He urged—and it was accepted—that the story be told from the point of view of a police captain, thus retaining the drama and excitement of the Prohibition era underworld and at the same time never losing sight of the fact that the gangster was an enemy of society.

One of the most trying rules that Shurlock has imposed on himself and his assistants is that of secrecy. No matter how sharply the Shurlock office is attacked by producers or pressure groups, neither he nor his assistants defend their rulings publicly. They do not even discuss the situation for publication.

Thus Shurlock was harshly criticized by religious and civic groups for permitting a bedroom sequence early in the Alfred Hitchcock thriller *Psycho*. This scene showed a man and woman— unmarried—in a rather sleazy hotel bedroom. They had obviously just completed an adulterous act and were still in bed when the scene opened. There was a great deal of embracing and impassioned behavior while they dressed to leave the hotel. Throughout the period when Shurlock was attacked for permitting this scene, he remained silent. Yet the truth was that the way the scene had been shot originally was so much more torrid that Shurlock had forced Hitchcock to reshoot the sequence to make it less sexy.

Periodically, whenever criticism of the movie industry is particularly heavy, Shurlock will discuss the situation discreetly with studio executives and producers, and with key persons in such organizations as the Catholic Legion of Decency. Shurlock also prepares confidential reports for the industry that will enable spokesmen and lobbyists for the movie business to answer its critics. At times he appears before legislators investigating movie morality. He does not, however, permit state or local censors to tell him how to censor scripts.

In appraising the purpose of his job—and of Hollywood censorship in general—Shurlock disagrees with those who think he need concern himself only with morality. "Taste," he insists, "must be considered as well as morality in our movies. It is not so much the subject of a picture that is important as the manner in which it is treated. Tennessee Williams' works are extremely moral. Unless you consider taste and treatment you can rule that many children's stories are too violent and that most of Shakespeare and the Greek tragedies should be banned forever from the screen."

Shurlock thinks the moral climate of the nation should be considered in judging movie scripts or films. He claims that the movies have been unjustly accused of subverting public morals when, in effect, they have been merely reflecting public morals. "The relaxation of morality in the movies," he contends, "has been much less than that of public morality. The movies are, to a large extent, based on those novels and plays that have won the widest approval. Those books and plays did not come out of a vacuum. They reflect changes in public attitudes. Homosexuality, for instance, would not have been considered a subject for movies in the early thirties."

Basically, however, the two major headaches for Hollywood censors are the same ones that led the field in the early thirties—sex and violence. "Nowadays," says Shurlock, "we might laugh at the objections to the Clara Bow, Jean Harlow and Mae West movies. But the men and women who criticized the movie industry at that time did not think they were funny. There was plenty of violence in such gangster movies as *Scarface, Little Caesar* and *Public Enemy*. And today, just as in the thirties, the majority of those who object to a movie have never seen it."

The fundamental guide for movie censoring, so far as Shurlock is concerned, is the same one that was followed in the thirties. It is the sentence among the general principles of the production code that says: "The sympathy of the audience shall never be thrown to the side of crime, wrong-doing, evil or sin." It is a corollary of this rule—the object of much ridicule by playwrights, novelists and even producers and directors—that requires cinematic punishment for criminals, sinning women, errant men. Shurlock feels no need to apologize for what is known as the retributive, or compensatory, theory of movie censorship.

"Our medium," he explains, "tends to develop the details of sin. The murders are shown on the screen. The sex affairs are shown on the screen. The details are graphic. The commission of sin in movies is vivid and dramatic. But repentance is purely internal. How often can you show someone kneeling in church? At the same time, some of our complainants ought to realize that to create sympathy for a sinner is not to sympathize with the sin.

"There is no hard-and-fast rule about any script. Each story has to be judged individually on the basis of morality and reasonable decency. Details of sin have to be balanced against details of compensation. There would be no sense in too much retribution for too little sin. This, of course, is not our problem. Ours is the other extreme of too much sin and too little retribution. Actually, we are not too far from the classic tradition. In the Greek plays, murder generally took place offstage and the play concerned itself with the results of sin, not with the details of sin. The idea of sin in detail was developed by Shakespeare. Corneille and Racine followed the Greek pattern of discussion of sin. But Shakespeare did not stint in his condemnation of sin and evil. His villains suffered. Compare the Shakespeare approach to villainy with that of our gangster movies. In gangster films the criminal lives high, wide and fancy. The police are dragged in at the end for a quick punishment. The gangsters in movies don't have the endless mental torment of an Iago or a Macbeth. I remember one day a producer came to me with a script about gangsters in which the chief gangster is killed by one of his own lieutenants. Where is the force of society in such a movie? You have gangsters operating in a vacuum. It is not even balanced drama. Producers and directors are sometimes so happy to get dramatic effects that they forget moral issues are involved."

At times, the star of a movie will fight for a word in a script because he believes it is dramatically correct, even if it is a little coarse. Thus, in making *Beloved Infidel*, Gregory Peck insisted that the word "bitch" was perfect for one speech. Shurlock refused to permit it, though Peck, a literate man of good taste, made a strong case. The main reason Shurlock rejected Peck's arguments was that it would have been construed as a precedent. "As soon as you let one producer use the word 'bitch' in a picture," says Shurlock, "there will be a horde of producers thinking of any sort of excuse to get the word into a picture. All the fast-buck boys will be trying to see how many times they can get 'bitch' into a movie."

Getting colorful—and off-color—words, expressions and situations into scripts has become a pastime, a minor industry, and even an obsession in Hollywood, depending on the man making the movie. It is common for producers to instruct writers to sprinkle their scripts with objectionable lines and situations in the hope that some of them may slip by the censor during an argument. "There is no doubt," says Shurlock, "that from 1960 to 1963, though the vast majority of pictures were unobjectionable, there were more pictures than ever that should not have been seen by children under sixteen, unless accompanied by adults."

Shurlock came into the movie censorship field almost by accident. Born in Liverpool, England, in 1894, the son of a sea captain, he was brought to the West Coast at the age of seven because his mother was fascinated by a school near San Diego run by theosophists. He remained at school until he went into the army in World War I. After the war he drifted into Hollywood as secretary to an extremely successful movie writer who needed someone fluent in French. But Shurlock quit when he learned the chauffeur was being paid more than he was. Then, with another man, he tried writing movie scripts and plays. "We never made a dime," he admits. In 1926 he became a script reader for Paramount. The movies were still silent. Three years later, after films had acquired speech, he was assigned to produce what he thinks is Paramount's last silent film. "It was badly produced," he recalls, "even for a western."

When it became known at Paramount that Shurlock was something of a linguist, he was told to produce Spanish-language films for the Latin-American market. But by 1932, as the nation's economic depression deepened, Paramount was in serious financial trouble and Shurlock found himself unemployed. Because of his knowledge of movies and his general cultural background, he was asked to take a job as assistant censor and did so. In 1954 he became chief censor, the fourth man to hold the job. The first was Jason Joy (1930-32), who hired him. The others were James Wingate (1932-34) and Joseph I. Breen (1934-54).

Over the years, Shurlock has evolved a methodical system of executing his censorship duties. Whenever a new script comes into his office, he hands a copy to each of two assistants. These men read the script separately, without comparing notes. Usually, the reading is done at home in the evening. Whenever a reader finds anything questionable, he turns down a corner of the page and marks the offending section. If the picture is important or suggestive of serious controversy, Shurlock also reads the script.

The second step is the film itself. The members of the Shurlock office often see segments of a movie shortly after they are shot if the script has indicated that there may be some question about how the scene will be interpreted on film. They always see a film when it is completed. For no matter what a censor says about a script or portions of a film, the seal of approval cannot be denied a producer until after a film is completed.

The censors make their headquarters in a covey of offices above a large Hollywood drugstore. Each censor has his own tidy cubicle, where he confers—or argues—with producers, directors and/or writers. On the same floor is an attractive screening room, where the censors may study filmed sections of a movie. Frequently, they see films at movie studios. They find it difficult to read new scripts in their offices because they are interrupted often to discuss other scripts.

The most secret ritual in gossip-riddled Hollywood takes place at 10 A.M. every weekday in the conference room of the censorship office. At these meetings Shurlock's assistants report verbally, in detail where necessary, on any script or film problem. It is at these sessions that the usually genial censorship chief's voice becomes metallic as he bounces up and down in his chair when provoked by a script or movie. "I think," he will say, "we should hit him hard on this one. He knows damn well he's not supposed to do this." Or, in a more judicious tone, he may suggest: "This is a real problem. The script is in good taste and the sex seems honestly motivated by the characters and the plot." More curtly, he may order: "Tell him five sex affairs are too many for this picture. He will have to cut down to two at the most." Or else: "I think we should explain to him that while he can get the seal with this script, he may run into trouble at these points with the Legion of Decency unless he makes some changes."

One day, when Shurlock was particularly disturbed at the close of a meeting concerning a rash of code violations in script and film, he sought out one of the film industry's most important producers and asked him bluntly: "What do you think my job is?"

The producer replied: "All I want is for you to operate so that when my picture is released it will have no difficulty with anyone, anywhere in the world."

This comment illustrates precisely what bothers Shurlock. "The danger is," he worries, "that producers may be getting into the habit of letting us do their thinking along moral lines. We want to make the producers do their own moral thinking. We want to throw them on their own, more and more. We want to make them grow up."

2 | Quality and control

Contrary to widespread belief, it is generally Hollywood's quality movies, not the tawdry "fast-buck" imitations of good movies, that exert the greatest influence toward changing the industry's interpretations of its own censorship code. The enduring values of the artistic models are discernible long after the rancor stirred by vulgar imitations is forgotten. The significance of such American cinematic landmarks as *From Here to Eternity, Double Indemnity* and *A Streetcar Named Desire* is revealed in a comparison of the original movie and the version finally seen by the public. Then there is that rare movie, the picture of little artistic merit that manages, in spite of itself, to exert noticeable effects on the entire industry. Such a film was *The Outlaw*, which, at first glance, seems remarkable only as an example of how much excitement and anger can be touched off by a film that could have been laughed out of existence. These cinematic trail-blazers all challenged aspects of the industry's censorship code. They defied or circumvented pressure groups and state and municipal censors. And one of them—*The Outlaw*—committed the most dreadful of Hollywood heresies: Its maker said the censorship code was not legal, thereby bringing into focus the moral as well as artistic and economic implications of voluntary censorship.

1. *Mammary Madness*

Jane Russell, a tall, robustly proportioned movie actress, created more frenzy over the question of movie censorship than any actress in history. Her breasts were to Hollywood what Eve's apple was to sin. She never attained major stardom, but with one movie, *The Outlaw*, she put the cleavage into new camera focus and paved the way to Hollywood fame for such full-bosomed Italian stars as Gina Lollobrigida and Sophia Loren.

The nationwide furor over this woman's 38-inch bust came to a climax in a vital court case that tested the right of the Motion Picture Association of America to bestow, withhold or revoke its seal of approval for movies. This movie had every kind of censorship trouble—over the script, the film and the advertising. Neither before nor since has there been such a triple threat to the industry's attempt to regulate morals, sex and violence in films and the ethics of film exploitation.

The Outlaw should not have created much fuss as a movie. It was another version of the adventures of Billy the Kid with guns and women. But it became the subject of one of the most celebrated censorship fights because that extraordinary industrialist, Howard Hughes, became intrigued with the script, with Miss Russell's appearance, and with proving he would not be contradicted. When Hughes, as producer of the movie, fired his director, Howard Hawks, and took over the direction himself in 1940, he was already an American symbol. He had multiplied about $250,-000 left to him by his father into hundreds of millions. He had set plane speed records across the country and had flown around the world. He had earned a ticker tape parade up Broadway. He had made a star of Jean Harlow, who became involved in one of Hollywood's major scandals. He had been linked in salacious gossip with a number of Hollywood actresses. It seemed incredible that, with this movie, the daredevil multimillionaire could become as famous for his cinematic exploits as for his earlier headlined feats. But he succeeded.

The result of his capricious behavior in connection with *The Outlaw* was a cross-country censorship controversy that became the bitterest in the annals of Hollywood. The battle offered badly needed comic relief to the press during the war years of the forties—and even afterward. *The Outlaw* marked the beginning of "mammary madness," a Hollywood fixation that has still not abated.

The sequences that caused the trouble were not extraordinary for anything in Hollywood's Wild West except the intended ironic touches of humor. The humor became overshadowed by sex when Hughes took over. Billy the Kid was a high-spirited lad with a good eye for women and horses, except that he treated the latter with more consideration. So when Billy met the lush Rio (Jane Russell) in a barn, he raped her with a zest that was tempered by his caution that if she kept making such a fuss her dress might become tattered. Now Rio had a boy friend, Doc Holliday, a notorious western gambler. Billy and Doc became friends without Doc's knowing that Billy had sampled his woman. So when Billy was wounded in one of his periodic gunning forays, Doc hustled him off to Rio who was to hide him out and minister to his wounds. Above all, Doc warned her, it was terribly important that he be kept warm. Then Doc rode off on Billy's horse. Rio, resentful of Billy's ungentlemanly conduct at their last meeting, considered revenge with a long knife. But she was a goodhearted girl. Therefore, mindful of Doc's medical advice, she kept Billy from cooling off by leaping into bed with him to apply sexual therapy. When Doc returned, saddle-weary and worried about his chum Billy, he learned of the perfidy in the sickbed. The ensuing row between gambler and gunman seemed to be nearing the gunplay stage when Billy made an offer no gambler could resist. He gave Doc a choice between Rio and the horse. The gambler, having tried both, chose the horse. Billy was chagrined. He said he'd become real fond of the horse. Rio sulked with injured pride.

When Hughes began transferring Jules Furthman's script to film, he was keenly interested in aspects other than funny dialogue.

Under his guidance the camera explored Miss Russell's cleavage during the rape, and even more in the bed-warming scene. He even put generous shares of her bosom on display when she was riding a horse, moving around a fire or bound for whipping. Hughes seemed determined to make a topographical survey with camera of Miss Russell. Persons close to Hughes during the shooting advised him to play it subtly for laughs. "But," said a responsible co-worker on the picture, "Hughes was a great student of the obvious. He believed in putting everything right on the floor. He had her bend over Billy and had the camera peering down to her navel. He claimed this shot had never been done before. He was right. No one else in Hollywood would have dared to try it."

The atmosphere in which the movie was shot was as incredible as the censorship hurricane it produced. There was the manner in which Hughes fired his director shortly after shooting began. The original director was in Arizona with the actors, props and equipment. One day, while the director was away scouting for locations for later sequences in the film, Hughes chartered a train and had the entire company, their costumes, equipment and props brought back to Hollywood. The director returned to find the troupe gone. Thereafter, Hughes was director. However, in this year of 1940 Hughes was greatly occupied turning out planes for the government. He had to spend many nights checking on his factories and was too tired to be very effective when he showed up early in the morning, the traditional time for movie shooting to begin. His solution was to arrange a schedule that began after lunch and ended for dinner. He deputized Furthman to act as assistant director and director pro tem when he was off on other projects. The hitch was that Furthman refused to work after 5 P.M. Hughes then began phoning Furthman at home at all hours of the night. The writer retaliated by leaving instructions with his maid not to call him to the phone after 10:30 P.M., particularly not to talk to Hughes. One night, when Hughes called long after the usual deadline, the maid, obeying Mr. Furthman's orders, told him she did not dare wake Furthman up. "He has a gun. He told me that if I woke him up he'd shoot me." Furthman had decided that only this kind of lie would deter Hughes.

Filming was kept lively with disputes between Hughes and

Thomas Mitchell, who played the sheriff. Mitchell told Hughes, with full-voiced oratory and hot-tempered invective, that he knew nothing about directing. Then there were the swarms of still photographers who collected periodically around Miss Russell for "art" shots for publicity. At one point, Miss Russell recalled many years later, there were twenty-five photographers working on her at once. "Sometimes the photographers would pose me in a low-necked nightgown and tell me to bend down and pick up a couple of pails. They were not shooting the pails. Or else they would tell me to jump up and down in bed in the nightgown while they shot from above and below. I didn't realize what they were doing. I was green as grass."

The crowning touch to this weird experiment in movie-making came when Hughes received a serious head injury in an auto accident. So he directed by phone from the hospital, with Furthman taking over on the set until Hughes appeared in person, wearing a turban of bandages, to take over the project. His head injury did not seem to affect his major purpose—sex. Thus, he was not satisfied at one point with the camera work on Miss Russell. He said: "We're not getting enough production out of Jane's breasts." Whereupon the designer of planes repaired to his drawing board. He designed a special bra for Miss Russell that would make the breasts more revealing than ever, but keep them from bobbing about too much and spoiling their contours.

On December 3, 1940, the first censorship clouds appeared in a letter from Breen, then head of Hollywood censorship, to Hughes. Breen wrote: "I 'see by the papers,' as Mr. Dooley used to say, that you have begun shooting on your picture and it occurs to me that you ought to let us have a copy of your shooting script, with a view to examining it, against the possibility that there may be some details in it, which will have to be deleted or changed in the finished picture."

The script was dispatched to Breen. This was the sort of material he read. When Doc learned how the ailing Billy had been kept warm by Rio, Billy told him:

"Well, you went off with my horse."
Doc stormed: "Well, you were not in any shape to use it."
Billy retorted: "A fair exchange is no robbery."

Billy's offer to Doc was phrased as follows:

"If you want her back you can have her and welcome. Now what d'you think about that?"

Doc: "I don't want her. Cattle don't graze after sheep."

During the rape scene, Billy said: "Hold still, lady, or you won't have much dress left." And when Rio prepared to keep Billy warm in bed, she said: "Be careful, your wound, you'll hurt yourself."

After reading this script, Breen wrote a much stronger note to Hughes. He said the script contained "certain elements" that would "render it unacceptable by us." He revealed a strong suspicion of the filming approach Hughes would take. He suggested that Miss Russell "be fully covered" and, if possible, wear a bathrobe over her nightgown. "Care will be needed," he pointed out, "in this scene with Billy pulling Rio down on the bed and kissing her, to avoid sex suggestiveness." All told, in addition to general cautions, the letter listed twenty-three specific objections.

Hughes undoubtedly read these letters. Nevertheless, on March 28, 1941, Breen sent off another missive to Hughes that indicated his earlier advice had not been followed carefully. "We had the pleasure this afternoon," wrote Breen, "of witnessing a projection room showing of your production, titled 'The Outlaw,' and, as I have already told you, the picture is definitely and specifically in violation of our Production Code and because of this cannot be approved." There was, he said, "inescapable suggestion of an illicit relationship between Doc and Rio and between Billy and Rio . . . the countless shots of Rio, in which her breasts are not fully covered."

Perhaps more important was the extraordinary letter he sent off the same day to Will Hays. For here, anticipating a major row, Breen was trying to line up the support of his boss and of the movie industry. "In my more than ten years of critical examination of motion pictures," he wrote, "I have never seen anything quite so unacceptable as the shots of the breasts of the character of Rio. This is the young girl whom Mr. Hughes recently picked up and who has never before, according to my information, appeared on the motion picture screen. Throughout almost half the picture the girl's breasts, which are quite large and prominent, are shockingly uncovered." He warned Hays that this was the most flagrant example of what seemed to be a trend to "undrape women's breasts."

Hughes refused to accede to Breen's suggestions. The fight was on. Hughes appealed Breen's decision to Hays. Although Hays supported Breen, he agreed to give a seal of approval to the film if Miss Russell's breasts were covered and if one line was eliminated. This line was one of the oddest aspects of the entire row. It had come into the script early in the shooting when Hughes rejected the sentence of Billy's, "A fair exchange is no robbery," to describe the swap of Rio for a horse. Hughes considered this too subtle. Instead, he wrote in: "You borrowed from me, I borrow from you." Breen took strong exception to the Hughes substitution. Furthman asked Breen if he would improvise a substitute. Breen offered: "Tit for tat." Furthman has never been able to understand what made Breen suggest this. Hughes was delighted. This was the line that Hays demanded stricken out. In its place went the line Hughes had written. As a final warning to Hughes, Hays wrote: "You understand, of course, that political censorship boards [state and local censors] are likely to insist upon additional eliminations." This proved to be a remarkable understatement. After considerable bickering and the appointment of committees to make studies, changes were made and a seal of approval was issued to *The Outlaw* on May 23, 1941.

This should have ended the trouble. With anyone but Hughes it would have. Actually this was only the beginning.

On February 5, 1943, Hughes opened *The Outlaw* in a single theater in San Francisco. The advertising accompanying this one-theater opening created more furor than the earlier censorship row. A women's group wrote to Hays: "A very disgusting portrayal of the feminine star was displayed throughout the San Francisco Bay section on large billboards."

Many who had never seen the picture and who were a long way from San Francisco began writing letters at the suggestion of Parent-Teachers' groups. Heads of the movie industry complained to Breen that their own advertising executives considered the Hughes advertisements a form of unfair competition. Darryl F. Zanuck, then head of the Twentieth Century-Fox studio, wrote to

Breen: "I have a hell of a job keeping the boys in line . . . The whole [advertising] campaign on this picture is a disgrace to the industry." The San Francisco police prepared arrest warrants. After conferences with the district attorney the advertisements were withdrawn. The picture, after closing in San Francisco, vanished. The relief in the movie industry was premature. Hughes had not given up. He was just too busy with war work.

Two years and eleven months later, on December 28, 1945, Hughes returned to his movie war with the censors. The movie industry code provided, as he knew, that advertising material must receive code approval. Accordingly, he began to submit, over a period of several months, advertising material for *The Outlaw*. Some of this material was rejected and changes were requested in other layouts.

Then, in February of 1946, three years after *The Outlaw* had "closed," Hughes began cutting loose with a lurid advertising campaign that contained material rejected and disapproved and also some text and pictures that had never been submitted. He used newspapers, magazines, billboards and even sky writing. The screams of protest exceeded by far anything heard before or since. *Life* magazine reported: "The unmitigated vulgarity of the movie itself was outdone only by the offensiveness of its advertising. This Hughes personally prepared or directed, and he has the dubious distinction of having authored the slogan: 'HOW WOULD YOU LIKE TO TUSSLE WITH RUSSELL?' " This invitation underscored pictures of Miss Russell that highlighted large, considerably exposed breasts. With other similar pictures of Miss Russell were such lines as: "WHO WOULDN'T FIGHT FOR A WOMAN LIKE THIS?" Or: "THE GIRL WITH THE SUMMER-HOT LIPS . . . AND THE WINTER-COLD HEART." Or: "WHAT ARE THE TWO GREAT REASONS FOR JANE RUSSELL'S RISE TO STARDOM?"

Whereupon the code authority, infuriated by this breach of an agreement by Hughes, took an unprecedented action. It revoked the seal of approval for the movie. It charged Hughes had "not submitted for approval to the association all advertising and publicity matter used in connection with the advertisement and exploitation of 'The Outlaw' and in that [he] had used advertising and publicity material unapproved by the association." Hughes appealed to Hays and was turned down. He then filed suit against the Motion Picture Association in the United States District Court of New York City. He charged the association with violation of the anti-trust laws by conspiring in restraint of trade. He asked the court to prohibit the association from revoking its seal and from interfering with his advertising campaign for the picture.

He lost his court fight when Judge D. J. Bright issued a precedent-setting decision on June 27, 1946, that held: "Experience has shown that the industry can suffer as much from indecent advertising as from indecent pictures. Once a picture has been approved the public may properly assume that the advertisement and promotional matter is likewise approved. The blame for improper, salacious or false advertising is placed as much at the door of the association as of the producer."

On July 7, 1946, there was a shift of sympathy toward Hughes. But not because of his movie. He was critically injured in an accident while flying an experimental plane. It was thought he would die. But early in September he was reported "recovered." A few days later he was ordered to remove the association's seal of approval from all prints of *The Outlaw*. There had been reports that at some theaters the picture was being shown with a seal. The seal, in those days, was particularly important, because very few theaters would show a movie unless it had one.

Hughes was still defiant. He showed his movie without a seal in those theaters that would take it. His publicity man, using a free tie-in with postwar conditions, boasted: "*The Outlaw* proves conclusively that sex has not been rationed."

Now the political censors struck hard at the film. State after state demanded and obtained elimination of scenes and changes of dialogue. In Maryland, when the state censors at first banned the picture, the case was fought in the courts. A Baltimore judge ruled in favor of the ban, saying that Jane Russell's breasts "hung over the picture like a thunderstorm spread out over a landscape." Australia, Canada and Great Britain joined the American censors in attacking the film.

One of the special dialogue targets of the censors in this country was the exchange between Doc and Billy after Rio had kept the gunman warm in bed. Ohio wanted this conversation deleted entirely. New York settled for deletion of "Cattle don't graze after sheep." In Massachusetts the entire movie was banned for Sunday showing.

In Alberta, Canada, deletions were even demanded in the sequence of "coming attractions." In Ontario, the censors deleted, from the rape scene, the words of Billy to Rio as they struggled on the barn floor. Over and over again there were objections to views of the Russell breasts.

The producer was, on the basis of this uproar, justified in advertising *The Outlaw* as "The Most Daring Picture Ever Made." When the movie opened in a Los Angeles theater in 1946, the sidewalk in front of the theater was jammed by ten in the morning and the theater did not bother to show a second feature. The *Los Angeles Daily News* reported: "What packed them in was . . . an opportunity for anatomical research." The *Los Angeles Herald-Express* said: "The audience reacts with sounds more appropriate to smoking room literature than a public theater." The *Los Angeles Times* said: "Sex passages . . . go as far as any since the establishment of censorship, or farther."

Censors were not the only ones who drew verbal beads on *The Outlaw*. In Philadelphia, a theater withdrew the movie after Cardinal Dougherty declared that if it continued, all Catholics in the archdiocese would be told to boycott the theater for a year. In New Jersey, because of the showing of the picture, the New Jersey Conference of the Methodist Church called for the formation of a state board of censors. In Harrisburg, the Most Reverend George Lee Leech urged parents to keep children away from *The Outlaw*, which he called "a destructive and corrupting picture which glamorizes crime and immorality." The *Philadelphia Record* attacked the advertising as "that of a bawdy show." In Washington, the Department of Justice denied it would prosecute the Motion Picture Association for anti-trust violation. The Justice Department condemned the movie and praised the Production Code Administration.

Finally, all the deletions and changes required by the Hollywood censors were made. In 1949, the Motion Picture Association restored a seal of approval to the movie. The Legion of Decency changed its "Condemned" rating to "B"—morally objectionable in part for all. "This reclassification," said the legion, "is in accordance with the policy in effect since the formation of the Legion of Decency under which the rating of an objectionable film may be changed when morally offensive elements in it are eliminated or substantially lessened."

And now *The Outlaw* was free to circulate in theaters throughout the country. It proved that bad publicity, if there is enough of it, can be good box office.

The Russell-type cleavage seen in *The Outlaw* is no longer unique in the movie industry. Such Italian films as *La Dolce Vita*, and *Boccaccio 70* went beyond *The Outlaw*. But Howard Hughes and Jane Russell were the pioneers. In the words of Shurlock the Censor: "The breast exposure that caused the uproar in *The Outlaw* would not create much excitement today. Still Hughes corrupted the whole world on this mammary gland business. He started the exploitation of big breasts. He started the cinematic avalanche of breasts."

Regardless of Hughes's motives, he brought some refreshing honesty to Hollywood's approach to sex. He made the American public laugh a little at its own prudery about the female breast. If ever a cinematic Rabelais emerges from Hollywood, he will be indebted to this unusual industrialist. Hughes lacked artistry. But he was not afraid to show, on a movie screen, that sex, even without a license, can be fun.

The most vital point raised by Hughes was obscured by the clamor about cleavage. Hughes said, in effect, that the censorship code is illegal, regardless of its voluntary nature. Neither the newspapers nor the magazines, so justifiably fearful of any censorship, explored this point in their editorial fulminations against Hughes and *The Outlaw*. Some extremely knowledgeable lawyers claim that a strong case can be made that the agreement setting up the code is a conspiracy in restraint of trade. It can certainly be argued, as we have seen, that the code was established by the industry only under enormous outside pressure and with extreme reluctance. That movie moguls agreed to a code of censorship for economic, rather than artistic, reasons is also immaterial. Suppose the country's newspapers were to set up a censorship code for the entire industry. Would that make censorship of the press legal? The test is not whether the signatories of a censorship code abide by it. Or even if it is voluntary. For volition is typical of conspiracy in restraint of trade.

For the time being it is easier for movie-makers to abide by the censorship code, forcing changes in interpretation or, rarely, in the code itself. But, inevitably, some producer or independent movie company will seek to determine in the Supreme Court, without becoming involved in peripheral sideshows, whether voluntary censorship by industry-wide agreement is more legal than censorship by the government. When that day comes it will be interesting to see how much, if any, credit will go to Howard Hughes and *The Outlaw*. It will be the height of irony, even for Hollywood, if consideration of the moral implications of voluntary censorship stem from this movie that was least likely to succeed in Sunday school.

2. *Indemity, Eternity, Plus Two*

While *The Outlaw* was grabbing headlines—and photos—another censorship fight was simmering behind the scenes in Hollywood. That it never attracted the attention *The Outlaw* did was partly due to the secrecy with which the intrigues were conducted. Face-saving for censors became easier, and an exciting saga of adultery and murder was served up on the nation's screens without any public awareness of the struggles that had gone on in the background or the censorship issues involved.

Any newspaper reader has run across stories about a wife and her lover who join to murder her husband. He has read it so many times it is a cliché. The only things he looks for are why and how the poor husband was dispatched. Was it for money? Love? Perhaps even out of boredom? And back in the thirites, when scandal, despite—or perhaps because of—the Depression and the Roosevelt Revolution, received more space and pictures than it does today, most adults and adolescents were almost experts on this type of crime.

Yet, when such a story was suggested as a movie in 1935, it started ten years of bickering between movie producers and Hollywood censors. Today *Double Indemnity* is just an exciting murder movie. It is not regarded as a threat to morality. It is difficult to imagine that *Double Indemnity* was a trail-blazer in movie history.

Double Indemnity is important in the story of American movie censorship—and movie trends—for two reasons. First, it was the first movie in which both the male and female protagonists were thorough villains. Second, *Double Indemnity* paved the way for America's twentieth-century successor to the erudite Sherlock Holmes—the tough-talking omniscient private eye. James M. Cain, author of the novel on which the book was based, must have been surprised at the Hollywood ruckus. For as a book it did not begin to create the stir of such other Cain novels as *The Postman Always Rings Twice*.

The plot as originally suggested for a movie went as follows. A married woman and her lover murder her husband for his insurance. Eventually, the woman confesses the murder to investigators from the insurance company who withhold the information from the police because the police have already called the death an accident and do not want to be bothered. The couple leaves the United States and later commits joint suicide.

Looking back on the hectic history of the conversion of this book into a movie, it seems as though it could not have taken place during the third and fourth decades of the twentieth century. The arguments raised by Hollywood's censors seem more characteristic of Victorian England than of the American literary ferment that produced the Group Theatre on Broadway and the incendiary realism of James T. Farrell's *Studs Lonigan* trilogy and John Steinbeck's *The Grapes of Wrath*.

The struggle over *Double Indemnity* in Hollywood began on October 9, 1935, when Maurice Revnes, of Metro-Goldwyn-Mayer, sent a letter to Breen asking him to read the book and to advise "at the earliest possible date, as to whether we will be able to make it as it stands or whether you could suggest any changes that would make it possible to get past the censors with it."

The very next day Breen rushed off a letter to Mayer, then boss of the Metro studio, saying: "I regret to inform you that, because of a number of elements inherent in the story in its present form, it is our judgment that the story is in violation of provisions of the Production Code and, as such, is almost certain to result in a picture which we would be compelled to reject if, and when, such a picture is presented for approval."

He summarized the plot and pointed out it was "replete with explicit details of the planning of the murder and the effective commission of the crime, thus definitely violating the Code provisions which forbid the presentation of 'details of crime.' "

Breen raised objections to the central characters themselves. "The leading characters are murderers who cheat the law and die at their own hands. . . . It may be argued that one of these criminals is, in a sense, glorified by his confession to save the girl he loves." This was a reference to the fact that the murderer falls in love with the stepdaughter of his accomplice and confesses when he realizes the circumstantial evidence points to the girl's sweetheart.

"The story," Breen continued, "deals improperly with an illicit and adulterous sex relationship. The general low tone and sordid flavor of this story make it, in our judgment, thoroughly unacceptable for screen production before mixed audiences in the theater. I am sure you will agree that it is most important to avoid what the Code calls 'the hardening' of audiences, especially those who are young and impressionable, to the thought and fact of crime."

Copies of this letter were sent to Paramount, Fox, Warner Brothers and Columbia, all of which were showing interest in the project.

The next chapter of this tale began on September 21, 1943, eight years later, when Paramount sent to the censors a new version that was part outline and part script. In this approach, prepared by Billy Wilder and Charles Brackett, the murderer kills his accomplice; then, though mortally wounded by her, talks his confession into a dictaphone at the insurance office. By this time the insurance investigator is closing in on him, and he collapses just as the investigator arrives.

Breen's reaction to this version was entirely different. Presumably, during the passing years, details of crime had become more common and adultery was no longer quite as objectionable in the movies. In addition, the suicide, to which religious groups usually take strong objection, had been eliminated and the insurance investigator had not, in effect, connived with a pair of murderers to permit their escape.

This time Breen's objections were minor and easily remedied. He pointed out that in one scene the wife was wearing a bath towel in a manner that was too revealing. He suggested that the towel "should certainly go below her knees." This was done. Then there was a line, in the lingo of the novel—and of the private eye brigades that were to follow—that the censor did not like. A lady, instead of being told to sit down, was asked to "park your south end." The more polite form was substituted.

What began as an argument about morals in *Double Indemnity* ended in a quibble about words, a pattern that is fairly common in censorship matters. However, it prepared the way for the next step in censorial tolerance. In *Double Indemnity*, though the adulterers were killed for their sins, their adultery was examined with an unusual degree of candor. How long would it be before neither party to adultery need be seriously punished? Before it was conceded that the shortcomings of the husband could justify adultery?

The answer came six years after *Double Indemnity* ended its censorship travails and became a critical and box office triumph. It was now 1951, and this time not only the censors but the literary and journalistic worlds became engaged in heated controversy. The movie was *From Here to Eternity*, based on the novel by James Jones. The furor became so loud and widespread that *Life* magazine wrote an editorial entitled "From Here to Obscenity."

The book, which dealt with life in the peacetime army before Pearl Harbor, was loaded with four-letter words, some of its action took place in a brothel and it included an adulterous relationship between an enlisted man and the wife of his commanding officer. It had brutality galore and, in general, offended the army's top brass. In short, this was hardly the type of book that anyone could imagine passing the Hollywood code in 1951.

Yet two years later the movie, produced by Buddy Adler, directed by Fred Zinnemann, written by Dan Taradash, was hailed by critics with ecstatic reviews. It went on to win eight Oscar awards and to become one of the big money-makers in movie history. What had seemed absurd even to attempt became the dream of all movie-makers—a film that was an artistic and financial success and broke new ground in the field of movie-making.

Looking back on the story of *From Here to Eternity* nearly ten years after the Oscar awards were gathered, Geoffrey Shurlock appraised the movie in terms of its significance in the history of movie censorship. "It was the first time," he declared, "that a novel of such notoriety, a novel considered by many reputable men to be obscene, was made into a movie. It proved that intelligent producers, directors and writers do not have to be afraid of any book. It proved that there were men in Hollywood who had good taste and an understanding of the artistic values of a book. We received a good deal of praise for the way the movie was made. Actually, the movie was a triumph for those who made it and for Hollywood. It gave to others the courage to try projects of which they might otherwise have been afraid. And it gave us the courage to work with such men."

The man who started the idea of making the book into a movie was the late Harry Cohn, then president of Columbia Pictures, a man notorious for his uncouthness, vulgarity, ruthlessness. Taradash recalls that at one of the many post-midnight sessions on the script, Cohn declared with his usual explosive energy: "We're going to get away with everything we can get away with." And yet, for some apparently inexplicable reason, he had selected as director the sensitive, artistic and tenacious Fred Zinnemann. This is one of those Hollywood paradoxes that can never be explained by pundits who reduce Hollywood to types and formulae. From the time that Cohn made his first inquiry of the Hollywood censors, until the movie was finished a year later, sixteen script revisions were required.

The first letter from Breen to Cohn about the original script was most discouraging. "We feel," he wrote, "that the adulterous relationship between Karen [the wife of the officer] and Warden [the enlisted man] is handled without any recognition of the immorality of their relationship. As we discussed the other day, we feel it will be necessary to have a strong voice for morality by which their immoral relationship will be denounced and the proper moral evaluation of it expressed."

During one of the discussions of this point Taradash exploded. "What do you want me to do?" he shouted. "Have her walk around with a sign saying: 'I have sinned'!" The solution, eventually, was to include a conversation between Karen [Deborah Kerr] and Warden [Burt Lancaster] in which she says the relationship was wrong, and another conversation between her and her rather loathsome husband in which she says she and her husband deserve one another. For reasons that remained mysterious to Mr. Taradash, no punishment was required for Warden. "I guess it was thought that the fact that he lost his love was punishment enough." The same sort of reasoning operated in connection with the whore who was making hash of morals with another enlisted man. He died, so it was adjudged that she was punished. Incidentally, the censor's objection to the inclusion of a brothel was met by making it a social "club." Curses were eliminated. "I felt," said Taradash, "that the vitality of Jones's dialogue did not need curses for the dramatic medium of film." However, the screen writer was chagrined when these hard-boiled soldiers were not permitted to say "hell" or "for God's sake."

One of the most vivid scenes in the movie was the sensual kissing, clutching and rolling of Karen and Warden on the beach. Breen suggested: "It would be well to have either Karen or Warden put on a beach robe or some other type of clothing before they go into embrace." The picture-makers fought and won this round and the lovers remained in bathing suits.

The handling of brutality in this movie was of particular significance because the entire subject of violence and brutality was to become a burning national issue in television during the sixties. The book had a good deal to say about brutality in army life. To demonstrate how sadistic it could be the author had one of the enlisted men fatally beaten by a guard in the stockade. During rewrites of the script Cohn insisted that there was nothing to do but to show this terrible beating in the movie. But Zinnemann and Taradash, who understood the impact of a camera better than the studio boss, worked out the idea that was finally used. The enlisted man was shown entering the stockade. He was shown leaving the stockade. The camera vividly caught his changed appearance. And the soldier quickly explained what had happened.

It is not often that Hollywood is a source of poetic justice. But in *From Here to Eternity* it was. When Dan Taradash was first approached to do the movie, he knew that throughout Hollywood nearly everyone believed it could never be done without ruining the book. As contract time neared, even Cohn seemed a bit dubious. Taradash was so convinced it could be made into a good movie that he offered to take a cut in his fee in return for 2½ per cent of the profits. Cohn jumped at this offer. The result was that Taradash received $32,500 for his work on the script—and more than $250,000 as his share of the profits so far.

For all their success in easing interpretations of the code and helping movies grow, *Double Indemnity, From Here to Eternity* and *The Outlaw* did not force actual changes in the code. That remained for Otto Preminger. It was fitting that this distinction should be his. For no man in the American movie industry has clashed more heatedly—and more successfully—with movie censors than this producer-director. Since Preminger is not popular in Hollywood, there are always persons in the movie industry who will insist that his disagreements on censorship are calculated as much for publicity as for integrity or art. The fact is, however, that Preminger is regarded with considerable respect by the Hollywood censors. This esteem was raised by his double victory, unique in Hollywood, over his movies *The Moon Is Blue* and *The Man with the Golden Arm*. The first film made the code and its censors seem ridiculous and the second, as we have already seen, forced a revision of the code.

The Moon Is Blue was an innocuous comedy, based on the play by F. Hugh Herbert. It was denied a seal because it dealt frivolously with the subject of adultery, though no adultery occurred in the movie. Nor was it salacious by any Hollywood standards when it was released in 1953. Its importance lay in the fact that Preminger, backed by United Artists, released the movie without a seal. This was extraordinary for an American producer, backed by a major American movie company. Until then, it had been assumed that this sort of rebellion spelled economic suicide because so many theaters in the United States refuse to show any movie that does not have a seal of approval. The movie grossed $6,000,-000 on an investment of $450,000.

What had been a suspicion, created by the success of some foreign movies that played in art houses without a seal, now became a certainty. There were very many Americans who did not care whether a movie had a seal of approval or not; who used their own judgment. And, in addition, as had long been known, there were many Americans who were attracted to any movie that was attacked for moral reasons by censoring bodies.

Then, three years later, Preminger turned out *The Man with the Golden Arm*. It too was refused a seal of approval. This was a movie about dope addiction, based on the novel by Nelson Algren. At that time the movie industry's censorship regulations forbade any picture dealing with dope addiction. This film also was financed and released by United Artists. It was distributed without a seal of approval and, though not as successful as *The Moon Is Blue*, showed a profit.

The arguments about these movies became furious within the industry at top executive echelons. Other major movie companies felt that United Artists was jeopardizing the entire censorship structure by violating a pledge. United Artists was a member of the Motion Picture Association of America. All members were committed not to release a movie unless it had a seal of approval. The furor became so bitter that United Artists quit the association.

United Artists and Preminger then carried the fight one step further. They demanded that the code be changed to permit movies on narcotics addiction. It was pointed out that the Catholic Legion of Decency had not objected to *The Man with the Golden Arm*. Furthermore, it was apparent that this restriction on movies had outlived its usefulness; it was acting as a deterrent to the making of films on a subject that had become an important social problem and that was dealt with frequently in other serious media such as newspapers and magazines.

This one picture brought about reconsideration of the code and it was changed to permit movies dealing with dope addiction.

A few years later, when the arguments about *The Moon Is*

Blue and *The Man with the Golden Arm* had subsided, United Artists rejoined the association. This should have ended the story of Otto Preminger's double defiance of the censorship code.

But very quietly, in 1962, United Artists began making strange moves. Through a friend of one of its top executives it sounded out Shurlock on the possibility of obtaining seals of approval for these movies so long after they had finished their runs. The head of Hollywood's censorship board said he could see no objection. *The Moon Is Blue*, he conceded, should never have been denied a seal in the first place. And the change in the code eliminated the objection to *The Man with the Golden Arm*. The late Eric Johnston, then head of the Motion Picture Association, said he saw no objection to granting the seals.

And so, late in July of 1962, the seals were quietly approved for the two movies. Preminger said later that he did not know the seals had been requested until after they were granted. Never before had the Production Code Administration reversed itself on movies after they had completed their runs in theaters.

United Artists wished to reissue the pictures as a double bill; and as noted previously with seals, the films could be shown in all movie houses and at a United States military establishment. United Artists was also thinking of leasing the pictures to television. Networks dislike handling a movie that has no seal. The company was also looking forward to the possibility that pay television might become a reality.

For all their differences in plot, style and subject, *Double Indemnity, From Here to Eternity, The Moon Is Blue* and *The Man with the Golden Arm* had one thing in common. They forced the watchdogs of the code to become more aware of the considerable changes in American morals, mores and educational standards since the early thirties when the code was written. The movie public was not shocked because a woman and her lover killed her husband. Americans were quite capable of being exposed, without subsequent trauma, to a movie that portrayed honestly the seamy side of life in the pre-Pearl Harbor army or that showed an officer's wife committing adultery with a sergeant. The movie public was mature enough to know the difference between harmless flirtation and seduction. It also knew that dope addicts suffered. All of these movies compelled enforcers and interpreters of the code to re-examine their own values and realize there was more to a marriage than a kiss; more to life's anguish than raised voices or an occasional fist fight. Even under voluntary censorship, these movies made clear, the censor must be guided by the spirit more than the letter of the code.

3. A Streetcar Named Milestone

Most important of all movies in forcing censors to broaden their interpretation of the code and to consider the realities of American behavior was *A Streetcar Named Desire*. This film was truly a Hollywood milestone. Now ordinarily movie-makers are not reluctant to use the word "milestone." If a movie is shown on a screen three inches wider than any previous screen, it is a milestone. If a star who has been playing ingenue leads for three decades finally plays a middle-aged woman, it is a milestone. If a new device is concocted to depict, with greater realism, a prehistoric ape carrying off a scantily-clad starlet, that too is a milestone. Short memory, self-deception and exaggeration are fundamental to Hollywood hucksterism, and the milestone is the glowing symbol.

How very odd then that on the one occasion when a studio could properly have claimed the right to a milestone, when all Hollywood, in fact, could have basked, by reflection, in extraordinary cinematic accomplishment, the reaction was one of secrecy and virtual terror. Not until Hollywood had paid its customary tribute of cowardice, not until the pressure groups had been appeased, did the movie capital publicly take pride in having made a fine movie from Tennessee Williams' Pulitzer Prize play, *A*

Streetcar Named Desire. And even after the critics had acclaimed this picture, Hollywood did not trumpet the point that made this picture a true cinematic milestone in the United States. For this was the first film to win a seal of approval from the movie industry's censors despite the conviction of the guardians of the movie code that this was not a "family picture."

"Whatever has been creeping in on us in the form of widening censorship pressures began with *A Streetcar Named Desire*," says Shurlock. "For the first time we were confronted with a picture that was obviously not family entertainment. Before then we had considered *Anna Karenina* a big deal. *Streetcar* broke the barrier. Other studios had asked us for advisory opinions on *Streetcar* and we had said we did not see how it could be done. *Streetcar* made us think things through. Tennessee Williams was something new to movies. Elia Kazan's approach was something new to us. We realized it was possible to treat rape on the screen. The code has never said that there was any book that could not be made into a movie. The stage got a shock from Tennessee Williams. We got twice the shock. Now we know that a good deal of what we decide in censoring movies is not morality but taste. It began with *Streetcar*."

The story of how *Streetcar* rode the labyrinthine Hollywood tracks is important for other reasons. It shows clearly how the twin forces of business and art can be in violent conflict in the American movie capital. It shows how much courage, determination and resourcefulness are required by those who would try something new in Hollywood. The story of the strange trip *Streetcar* made from Broadway to Hollywood to the nation's movie houses reveals how different groups, all of them with good intentions, can thwart the artistic convictions of the most talented writers and directors. It demonstrates also how hypocrisy and cynicism can flourish or be conquered. No one can pretend to appraise movie censorship without knowing the story of *A Streetcar Named Desire.*

During the late spring and early summer of 1949, a number of producers and movie studios showed great interest in making a movie of the Broadway smash hit. But they were also fearful that, in the transition to the screen, the play might have to be altered so drastically to win a seal of approval from the censors that it would become a box office failure, let alone an artistic mockery. They were worried about the plot that Williams employed as a sort of clothesline on which to hang the poetic language in which he deplored the destruction of the beautiful by the bestial.

The play is the story of Blanche du Bois, a sensitive woman from the South, whose fiancé commits suicide when she learns he is a homosexual. She becomes a teacher after his death and, in her misery and loneliness is promiscuous in seeking out the companionship of young men. The play opens when Blanche, now middle-aged, has been fired from her job and virtually run out of town. She seeks refuge with her married sister in New Orleans. While her sister is giving birth in a hospital, Blanche, already on the verge of a complete nervous breakdown, is raped by her sister's husband and becomes deranged.

Torn between the desire to produce a money-making and artistic movie and the fear of offending powerful pressure groups, interested studios and producers sought the advice of Breen, who had not yet retired as administrator of the industry's self-censoring body. His responses were discouraging. Thus, he told Paramount that, if it tried to make *Streetcar* into a movie, the homosexuality and rape would have to be eliminated. More significant was his letter to Irene Selznick, who had produced the play and was interested in the movie prospects. "You will have in mind," Breen wrote to Mrs. Selznick, "that the provisions of the Production Code are quite patently set down in the knowledge that motion pictures, unlike stage plays, appeal to mass audiences; to the mature and the immature; the young and the not-so-young.

"Because these motion pictures are exhibited rather indiscriminately among all kinds of classes of audiences, there is a frank acknowledgment on the part of the industry, of a peculiar responsibility to this conglomeration of patrons. Material which may be perfectly valid for dramatization and treatment on the stage may be questionable, or even completely unacceptable, when presented in a motion picture."

Here, clearly stated, by the leading authority on movie censorship at that time, was a variation of the philosophy that movies are suited to the mentality of twelve-year-olds. Here was the conviction that some material is not for the American screen, regardless of its artistic merit or the taste shown in making the movie. The subject itself was censorable, regardless of the film's beauty or sensitivity. The concept of the adult movie was, obviously, not yet acknowledged by Hollywood's chief censor in 1950.

Nevertheless, one man was determined to take a chance. He was Charles K. Feldman, a leading talent agent, a Hollywood profession that is often greatly scorned as "flesh peddlers." Feldman persuaded Warner Brothers to join him in the project. It was agreed that the screenplay would be done by Tennessee Williams and directed by Elia Kazan, who had staged the play.

Before the shooting began, Kazan suggested to Williams that he make the script more suitable to movie technique. The director's idea was to open the film in Blanche's home town. But he soon realized that in his desire to make the play more cinematic he would weaken the drama. This script was discarded and it was decided to adhere closely to the play.

At first there was little trouble with the Hollywood censors— merely a matter of eliminating damns and hells. Then Breen turned to the more serious matter of homosexuality. He won his point. In a letter to Breen, Kazan wrote: "I wouldn't put the homosexuality back in the picture if the code had been revised last night and it was now permissible. I don't want it. I prefer debility and weakness over any kind of suggestion of perversion."

This concession did not end Breen's request for changes. He then attacked his second major point, rape. He insisted the rape must be thrown out of the film. It was at this point that Williams, who had reluctantly agreed to other changes, decided he would not permit his play to be shattered or branded as smut. In the countless bitter exchanges between movie censors and movie-makers, it is doubtful whether there is any letter that expresses more movingly the anguish an artist faces when he considers his work unjustifiably censored. Here Williams confessed the humiliations he had endured and the compromises that had been extorted from him and displayed a ferocity of attack unique in a Hollywood where writers are purchased like so many word carpenters.

" 'Streetcar,' " the playwright wrote to the censor, "is an extremely and peculiarly moral play, in the deepest and truest sense of the term. . . . The rape of Blanche by Stanley is a pivotal, integral truth in the play, without which the play loses its meaning, which is the ravishment of the tender, the sensitive, the delicate, by the savage and brutal forces of modern society. It is a poetic plea for comprehension. . . .

"Please remember, also, that we have already made great concessions which we felt were dangerous, to attitudes which we thought were narrow. In the middle of preparations for a new play, I came out to Hollywood to rewrite certain sequences to suit the demands of your office. No one involved in this screen production has failed to show you the co-operation, even the deference that has been called for.

"But now we are fighting for what we think is the heart of the play, and when we have our backs against the wall—if we are forced into that position—none of us is going to throw in the towel! We will use every legitimate means that any of us has at his or her disposal to protect the things in this film which we think cannot be sacrificed, since we feel that it contains some very important truths about the world we live in."

With Williams and Kazan fighting hard, Breen yielded on this major issue. But he then proceeded to harry the director and author for lesser, but still important, changes. He wanted the ending changed. In the play Stella (Blanche's sister) refuses to accept Blanche's (Vivien Leigh) story of rape. She (Kim Hunter) forces herself to believe that this is the hallucination of an insane woman. In this she is supported by her upstairs neighbor who assures her: "Life has to go on. No matter what happens, you've got to keep on going." She is then consoled by her husband (Marlon Brando), who caresses her lovingly while soothing her with endearments. In a mood of sensuality, supported by background music of piano and trumpet by Alex North, it becomes clear that the episode of Blanche du Bois is to be put behind them and life is to return to normal, with the bestial unpunished for its annihilation of the beautiful.

This ending was unacceptable to Breen. The husband had to be punished for the rape. Williams finally came up with a compromise.

He suggested that Stella deliver the following speech to her infant when Blanche is led off to the asylum. "We're not going back in there," she murmurs to the baby. "Not this time. We're never going back. Never, never back, never back again." Thus the twelve-year-olds could believe Stella was leaving her husband. But the rest of the audience would realize it was just an emotional outburst of the moment.

Williams and Kazan were now convinced that the censoring of *Streetcar* was finished. Kazan began work on another picture. Williams returned to New York to work on his other play. What they did not know was the censoring power of pressure groups. This is an often ambiguous and covert power that prefers not to call itself censorship. But the result is often the same. The pressure group says it finds something objectionable in a picture. It makes it clear it will try to hurt this picture at the box office because of the obnoxious material. Then the bargaining begins. The producer and studio first try to defend the picture. If this fails and the pressure is great enough, possible changes are discussed. If this does not work, the producer and studio may agree to delete the offending sections. In some cases the pressure group can be assuaged by an agreement that the picture will not be shown to children unless accompanied by adults. At the other extreme the pressure group may find the picture so thoroughly vulgar it will not bargain.

In the case of *Streetcar* there was obviously room for bargaining. So when it became known to Warner Brothers and Feldman that the Legion of Decency was unhappy and planned to give the picture a "C" or "Condemned" rating, studio and producer were terribly upset. They were convinced that a "C" rating would keep many Catholics away from the film. So negotiations began. Feldman asked Kazan to meet with representatives of the Legion of Decency. Reluctantly, Kazan went to the session.

"We did not see eye to eye," he recalled afterward. "At the meeting I had a hostile attitude. It is hard to suppress anger when you are being judged about something you think worthwhile. The leader of the legion group at these talks was always stressing that he was not a censor; that he was not demanding, just asking. He had a sorrowful attitude. Very soft-spoken. So sorrowful. He was damned patronizing. 'I am not asking you to do anything,' he would say. 'I'm just telling you what we think.' I had the impression that they had watched the picture in a different way from anyone else. Williams and I told Feldman we were not going to do what they wanted."

Once more Kazan thought he had won. But there is another phase of movie censorship that neither Kazan nor Williams had apparently considered. In the movie business, the studio does not need the permission of a writer or director to make cuts in a film after it has been shot. The power to make changes in the movie after the filming is known as "the right of the final cut." A very few movie directors can reserve this power for themselves. And Kazan was not one of them. Consequently, a short time after his conference with Legion of Decency representatives, he was surprised to hear a rumor that the film cutter who had worked with him on the editing of *Streetcar* had been sent to New York from Hollywood. Curiously at first, then anxiously, he began trying to learn why the cutter was in New York. The answers were reluctant and evasive, though Kazan was in Hollywood and presumably in a position to get information from those in authority.

"I decided to go to New York," he wrote later in *The New York Times*. "Here I was introduced to a prominent Catholic layman who informed me that he himself, giving time and thought and great care to the matter, had suggested the cuts in my picture. His presence was at the invitation of Warner Brothers and he had striven to build a bridge between the picture's artistic achievement —which he praised highly—and 'the primacy of the moral order,' as interpreted by himself, in conformity with the legion's standards. There had been no overt involvement of the legion, which had then passed the cut version."

All told, twelve cuts suggested by the Catholic layman were accepted by Warner Brothers. Thus "on the mouth" was deleted from the line: "I would like to kiss you softly and sweetly on the mouth." Some close-ups were deleted because they allegedly indicated that Stella's relationship to her husband was "too carnal." Just before Stanley rapes Blanche he says: "You know, you might not be bad to interfere with." Kazan considered the deletion of this line particularly thoughtless because it showed for the first time that Stanley meant to harm his sister-in-law. "This obviously changes the interpretation of the character," Kazan still believes, "but how it serves the cause of morality is obscure to me, though I have given it much thought.

"Now Warner Brothers, as the owners of the film, had the right to make these—or any other—cuts," Kazan concedes. "From a business standpoint it is easy to understand why they acceded to them. The legion's point of view is also clear: they believe that certain things should be seen and others should not be seen by those who follow their dictates. If a picture, especially an important picture, can be brought into line with their code, they are naturally pleased. That leaves the public, the author and myself to be considered.

"I could not help wondering where this process left the moral responsibility of the makers of the picture, including the author and myself, or how the end result differed from direct censorship by the legion.

"I was more naïve then than I am now. I know now that they are not fighting monsters. They are just men. They are just worried about how much trouble they might get into and they want you to help them find a way out. If you put up strong resistance to studio executives they will give. Our attitude helped Warners fight against more changes. Warners just wanted a seal. They didn't give a damn about the beauty or artistic value of the picture. To them it was just a piece of entertainment. It was business, not art. They wanted to get the entire family to see the picture. They didn't want anything in the picture that might keep *anyone* away. At the same time they wanted it to be dirty enough to pull people in. The whole business was rather an outrage."

Out of this act of defiance of censorship and hypocrisy came a Hollywood concept new to talking movies—the idea that movies for adults were not only feasible but could be extremely profitable. This was a powerful blow at the undisputed king of American movies, the "family" picture, that syrupy, maudlin combination of pseudo conflict and stock characters that reached perfection in the

Andy Hardy movies of the forties. Neither the code nor the Legion of Decency could be given as excuses any longer by those who said it was useless to try to make good movies. The way was now open for men of courage, taste and artistry to make films that could elevate a business commodity to art.

3 | Pressures and politics

Censorship would be neither created nor sustained without pressure groups. Today these organizations are on the increase and one of their prime targets is the American movie. They constitute a form of censorship that is, in some ways, more dangerous than a code, because it can operate in secrecy with rules of its own making. These associations for persuasion may number either many millions or just a few hundred. Almost every adult American belongs to at least one pressure group that has influenced movies. Like all forms of censorship, these societies justify themselves by showing how they curb vulgarity, tastelessness, offenses to a minority. They all claim to have been formed for the loftiest principles. But they have also stifled Hollywood's artistic freedom and growth beyond estimate. And there is no limit to how powerful the nations's pressure groups can be when it comes to the movies. Highly developed publicity and advertising techniques, magnified by mass communication, have given them terrifying weapons against any art form and particularly one that caters to a mass market. They can concentrate with enormous impact on a single movie, or, more often, a single scene from a movie. Curiously, government departments and agencies, themselves so often badgered by such organizations, are showing an increasing tendency to interfere with the movies.

1. *Legion of Decency*

In the late summer of 1933, a visitor to the United States from Rome issued a statement that hit the nation's film-makers like an earthquake and has continued to reverberate in American movie circles. The speaker was the newly arrived Apostolic Delegate, the Most Reverend Amleto Giovanni Cicognani, making his first public talk. He said: "Catholics are called by God, the Pope, the bishops and the priests to a united and vigorous campaign for the purification of the cinema, which has become a deadly menace to morals."

By November of that year, a meeting of Catholic bishops had named an Episcopal Committee on Motion Pictures to implement the Apostolic Delegate's wishes. From this emerged the most important and effective pressure group the movie industry has to contend with—the Legion of Decency.

The power of the Legion of Decency has made it an instrument of fear in Hollywood and New York. The legion has also become a magnet for national controversy. It is conceded that the legion has the right to speak out on movie morality for Catholics. But millions of Protestants and Jews think they are being deprived, by the legion's intimidation of the movie industry, of opportunities to see certain subjects handled in a manner less offensive to them than to the legion. Then there is a smaller, but highly articulate contingent that regards all pressure groups in the arts as censors and all censors as evil. This element argues that if a movie violates the law it is up to the authorities to try the movie-maker in open court. Condemnation of a movie by extralegal or *sub rosa* methods worries these enemies of the legion.

Behind the arguments are certain basic questions. Are the activities of the Legion of Decency simply a case of narrow-mindedness and a grab for power? Or do they reflect an honest and respectable philosophy that conforms with accepted democratic tradition?

The bitterness—and sometimes bigotry—behind disagreements over the Legion of Decency has obscured two important facts. First, there was nothing haphazard about its formation. Second, many important non-Catholic groups aided in its organization, and Protestant leaders in particular extolled the legion after it went into action.

The legion was born of the same conditions we saw create Hollywood censors and a censorship code. It stemmed from the widespread discontent of American religious leaders with what they considered the immorality and irresponsibility of movie producers. In fact, Martin Quigley, one of the two men who, as we have seen, drafted the Hollywood censorship code in 1930, played an important part in the formation of the legion. It was Quigley who asserted the code could not work unless there was "sufficient pressure and support of public opinion to encourage or compel the industry at large to conform with the letter and spirit of the regulations." According to a doctoral thesis by the Rev. Paul A. Facey, a Jesuit, one of the lay Catholic leaders in the movement to set up the Legion of Decency was the same Joseph I. Breen who was appointed chief Hollywood censor by Will Hays in 1934, the year the legion went into action.

"It was no accident," wrote Father Facey, "that the Legion of Decency was directed and principally located with the Catholic Church; and it was not by chance that the Episcopal Committee directed the pressure of the Legion toward supporting the film industry's system of self-regulation according to the Production Code." In fact, a small group of American Catholic clergy and laymen persuaded the Apostolic Delegate to make his explosive statement in 1933.

It was important for the legion to win support of non-Catholics with similar aims. At that time the leading Protestant organization formed because of dissatisfaction with movies was the Federal Motion Picture Council in America, with the Rev. William Schaefe Chase as its general secretary. This group was mentioned favorably by Bishop John F. Noll, a member of the Catholic Episcopal Committee, and the chairman of the Committee, Archbishop

John T. McNicholas, wrote: "From all sections of the country, from all groups—Protestant, Jew, and those affiliated with no organized religion, and from countless Catholics—comes the word that the movement against the immoral cinema was too long delayed. It has not been possible to acknowledge all the communications expressing this thought which were sent to the members of the Episcopal Committee."

Father Facey noted that fifty-four Protestant and Jewish groups were helping the Legion of Decency campaign in this early period. *The Christian Century*, a Protestant Publication that has at times expressed views unpopular with Catholics, wrote: "It has been heartening to see the Protestant reaction to the launching of this Catholic crusade. . . . Thousands of Protestant ministers and laity . . . say 'Thank God that the Catholics are at last opening up on this foul thing as it deserves! What can we do to help?' "

That Protestant groups were astir in the campaign against immorality in movies before Catholics became active is conceded in a study of the Legion of Decency by two Jesuits, Father Gerald Kelly and Father John C. Ford. In an article in the September 1957 issue of *Theological Studies*, they wrote: "And it may be said to the credit of non-Catholics that their own efforts toward this goal antedate the efforts of organized Catholic bodies. The Catholic contribution was that in the very structure of the Church there existed a power of mobilizing opinion that no other religious or social group possessed."

The legion's power was so great that it mobilized more than opinion. It poised an economic threat. This was done by a pledge that committed supporters to avoid certain movies. Father Facey estimated that the pledge of the Legion of Decency, introduced in April 1934, had between seven and nine million signers. The first pledge was long and it was shortened by the bishops in November 1934 to read as follows:

"I condemn indecent and immoral pictures, and those which glorify crime and criminals.

"I promise to do all that I can to strengthen public opinion against the production of indecent and immoral films, and to unite with all who protest them.

"I acknowledge my obligation to form a right conscience about pictures that are dangerous to my moral life. As a member of the Legion of Decency, I pledge myself to remain away from them. I promise, further, to stay away altogether from places of amusement which show them as a matter of policy."

The next question was: who was to decide which movies were contrary to the pledge of the Legion of Decency? At the same time there arose the question as to whether lists were to be prepared with various categories of movies. Catholic clergy and laymen found these matters a subject for disagreement. "There is no doubt," wrote Archbishop McNicholas, "that the great anxiety of bishops and priests is to keep their people away from evil pictures. They have the obligation of instructing them to avoid the proximate occasion of sin. There is no difficulty from the standpoint of moral principles of publishing blacklists. There is, however, the practical question: Does the blacklisting of pictures bring people to see them in greater numbers, thereby making them more successful financially?"

The International Federation of Catholic Alumnae was already listing "recommended" movies, but not objectionable pictures. In Chicago, a diocesan group began listing both kinds of movies. Many Catholic diocesan papers began to reprint these lists. However, though the Catholic bishops recommended the list, it suggested it remain "informal" and "unofficial." By 1936 this job had been taken over by the International Federation of Catholic Alumnae and its reviewers became the official critics for the Legion of Decency. The federation was directed by a permanent executive secretary from the Archdiocese of New York who was directly accountable to the Episcopal Committee. The reviewers of the Catholic Alumnae were assisted by consulters of priests and laymen. The consulters reviewed the film when there was disagreement among the Catholic Alumnae. The final decision was made by the executive secretary. This is the method still in use today.

The classifications prepared by the Legion of Decency, as amended in 1957 and in 1963, are:

A-1: Morally unobjectionable for general patronage.
A-2: Morally unobjectionable for adults and adolescents.
A-3: Morally unobjectionable for adults.

A-4: Morally objectionable for adults, with reservations.
B: Morally objectionable in part for all.
C: Condemned.

The Legion of Decency points out "that, in deciding the ratings of the films, no consideration is given to artistic, technical or dramatic values. Only moral content is weighed."

By the end of 1934 the force of the Legion of Decency had already become apparent. The late André Sennwald, then movie critic of *The New York Times*, wrote: "The Legion of Decency has exerted a profound influence upon the activities of the film city, and it has performed a service to filmgoers everywhere by crippling the manufacture of such feeble-minded delicatessen as 'All of me,' 'Born to Be Bad,' 'Enlighten Thy Daughter,' 'The Life of Vergie Winters,' 'Limehouse Blues,' and a number of others which will hurt nobody by their presence on the Legion's blacklist. . . . There has been an obvious improvement in themes and a noticeable diminution in the kind of appalling cheapness and unintelligence which filmgoers deplore without regard to private allegiance of faith or creed." And in 1936, Pope Pius, in his encyclical *Vigilanti cura*, praised the Legion of Decency and declared that "the motion picture has shown improvement from the moral standpoint." He noted, at the same time, that artistic values had not been impaired by the campaign of the Legion of Decency and that predictions of financial suffering by the movie industry because of the reforms had not materialized.

This encyclical, which is of enormous importance in determining the Catholic position toward a film further asserted: "The bishops of the whole world will take care to make clear to the leaders of the motion picture industry that the force of a power of such universality as the cinema can be directed with great utility to the highest ends of individual and social improvement. Why, indeed, should there be a question of merely avoiding evil? Why should the motion picture simply be a means of diversion and light relaxation to occupy an idle hour? With its magnificent power, it can and must be a light and positive guide to what is good."

The harmonious relationship between Hollywood and the Legion of Decency began to degenerate after the war. It was in the postwar period that movies began to be produced that made the legion—and many non-Catholic clergy and civic groups—increasingly indignant. These were the films that dealt with violence, sex and moral degeneracy.

The new kinds of films were brought on by several causes. First, as in most postwar periods, there was a decided change in public morals, with a greater tolerance for what had been condemned in the thirties and early forties. This was similar to what had happened after World War I. Second, television replaced movies as the chief mass medium of entertainment and movie attendance fell from nearly 80 million a week in the United States, to about 40 million a week. To win back the former moviegoers from television, Hollywood tried making sensational films. In this field television could not match movies. Third, foreign films, which treated sex and morals with more maturity, began making inroads into American movie audiences. Fourth, as Americans began making an increasing number of movies abroad, they became less dominated by the letter of the Hollywood code. Fifth, the courts, in judicial decisions, accorded movie-makers greater latitude. Sixth, as we have seen, the Hollywood censors, reflecting this entirely new atmosphere, began judging movies, not so much by individual lines or scenes, but by the over-all taste with which a subject was handled.

All of these factors influenced the legion in turn to show an increasing tolerance for adult movies done in good taste. Catholics as well as Protestants were saying that the legion had fallen behind the times. The legion became increasingly aware that outside the church it was becoming a subject of some derision. For quite frequently the legion was forced to give its A-1 classification to simpering comedy or domestic drama little better than soap opera simply because those movies were unobjectionable. Thus the legion was being placed in the embarrassing position of seeming to suggest that such movies were what it considered best for the movie industry and for Catholic entertainment.

It was to avoid, or at least minimize, this ridicule that the legion amended its regulations in 1957 and 1963 to permit itself to give special classification to such movies as *La Dolce Vita, Martin*

Luther, Anatomy of a Murder, Lolita, Advise and Consent and *Suddenly Last Summer*. It thus did not have to condemn them outright.

The growing tolerance in the legion's classifications did not ease the friction between Hollywood and the Catholics. Thus, in November of 1960, the Catholic bishops of the United States issued a statement noting that "the increased emphasis which films are placing upon unhealthy sex and brutal violence has aroused the deep social concern of religious leaders of all faiths, of public officials, and of respected critics and journalists in the secular and religious press." The bishops added: "Not insignificant has been the insistent cry, heard within the very ranks of the motion picture industry itself, for a reform and for a return to the letter and spirit of the Production Code. We hope that these cries will not fall on deaf ears, for the Code can be and should be a bastion of strength for the industry against morally and socially irresponsible producers and exhibitors who, if unchecked, will feed and pander to the baser instincts of the public."

Priests and educators were advised to urge Catholics to study carefully the Legion of Decency's classifications of films before going to a theater. "Parents particularly," said the bishops, "must be reminded that they are seriously delinquent in the fulfillment of their parental duties if they permit their children to attend films not approved for them. Indeed, indiscriminate attendance at any film by young or old can only manifest a pathetic disregard for good moral and artistic taste."

Between the pressure of the Legion of Decency to raise moral standards and the apparent appeal of the box office for greater latitude in morals and sex, the movie industry and the Legion of Decency found themselves, with increasing frequency, involved in bargaining discussions about the classification of movies. These meetings are held in secrecy and, though they deal with only a minority of the total of American films, they concern the most controversial of movies.

According to Msgr. Thomas F. Little, executive secretary of the legion, his organization never initiates such negotiations. The producer of the movie, or his representative, generally approaches the legion, either directly or indirectly, when it is obvious the film may not get a favorable classification by the legion. Very frequently the producer is alerted to this possibility by the movie industry's censors. Sometimes either Shurlock or Vizzard, his chief assistant, will act as intermediary between the producer with the Legion of Decency. Often the go-between is Quigley. This is most always at the request of the producer. Such talks get under way a few months before the movie is ready for release so that the producer will have time, if necessary to make changes to placate the legion and thereby get a more favorable rating. Privately, producers, when they make changes to suit the legion, may say harsh things. But publicly they prefer not to let it be known that they yielded to the legion. They may even speak admiringly of the legion.

Lolita underwent what Msgr. Little called "changes of a vital nature" in order to avoid a "Condemned" rating. In the case of *The Chapman Report* Warner Brothers, long before the picture was released, opened discussions with the legion. "They realized," said the head of the legion, "that they had a hot potato." Important alterations were made and the film avoided being condemned by the legion. *Elmer Gantry* also would have been faced with a "Condemned" rating if United Artists had not agreed to label the picture as not suitable for children.

Spartacus as it was shown to some reporters before its release contained a scene that indicated a Roman general (Sir Laurence Olivier) was a homosexual who wanted to acquire a male slave (Tony Curtis) for sexual gratification. This scene was killed because of the legion. Some of the bloodiest violence was also eliminated for the same reason.

The Nun's Story had no trouble with the code. The script was sent to the legion, which urged elimination of a scene showing a mother superior urging a nun to flunk her exam. Robert Anderson, who did the screenplay, argued against it. "They were afraid," he recalled, "this scene might, when shown in a movie, create the impression that this behavior by the mother superior was typical. Vizzard acted as mediator, trying to help us. It was a long, heartbreaking battle. The legion agreed to let it stand."

Then the argument got down to dialogue. "At times the discussion narrowed down to a single word. Thus, there was one line saying: 'We can always cheat our sisters and ourselves, but we cannot cheat God.' The legion wanted 'cheat' changed to 'trick'." Both the writer and Fred Zinnemann, the director, remained obdurate and "cheat" remained. Recalling his meetings with members of the Legion of Decency, Anderson said: "They were nice, but adamant."

The late Jerry Wald, one of the most prolific of Hollywood producers, insisted he had little trouble either with the code or the legion. He pointed out that his *Peyton Place* received an "A" rating. "The big problem," he once said, "is how not to offend the innocent and yet not antagonize the intelligent. Still, the Catholic Church has a tendency to magnify things sometimes."

The Rev. Harold C. Gardiner, in his lucid book *Catholic Viewpoint on Censorship,* presents the Catholic argument for the legion. He starts by pointing out that man has God-given tendencies to live a communal existence and at the same time to exercise his individual will. The impulses can conflict and therefore an authority is needed to make compromises. This authority, also instilled by God, must be loved as well as respected. Authority imposes regulations and penalties. It can, by abuse, become coercion and tyranny. But it is the law, not the legislator or enforcer, that is important because the ultimate purpose of law is to assure just freedoms.

"It is hard, indeed impossible," he writes, "to see how any community could exist if freedom consisted not merely in the innate 'ability' of everyone 'to do as he pleased,' but in the actual carrying into social operation of that principle of utter individualism." To Catholics, freedom means the "freedom to act as I ought." The "oughtness" comes from the reasonableness of law.

"Prudence, charity, respect for individual freedom and other qualities evident in the Church's legislation might well be a model for all official censoring bodies (the courts and so on)," says Father Gardiner, "and must be a model for groups of Catholics who feel impelled to do something to meet this very human desire and need of keeping the printed word and the films under some control, especially as they are spread before the young today."

The Ten Commandments sum up morals. The Catholic Church "by reason of its Divine mandate has not only the right, but the duty, of safeguarding the faith and morals of its subjects." The church believes that books and movies can seduce the mind—or inspire it. It believes it is better to restrict the freedom of one person than to permit each person to be his own body of law. The law must consider the community, not the special gifts of one person. The United States Supreme Court has held that freedom of speech and the press do not include obscenity. Neither the court nor canon law define obscenity. It is not, however, to be confused with vulgarity. Obscenity, Father Gardiner contends, "consists of the intrinsic tendency or bent of the work to arouse sexual passion." Obscenity is in the work itself, not in the reaction of an individual who may be a genius, moron or degenerate. The work must be considered as a whole, which is also the position of the American courts. It is because the courts are slow and because, in the view of many Catholics, they have become lax that the Legion of Decency is necessary.

The legion does not consider itself a censoring agency, but a source of guidance to the public. It looks upon itself as critical rather than suppressive. That its classifications may hurt a movie, it believes, does not make it coercive.

Whether one agrees or disagrees with this explanation of the Legion of Decency, there is no longer any doubt that the legion is far more flexible than it used to be. This was proven by the decisions of the legion to ease its regulations in 1957 and 1963. Today the Legion of Decency, for all its surface assurance and stability is in a state of flux. It has decided to risk offending strict Catholics by making allowances for artistic values in movies. This seems to be a departure from the original idea that "only moral content is weighed." Quite possibly a matter more serious than the wishes of American Catholic prelates may decide the future position of the Legion of Decency. Its ultimate position may have been shaped by the late Pope John XXIII, who introduced a spirit of liberalism into the Catholic Church that is being pushed by his successor, Paul VI. The purpose is to ease the way for Protestants to return to the Catholic fold. One way to overcome the suspicion of Protestants is to soft-pedal the pressures brought by Catholic groups in the arts. Since the movies are so conspicuous, Protestants will be watching the Legion of Decency very carefully.

2. Protestant Pressure

Many Americans think there is very little difference between the Protestant and Catholic attitudes toward "objectionable" films. Others think they have nothing in common. Both thoughts are wrong. There is a strong difference between the Protestant view of undesirable films and that of the Catholic Legion of Decency. But what both Protestants and Catholics have in common is that they are pressure groups. They differ in the manner in which the pressure is applied; in the degree of pressure; in the points at which pressure is applied. But they are pressure groups in the sense that they try to exert influence on a private industry and an art form to meet certain standards they consider of vital importance—of greater importance than whether a movie makes money or not. Sometimes of greater importance than whether a movie is artistic or not.

One reason for the failure of Americans to understand the difference between the Protestant and Catholic approaches to film censorship is that, periodically, when it seems that Hollywood has gone berserk in its quest for sensationalism, both groups seem to be in agreement in their sense of outrage. This was true in the early twenties. Then again in the early thirties. In the sixties it seems to be true again. But beyond the similar indignation there is a considerable difference between the Catholic and Protestant positions toward movies. This difference becomes clear when one examines what leading Protestants have said about movies; about Catholic clergy; and about one another.

To begin with, members of the Protestant clergy go to considerable pains to make certain the public will understand they often disagree with the Legion of Decency. For example, in 1960, the National Council of Churches, which represents many Protestant churches, issued a blistering attack on American movies that sounded, at times, very much like sentiments of the Legion of Decency. The council, in a detailed report, accused movies—and television—of creating an image of man that was frequently "poles apart from the Christian understanding of man and his purpose." The council berated movies for displaying a "pathological preoccupation with sex and violence." The council was angry that movies were devoted entirely too much to assuming "that man's end is material advantage, power and pleasure to be achieved through competing with, manipulating and exploiting his fellow man." And, in another section, the council asserted that churches were "under the mandate of Christ to bring the judgment of the Gospel to bear upon the policies and practices of the organizations which operate the mass media, as well as upon the total use which men make of the media."

But after the report was released to the public a reporter for *The New York Times*, John Wicklein, questioned a member of the group that made the report and was told: "We want to stay as far away as possible from Legion of Decency techniques." And the Rev. Dr. Murray S. Stedman, in presenting the document to the 250-member general board of the National Council, said: "We want to draw attention to good film fare, while avoiding the error of certain groups of singling out bad pictures and therefore giving them particular attention."

These comments constituted more than an obvious disagreement with the Legion of Decency and the position of the Catholic Church. They were, in effect, an attack on the attitude of Cardinal Spellman, head of the New York Archdiocese. For the Cardinal had made it clear he thought there was nothing wrong in singling out a picture for special condemnation. For instance, after *Baby Doll* was released he went to special pains to denounce the movie from the pulpit of St. Patrick's Cathedral midway through solemn mass, at which he was presiding. This film had been made by Elia Kazan from a script by Tennessee Williams. It had been condemned by the Legion of Decency. Cardinal Spellman said that Roman Catholics would commit a sin if they saw the movie.

The following Sunday the Very Reverend James A. Pike, then Dean of the Protestant Episcopal Cathedral known as St. John the Divine, delivered an extraordinary sermon, taking issue with Cardinal Spellman. He said neither he nor his wife had found the movie pornographic. He suggested that "those who do not want the sexual aspect of life included in the portrayal of real-life situations had better burn their Bibles as well as abstain from the movies." The Cardinal had declared his condemnation of *Baby Doll* was based on patriotism as well as his position as a Roman Catholic archbishop. To this Dean Pike retorted: "The true patriot defends freedom against governmental authority and against majority or minority pressure groups, against volunteers in the cause of thought control. It would take a fairly subtle and independent mind to interpret this picture aright. Maybe many adults are ill equipped to see the picture. But it is one of the privileges of adulthood in a free country to expose oneself to picturization of life and make one's own interpretations. The task of the church is not to spare adults this experience, but rather to provide them with the right canons of interpretation and to furnish them with answers in depth to questions asked in depth."

At the root of the Protestant position is its opposition to church censorship. Though the Legion of Decency protests it is an advisory rather than a censoring body, Protestants for the most part do not accept this claim. When the Legion of Decency claims that any boycott that may follow its condemnation is a by-product for which it is not responsible, Protestants consider this specious reasoning. Repeatedly, Protestant leaders have attacked the boycott which is used to enforce opinions on mass media. Just as often, Protestant spokesmen have resisted pressure to "rate" movies.

However, the difficulty in establishing the Protestant position is that there have been occasions on which there was strong—and public—disagreement among Protestant leaders. This disagreement has created disunity in the Protestant position on movie censorship.

For example, in 1959 the Protestant Film Council was forced to repudiate its West Coast representative, who accused the movies of overemphasizing violence and sex. The West Coast representative of the commission, established by the National Council of the Churches of Christ, George A. Heimrich, had insisted that leaders of his church would have to do something and had hinted at boycott. Less than a month later the Reverend Dr. Robert W. Spike, vice president of the Protestant commission, said that Heimrich had not represented the thinking of Broadcasting and Film Commission of the National Council of Churches. In a letter to the late Eric

Johnston, Dr. Spike said: "Boycott and censorship are most reprehensible to traditional Protestant thinking."

Nevertheless, three years later, Methodist Bishop Gerald H. Kennedy, of Los Angeles, made an even stronger attack on Hollywood than had Heimrich. The bishop even attacked movie stars for immorality off the screen.

And about the same time, the Rev. Malcolm Boyd, Protestant Episcopal Chaplain at Colorado State University, said there was more religion in Tennessee Williams' *Cat on a Hot Tin Roof* than in such religious spectaculars as *The Ten Commandments*. In an interview with George Dugan, religious news editor of *The New York Times*, he cited *Room at the Top, La Strada, Hiroshima, Mon Amour* and *La Dolce Vita* for "decided religious dimension." He said that churches had "frequently stood by and witnessed the spectacle of churchly kudos being bestowed upon artistic and religious trash in the form of very bad movies that are dubbed 'religious' merely because they deal with Biblical subjects or sentimentally pseudo-religious themes."

But in the South, Protestant thinking seems to be somewhat different from that of New York or Colorado State University. Some of the most bitter attacks on *Inherit the Wind* came from Protestant churchmen in the South. Stanley Kramer, producer-director of this movie based on the Scopes trial about evolution, said that Fundamentalist clergy told their congregations to avoid the movie. "They called it antireligious and there were some who tried to give it a Communist tinge by saying it gave comfort and support to the godless world."

A contrary position was taken by Mrs. Jesse Bader, president of the Protestant Film Council. At a hearing in New York City in 1959, she told the Joint Legislative Committee to Study Publication and Dissemination of Offensive and Obscene Material: "We are opposed to censorship of the movies and every other form of mass communication because primarily we regard it as a violation of our basic constitutional rights."

In the words of one of the leaders of the National Council of the Churches of Christ: "The very nature of Protestantism makes it impossible to get one spokesman who can represent a single view fair to all."

The majority of Protestant leaders think they come close to agreement on certain basic points of theory. They think Protestants are less likely to take orders from their church than are Catholics. They claim that it is better to educate the people so they can decide for themselves than to give them orders on what is best. They do not favor the boycott used by Catholic groups. Protestants say it is improper to threaten if their advice is ignored. They believe it is important to have the right to disagree and discuss. Those who fear discussion, they say, either have closed minds or do not care about the subject being considered. On one important point Protestants agree completely with Catholics. They say that movie-makers are much more interested in box office than in art and that they are therefore much more responsive to any threat to the box office than to any other kind of objection or criticism.

The dissent within Protestant ranks is indicated by the history of Protestant organizations dealing with films. Actually, they were started by the movie industry, through its production code. Shurlock became concerned because he was receiving many complaints from Protestants who said that Catholic clergy were treated more favorably than Protestants in movies. Protestants cited *Going My Way* as an example. The objectors did not realize that many Catholic clergy were angry about *Going My Way* because, in its sentimental fashion, it created the impression that Catholic priest spent very little time on religious matters and seemed mainly concerned with arranging romances and running shows.

To placate Protestants, Shurlock urged them to organize their own group in Hollywood as a sort of clearance house through which Hollywood could obtain expert advice on movies dealing with Protestant groups and clergy. Ironically, it was Shurlock who suggested George A. Heimrich as spokesman for the Protestant group. This was the same Heimrich who later clashed with his superiors in the National Council of the Churches of Christ.

One point some Protestants find difficult to answer. Suppose Catholics had never taken so strong an interest in the morality of movies. Would the Protestants have to become more aggressive? This question was put to one of the most important Protestant authorities in the field. He replied: "I do not know what would happen if the Catholic pressure were withdrawn. The Catholics have carried the ball pretty much by themselves a good deal of the time. They deserve a pat on the back."

This comment is indicative of a development that has been obscured by the differences between Protestants and Catholics, and among the Protestants themselves. The fact is that for all their differences Protestants and Catholics are drawing closer in their attitude toward movie censorship.

Protestants no longer see any objection to rating movies. The Protestant Film Council, for example, rates films; it says these ratings are for the guidance of parents. They do not question its right to appraise movies for others.

Indications are that there is greater unity among Protestants than there used to be. In this approach to a single voice, the Protestants also come closer to the Catholic attitude.

At the same time Catholics have accepted the idea that artistic values must receive greater importance in judging the morality of a movie. They are increasingly reluctant to apply the boycott or utter threats of economic pressure. Finally, in a manner similar to that urged by Protestants, the Catholic groups are placing greater stress on praising movies they like than in attacking those they do not favor.

It is impossible to know how much closer the Catholic and Protestant points of view will come. But one thing is certain, the greater the harmony between them, the greater their combined influence over the kinds of movies that will be made.

3. *Sweet Minority Persuasion*

Self-ordained movie censors among Catholics and Protestants give the impression that morality in the broad religious sense is the main concern of all pressure groups. This is far from true. The preponderance of such organizations are formed to espouse more practical causes. They do not concern themselves with whether sin triumphs over virtue in a film; that a décolletage is too low or lingerie too sheer; that a subject is degenerate or a word too purple. These other groups are specialists; each of them is dedicated to a single purpose that may be important or trivial to the rest of the nation but is of consuming interest to the society that guards that particular cause. These blocs, because of their comparatively limited objectives, do not look upon their influence as pressure but rather as persuasion.

The most dramatic exemplar of such exhortation is the National Association for the Advancement of Colored People. Here is a clear illustration of an organization with a cause and tactics used to make its point with the movie industry.

If ever there was an evil that invited the retaliation of a pressure group it was the plight of the Negro in movies as late as May of 1963. Negro actors had a priority on unemployment and hunger. Movie scripts about Negro subjects were almost taboo. Craft unions shunned Negro applicants. Integration, a burning issue in the rest of the nation, was still ignored in Hollywood, wrapped in the dreams of unreality from which producers fabricate so much of their films. The film industry's discrimination humiliated the Negro, not only as a person, but it also used its vast power as a mass medium to minimize and deride his race. It is bad enough when a business is intolerant. But when an art form carries its prejudice into its own creation it vomits upon itself.

To abate these evils Negro representatives in Hollywood had pleaded with movie studios for twenty-five years. They were put off with oily promises that usually resulted in little more than a token increase in the number of Negroes used as extras in movies. The craft unions did not even bother to talk to Negro spokesmen. The law, public opinion, reason, all were on the side of the Negro. Still he was helpless in Hollywood. The trouble was that his persuasive power was almost nil.

On June 25, 1963, a radical remedy was tried. The full strength of the NAACP, instead of only the local chapter, was thrown into the fight against racial bias in movies. The organization's national labor secretary, Herbert Hill, flew out from New York to sit beside the head of the Beverly Hills-Hollywood chapter, James L. Tolbert. This day, when equality was sought, there was no meekness. Hill bluntly accused movie studios of "artistic and moral dishonesty." He asserted they had been depicting the American Negro either as a "caricature" or as an "invisible man." He denounced the craft unions for their "lily-white" tradition. Then came the trump—the threat. He vowed that unless there were substantial changes in Hollywood's attitude toward the Negro, 20 million Negroes in the nation would be mobilized in mass demonstrations and in economic and legal offensives. During succeeding weeks this powerful persuasion was maintained. The unions of actors, writers and musicians, which had not practiced discrimination, but which had been silent, began to speak out for fairer treatment for the Negro. Stars of the magnitude of Marlon Brando, Paul Newman, Tony Curtis and Charlton Heston espoused the cause of the NAACP.

Changes came quickly in Hollywood. Movie companies rushed to hire Negroes as extras or bit players. No longer would crowds at baseball parks or in city streets be all white. There was a sudden awareness that Negroes could, in all honesty, be portrayed as teachers, nurses, doctors, lawyers, government officials and politicians. During July and August of 1963 Negroes earned nearly $27,000 in the movies, as compared with $3,600 in the same period of 1962. A few craft unions took in Negroes. By early September, Warner Brothers was boasting it had cast forty Negroes in *Kisses for My President*.

Both Hill and Tolbert insisted that the NAACP had no desire to censor scripts. The NAACP had no intention of setting itself up, like the Legion of Decency, to "rate" movies according to their treatment of Negroes. But there was no doubt in Hollywood that any movie that treated Negroes unfairly, either by portrayal or by ignoring them, would face retribution from the NAACP. Whether it wished to or not, the NAACP had followed the inevitable pattern of all pressure—or persuasion—groups and was being forced to play a larger role in movie censorships.

The truth is that the NAACP already had a history of censorship by persuasion.

One of the most celebrated movies in the world, D. W. Griffith's *The Birth of a Nation*, was a hateful thing to Negroes since it portrayed them as vicious and stupid and the Ku Klux Klan of the Reconstruction period as heroic. The fight against the film was spearheaded by the NAACP. Leading non-Negro educators spoke up for the Negroes when this movie was released. Another famous film, *Gone With the Wind,* also caused uneasiness among the Negroes. Before it was released the Neighborhood Council of Washington, D.C., wrote to the Motion Picture Association of America, saying that unless the movie tried to foster the idea of race tolerance and good citizenship, "we fear it will create race antagonism, race prejudice and great humiliation to a minority group struggling to reach the high levels of democracy." Another Negro group pointed out that *Gone With the Wind* did not show any repentance "for the selling of human beings as cattle." The Hollywood censors banned the use of "niggers" unless used by Negroes. Scarlett's reference to "free niggers" was changed to "freedmen."

A second major point of attack by Negro groups has been the kinds of roles assigned to Negroes. There were too many movies, it has been argued, that showed the Negro as a lazy but amusing servant; as an employee who delighted in his own slavishness. These are the so-called "Uncle Tom" roles so irritating to most Negroes. This issue was raised by the Los Angeles chapter of the NAACP late in 1961. Edward D. Warren said: "All we ask is that movies show the truthful American image. And that means show the Negro as he is in American life, good, bad or indifferent. Any time they have a crap game they show plenty of Negroes. But when do you see a Negro doctor or lawyer except on some Amos and Andy show? We are not arguing for Negroes alone on this matter. We want fair treatment for Mexicans, Jews or any other group."

The irony of the situation is that this attitude cost Negroes jobs as actors. For example, the original script of *The Egg and I* called for a Negro railroad porter and a Negro maid in two sequences. Both were shown sympathetically, but they were menials. So the maid was converted into a Caucasian. A Negro actress lost a job.

One of the angriest demonstrations by Negroes against a movie was directed at Walt Disney's *Song of the South.* This was an adaptation of Joel Chandler Harris's "Uncle Remus" stories, with the picture set in the 1870's. To many Negroes this was pure

"Uncle Tomism." The movie was picketed at a number of theaters by Negroes.

No matter how strongly an organization dislikes the concept of censorship, it seems incapable of resisting the temptation to apply pressure on movie-makers at some time or other. It is as though every organization—religious, racial, labor, industrial, social or political—has at least one raw nerve which, if touched, will create a reflex action in the thinly disguised form of censorship known as the pressure group.

For example, it would be difficult to find any group that hates censorship more than the Jews. To Jews, censorship is the first step toward tyranny and often a characteristic of incipient anti-Semitism. The opposition of Jews to censorship is as much emotional as it is ethical. As individuals and as groups, Jews are constantly very active in trying to block or destroy censorship. The Jewish position on censorship was stated during the summer of 1962 by the National Community Relations Advisory Council, which represents six major Jewish organizations and sixty-two independent local Jewish community councils. The advisory council said: "Under both the Judaic concept and the principles underlying American society, the ultimate purpose of a free society is to further development of the individual and to strengthen the dignity of man . . . History demonstrates that social progress in a free society can be made only through the efforts of the questing mind, through the clash and contest of ideas . . . But in the clash of ideas, the only weapons must be the ideas themselves. The ideas or positions of an individual or a group must not be spread through the use or threat of economic or political power . . . These concepts require that there be no limitations in advance, no "prior restraints' on what may be spoken or said or shown."

However, Jewish groups become as aroused as the Legion of Decency if there is a possibility that any movie may show a Jew in an unflattering light. Thus Jewish organizations fought against the showing of the British movie *Oliver Twist* in this country. Jewish pressure was probably the main reason that the picture, with the notorious Dickensian caricature of Fagin, the Jew who has children steal for him, was never shown widely in this country.

Jewish groups worry that Biblical pictures will depict Jews as "Christ-killers." They make a point of explaining to producers that crucifixion was a Roman form of punishment. This situation caused a misunderstanding in connection with the filming of *The Greatest Story Ever Told*. George Stevens, director-producer of the carefully researched movie about Christ, hired the Imbal dance troupe of Israel. Some Israeli groups were fearful that the movie would tend to perpetuate the Jews in the role of "Christ-killers" and demanded that the dancers be forbidden by Israel to participate. However, after Mr. Stevens assured the Israeli government that the movie was being done honestly and artistically, the dancers were permitted to work in the movie.

Sometimes Jews will bring pressure to bear before a movie is released. For instance, in *Freud* an anti-Semitic remark was directed at the analyst in the film before it was released. The man making the comment was obviously psychotic. Nevertheless, Jewish organizations asked that the line be deleted. They argued that even if anti-Semitism were attributed to an unbalanced person it would help keep anti-Semitism alive. The anti-Semitic remark was dropped.

This understandable terror of anti-Semitism takes another form —the reluctance to see anyone associated with anti-Semitism portrayed in a favorable light. The fact that German Field Marshal Rommel was depicted as an honorable professional soldier in the British movie *The Desert Fox* angered a number of Jewish groups and they tried to have the film's showing limited in the United States. They had some success. And yet, when in 1962 *The Longest Day*, which showed Rommel even more favorably, was released there were no protests from Jewish groups. The reason seems obvious. The first picture was put on the screen when the Nazi atrocities were much more vivid to Jews than when *The Longest Day* was released.

When Dore Schary, himself a religious Jew, was planning to make *Crossfire*, which dealt with anti-Semitism, he was approached by a representative of the American Jewish Committee, who suggested the movie might provoke anti-Semitism. Mr. Schary scoffed at the idea and went ahead with the film. A somewhat ludicrous situtation arose when Mr. Schary was making *Ivanhoe*. Some Jews asked him to make Isaac of York, the moneylender, a non-Jew. He refused.

A different aspect of the fear of anti-Semitism is seen in the reluctance to use Jewish characters even when it is mandatory. Thus, when Jerome Weidman's *I Can Get It for You Wholesale* was made into a movie, New York's Jewish-dominated garment center lost its Jewish atmosphere in the film. Far from being displeased by this distortion of a nationally known fact, Jewish groups liked the idea of Gentiles becoming kings of the clothing business. There is also, for the most part, a careful avoidance of using Jewish actors to play Jewish roles. When *Majority of One* was made into a movie, Gertrude Berg was obviously perfect for the part of the dumpy middle-aged Jewess she had created on Broadway. She wanted the part. It was given to Rosalind Russell. The movie *Having Wonderful Time* was about the Borscht Belt in the Catskills. The leading roles were played by Douglas Fairbanks, Jr., and Ginger Rogers, both non-Jews.

This kind of dishonest casting delights Jewish organizations. One spokesman for a major Jewish organization said: "We don't want people to cling to the idea that Jews all look a certain way. We want to get away from the vaudeville caricatures of the Jew as 'Ikey' with a long nose, greasy face, beard and derby."

Part of the explanation is that many producers and studio executives are themselves Jewish and are acutely sensitive about their Jewishness. They try to avoid the entire subject whenever possible. They realize such an attitude is a form of dishonesty. One of them summed up his hypocrisy when he was approached by a director, a Jew, who wanted to make a movie based on a novel about Jews. The Jewish executive said, sardonically: "Jews are for killing, not for making into movies."

The basic difference between the Jewish approach to movie censorship and that of Catholic and Protestant organizations is that the Jews, like the Negroes, are much less concerned with the morals or sociological themes of films.

Italians also have a pressure group. One of their prime targets is the film that shows nearly all gangsters as Italians or of Italian descent. They resent even references to organizations such as the Mafia. Their resentment is no less if the movie is a comedy. For instance, in *Some Like It Hot,* in which nothing was intended seriously, there are some gangsters who are, in effect, satires of movie types. But the resentment among Italian organizations was so great that when Marilyn Monroe, who starred in the film with Jack Lemmon and Tony Curtis, was to have received some sort of publicity award from the Italian consul's office in New York, the consulate refused. Said Billy Wilder, who co-authored the spoof with I. A. L. Diamond: "We should invent some Kurdish tribe for these parts."

Actually, he could have settled for Greeks. Because, for the time being, the Greeks do not seem too concerned about someone with a Greek name playing a villain. This is the explanation of a name change that may have puzzled some connoisseurs of Tennessee Williams who saw the movie version of *Summer and Smoke.* The Mexican who owned the casino and gambling joint and later killed the hero's father turned up in the movie with a Greek name. In the original screenplay by James Poe, he was Mexican. But executives at Paramount, which released the movie, thought Latins might object. The Greek name was substituted.

All sorts of professions and trade associations are quick to apply pressure. The American Medical Association is among the most active professional pressure groups, and it keeps up a busy check to see that no movie doctor is shown in a bad light. The Bar Association, though off to a later start, is catching up fast. So far as movies are concerned there is no fee splitting among doctors and no "shyster" among lawyers. In fact, the words have been drummed out of the movie industry.

Among complaints that the movie industry has had to consider from pressure groups are the following. Bourbon-makers protested that movie heroes are constantly ordering Scotch and soda. Some women assailed a short about poppies because poppies produce opium. Manufacturers of doughnuts became wroth because movies ridiculed doughnut dunking. Aviation associations have become exercised at portrayals of plane crackups. Milliners complain about hatless stars. Glass blowers have objected to scenes showing canned beer. A billiard association resented scenes showing poolrooms in an unfavorable light. Temperance groups frequently object to drinking scenes, and hotel owners become vocal about movies that show hotel guests smoking in bed. A manufacturer of fraternity pins objected to a movie that criticized fraternities and sororities.

This endless flood of "persuasion" groups once prompted Joe Breen to say sarcastically: "Movie villains should be unemployed, white Americans, without religious, professional, labor union or other affiliations."

4. *Pressures from Bureaucracy*

Edward R. Murrow was the new head of the United States Information Agency in 1961 when he decided to make an official visit to Hollywood. As one of the most famous of radio and then television news commentators, as a celebrated television personality in his own right, as a man of liberal tendencies, Murrow was welcomed with an enthusiasm beyond that usually accorded a government official of his rank. A private dinner was arranged for him at the now defunct Romanoff's Restaurant that was attended by carefully selected top brass of Hollywood. An air of expectancy as well as festivity surrounded the affair. For Murrow was going to talk about the relationship of Hollywood and the federal government. And questions were to be answered afterward.

It did not take his audience too long to realize that Murrow was somewhat naïve about the movie industry's dealings with Washington. For he said, without qualification, that the federal government did not censor movies and did not intend to. This is a myth. The fact that it is believed by almost every moviegoer in the United States does not change its basic inaccuracy. No one at the dinner challenged Murrow's assertion. Many of his listeners knew, from personal experience, it was not true. Perhaps Murrow was spared because he was considered an innocent. Or maybe out of politeness to a guest. Maybe it was because, as a government official, he was thought to be of possible future use to Hollywood if he were flattered.

The fact is that Washington has censored American movies for many years. It has done so without legal support. Sometimes this censorship has been construed as "guidance" or "technical assistance" or "putting a subject in proper perspective." But it has been coercive. Frequently it has meant that an agency or representative of the government had the power—and exercised that power— of changing a movie script before it was shot. It is precisely because federal censorship is invisible—and almost always done in secret—that it is so insidious. That movie-makers put up with it is an example of their own cowardice and their inability to realize that this sort of practice, no matter how limited it may be at first, can become a plague that, in effect, denies constitutional rights.

It is virtually impossible for anyone in Hollywood to make a movie about the armed forces, the Department of State, American diplomacy, bureaus dealing with narcotics, immigration, crime, counterfeiting—and many other subjects—without running into federal censorship. For, to make a movie on such subjects, any intelligent producer or director will seek information from the proper governmental agency.

More than that. He may need assistance from the government. For example, he may be making a movie in which he wants to film sequences aboard a warship. He will find this impossible unless he gets permission from the navy. Such permission will be granted in return for the producer's agreement to allow the navy to censor the script. The theory behind governmental requests of this sort is that the agency involved wants to be sure it is not presented in a ridiculous light. Actually, it wants to be certain it is presented in a flattering light—whether it deserves to be or not.

Among those at the Murrow dinner was Stanley Kramer, one of the few producer-directors who has fought this invisible censorship. It has cost him a great deal of anguish. But he has proved that if a producer is determined he need not submit to federal censorship. He did not discuss the matter with Murrow. But he could have cited some very dramatic episodes of resistance to federal censorship.

Kramer wanted to make a movie of *The Caine Mutiny*, the best-selling novel by Herman Wouk about the trial of an officer who took over the control of a ship during wartime because the captain was incompetent to the point of near insanity. He had to photograph scenes aboard navy warships at Pearl Harbor. He asked permission from the navy, dealing eventually with an admiral.

The navy refused. He was told the navy did not think that a movie based on this widely read book was in "the best interests of the navy." He was informed there had never been a mutiny in the American Navy. When he offered to eliminate the word "mutiny" from the title the navy was still obdurate. It pointed out that such a movie might hurt recruitment. Fathers and mothers might become distraught at the thought of their boys serving under a neurotic skipper. When news of the navy's coolness reached Hollywood, Metro-Goldwyn-Mayer and Twentieth Century-Fox lost all interest in the project. The movie was eventually released by United Artists.

"The refusal to give me help," said Kramer, "was definite and specific. I got nowhere. Then I did the unpardonable. In sheer frustration, I sent a telegram that created an emotional upheaval. I sent a telegram to the Secretary of the Navy. This was unforgivable because I had jumped the chain of command."

In the telegram Kramer asked if he could meet with the Secretary of the Navy and if the navy's chief of operations could be present. Twenty-four hours later the producer-director received a phone call to be in Washington. There he conferred with the Secretary of the Navy, his chief of naval operations and with some of the top brass of the navy's public relations setup.

"I tried to explain that this was not an anti-navy picture. That in order to show white, you have to show black. I got approval from him, and the navy was told to give full cooperation." While the movie was being made many naval officers told Kramer they were sure the villain of the film was someone they had served under. When the film was screened in Washington, before 2,700 navy officers, it received an ovation. Nevertheless, the navy brass got a bit of revenge. It refused to allow Kramer to use, in the screen credit, the statement that the movie was "made with the co-operation of the United States Navy."

Long after the movie finished its run Kramer said: "I do not regard myself as a knight in shining armor. I won't say I don't have to fight. But basically, I am convinced the situation is loaded in my favor. For, while we tinker with freedom, we believe as a nation in freedom. And I don't believe in government censorship in any form."

Kramer's attitude is rare. The usual pattern is what happened to *The Young Lions*. To please the army, the script was altered so that the subject of anti-Semitism among army officers was toned down. It still showed the Jewish soldier (Montgomery Clift) being treated unfairly by one officer because of his religion. But it also showed the officer being punished severely by the army for his behavior. Three rewrites of this script were submitted to the Pentagon before it won a pledge of co-operation from the army.

Then there was the case of *From Here to Eternity*. Since the novel was outspoken about unfavorable aspects of army life in peacetime—as noted in Chapter VI—the Pentagon had to be appeased before it would co-operate. In the book, the sadistic captain is promoted to major. In the movie he was cashiered out of the army. "The army would never have allowed us to shoot the picture at Schofield Barracks if we hadn't done this," said someone who followed the negotiations between Columbia Pictures and the army closely. "And it would have been awfully expensive to build a set like Schofield Barracks." The army saw every draft of the script before shooting began. Repeatedly, the producer, the late Buddy Adler, went to Washington to dicker with the army about the script. It is significant, in illustrating the censorship power of the government, that this famous film had more trouble with the military than with decency groups.

Francis the Talking Mule had been the subject of several successful movies when he tangled with the army. Since mules are accredited mascots of West Point, Hollywood thought it only natural to make a picture called *Francis Goes to West Point*. The West Point brass became balkier than a mule. Permission was refused to make the movie at the Point. The issue became so important that it was bucked along to the Pentagon, where it became mired in conferences. At last a solution was reached. General Robert Eichelberger was hired as technical adviser to protect the interests and sensitivities of the U.S. Military Academy.

The Ugly American created animosity in the State Department when George Englund announced he was making a movie of the book by Eugene Burdick and William J. Lederer. The issue was joined when Englund approached State for technical assistance. Since the book showed American diplomacy in a poor light in Southeast Asia, the Department of State suggested that the movie did not further the American image abroad. The United States Information Agency in particular regarded it as a sort of enemy in film.

"It was not," said Englund, "that they demanded I make this change or that. It was more a sense of being immersed in bureaucratic smog. I could not help notice that our embassy in Thailand was strongly opposed even to our going there to shoot part of the picture. I made many changes. But they were not made to placate State."

Stewart Stern who, as author of the screenplay, sat in on some meetings in Washington, was astonished at the arrogance of government officials. "At least one official thought he had the right to tell us what we must do and must not do. Some felt they had the right to threaten." In some ways, said Stern, the government men showed appalling ignorance. Another person close to the situation said that State dropped a strong hint that if Universal persisted in making *The Ugly American* it might encounter difficulties in freeing box office revenues abroad. Stern, like Englund, insisted that none of the threats had been effective. He disagreed with the comments of such critics as Bosley Crowther of *The New York Times*, who pointed out that the movie was less skeptical than the book.

State tangled more openly with Kramer after he made *The Defiant Ones*. This film was about a Negro (Sidney Poitier) and a white man (Tony Curtis) who break out of a southern jail handcuffed to each other. The movie shows how senseless is the white man's bigotry. Kramer decided to make the movie after the outbreak in Little Rock, Arkansas, over school integration had become an international headline. He had no trouble with the Hollywood censors.

Kramer, who is shrewd in exploiting a movie, decided to enter *The Defiant Ones* in the Berlin Film Festival. He sent it to Germany and was invited by the festival staff to exhibit it. "The

State Department," said Kramer, "was upset. This was not the kind of film that the State Department thought should represent the United States. I could not help but be intrigued by the irony that a picture about race was being invited by the Germans to the Berlin Festival and opposed by our State Department."

The movie was shown at the festival with German subtitles. It aroused considerable favorable comment and Sidney Poitier won an award for his performance. This did not deter the American bureaucracy in foreign affairs from continuing its foolishness. Months later—by this time the movie had become successful in the United States—it was time for the film festival in Mexico City. Washington tried to block the entry of *The Defiant Ones*. During the festival's first few days the Russians became the favorites. They had brought along a ballet company, top stars and directors for cultural propaganda purposes, Mexicans literally threw rocks at the U.S. embassy. Despite United States objections *The Defiant Ones* was shown at the festival. The American ambassador did not attend. The film was the hit of the festival and a source of substantial good will for Americans.

The weapon of the State Department, says Kramer, is to say that a movie "is not in the best interests of the United States." This label, he believes, is reserved for any film that tries to make any commentary on the American scene.

Illegal Entry was a movie about immigration. To make the picture the producer obtained the co-operation of the Immigration and Naturalization Service of the Justice Department. Case histories from government files were even made available for dramatization. But there was a payoff. A man close to the situation confided: "Because of the nature of the subject matter, the Department of Justice set up rather stringent requirements with regard to department approval of various stages in the making of this film." Also, the Commissioner of Immigration appeared in a prologue to the movie.

Johnny Stool Pigeon was about narcotics and, inevitably, about the work habits of the Federal Bureau of Narcotics. The bureau agreed to help. In return it was allowed to check all scripts before shooting started. Before the movie was made available in theaters it was screened in Washington before the Secretary of the Treasury and officials of the narcotics and customs agencies.

When Metro-Goldwyn-Mayer bought Franz Werfel's best-selling novel *The Forty Days of Musa Dagh* in 1934, it had every intention of converting it into an important feature attraction. But the years passed and no movie was made. None was even started. Not until 1962 did Metro say it was planning to make the book into a movie. It was still planning in 1963. The delay was not caused by the usual reasons—inability to get a good script or certain stars. The reason was the State Department. The book dealt with the shameful massacre of Armenians by Turks. The Turkish government found the subject objectionable for a movie. The State Department interceded in behalf of Turkey only once. That was enough. The movie was shelved.

A strong argument can be made for the concern of the government, or any of its agencies, about the kind of movie that will be made about its work. Movies have been known to distort reality beyond all dramatic necessity. Thus, when Budd Schulberg was preparing a movie script based on *The Enemy Within*, it made sense that he should confer with the author of the book, Attorney General Robert F. Kennedy, brother of the then President. That was as much a part of his research activities as his examination of union problems in this book about labor racketeering in trucking. He did not, however, confer with James R. Hoffa, head of the union.

There have been occasions when the army has been criticized unduly for co-operating with movie-makers. This was true in the case of *The Longest Day*, a movie about the D-Day invasion of Normandy in World War II. The army helped the producer, Darryl F. Zanuck, get American troops for the filming, and American equipment. At the same time that the movie was being shot in France, however, Jack Paar attracted a great deal of attention by being filmed with American troops at the wall separating East and West Berlin. It was alleged the troops had been expressly supplied for the television star's filmed appearance. The reaction in Congress to this episode carried over to the movie *The Longest Day*. The question was raised: why should American soldiers be put to work for Hollywood? There were two answers. First, to help straighten out the misconception in Europe about the D-Day invasion—that Americans played only a small role. They played a very important part. Second, to help give a serious movie a chance to be honest and dramatic at the same time.

But because of the controversy aroused in Congress the number of American troops allotted to *The Longest Day* was cut. Since the British government had already made 500 soldiers available for the movie, and the French another 500, the Americans were outnumbered. George Stevens, one of Hollywood's most respected directors pointed out the unreasonableness of cutting the American soldiers. "The Americans," he observed, "outnumbered all other troops on D-Day. But they never received the credit they deserved. The impression was created that the British did all the work. Now, by cutting the American troops to be permitted in the film the British will have twice as many men as the Americans in the movie. And the fallacy will remain."

Since most of the forty stars in the film were Americans playing American roles, the impression was corrected by the number of close-ups of American performers.

Indirect government censorship, though only in its infant stages, is most dangerous of all. Part of its menace is that it does not look like and may not be intended as censorship. The government puts forth its position in so reasonable a manner that it seems as though it is trying to do the movie industry the favor of saving it from possible obloquy. This new approach could be called "image control." Murrow, who probably does not consider it to be government pressure, outlined the idea during his appearance in Romanoff's. He said: "Films may provide a high level of audience enjoyment and at the same time convey an equally high level of negative impressions about the United States. Because audiences like the extremities of storytelling is no reason to feed them to the exclusion of all else. . . . I suggest that the image conveyed abroad of our land is not always a healthy one and self-restraint may nowadays be a good prescription. . . . I trust this will not be regarded as in any way a plea for a great outpouring of films of social significance designed to improve the image of the United States abroad. Merely to entertain is to create a favorable climate of opinion. But it is not a totally entertaining world in which we reside. You have the overwhelming power both to entertain and inform."

The movie industry, as might have been expected, retorted through Eric Johnston, its official spokesman at the time. He insisted that American movies create a favorable image of the United States.

The danger arises when it is asked: who is to judge whether the "image" projected by a film is favorable or unfavorable to the United States? Is it to be the movie-maker or an agency of government? Obviously both the USIA and the State Department believe they know more about such a delicate subject than some Hollywood producer. The first official step along what may be the road to federal censorship of movies was taken in 1962. George Stevens, Jr., left Hollywood to work for the USIA as the liaison between Washington and Hollywood. Stevens, it was agreed in Hollywood, was an excellent choice for the job. He had grown up in the movie business. He had the honest movie-maker's resentment of government censorship. And he had good taste.

But there was no guarantee that his successors would be as capable. And the lesson of governmental bureaucracy is that it tends to increase its power wherever possible. Eventually, what began as a well-intentioned exchange of opinion could become something else. It is easy to imagine some successor to Stevens becoming angry when his advice on a movie is disregarded and using his own prestige and connections in Congress to question the sincerity, even the patriotism, of a producer. The next step becomes the assignment by the government of a man at each studio to be sure each movie has a satisfactory "image."

To guard against growing federal censorship, the movie industry must do two things. First, it must not make secret deals with government agencies. Every producer who is seeking the co-operation of the government must make his intentions public. And he must also make public any changes that are forced upon him by the government. This will enable the government to defend itself and explain why changes are being requested. For while Hollywood, like the press, has the right to portray truth, it does not have the right to villify or ridicule public officials.

The second precaution that Hollywood must take is to make it clear that, so far as the image of a movie is concerned, it is reasonable for the government to make suggestions but it is not shameful for a producer to refuse to accept the suggestions. Here again there must be no secrecy so that the public can be allowed to judge. Unless the movie industry insists on its rights and carries them out in an open and tasteful manner, there is a good chance that the present federal curbs on movie-making will grow rather than diminish.

MACK SENNETT'S BATHING GIRLS: Their risqué costumes steamed up censors of the World War I era.

left:
THEDA BARA: The *femme fatale* of the twenties, in *Salome*.

right:
CLARA BOW: The "It" girl, symbol of fast living in the twenties, in
Red Hair.

THE VICTORS: This nude scene was never shown to U.S. audiences—not even to the official censors of the movie industry. Naked star is Elke Sommer.

LES LIAISONS DANGEREUSES: The Gallic touch with telephone. The unusual phone pedestal is Jeanne Valerie. Holding her in place is Gerard Philipe.

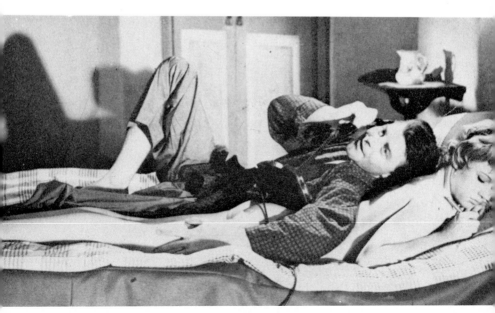

FATTY ARBUCKLE: The scandal that destroyed his fabulous career as a comedian of the silent screen was front-page news for months and spurred those who demanded movie censorship on moral grounds. Arbuckle was accused of killing an actress during a hotel-room orgy. He was acquitted.

MALE AND FEMALE: One of the major contributions of Cecil B. De Mille to this film was a sensual bathtub scene. Gloria Swanson is in the tub back in 1919.

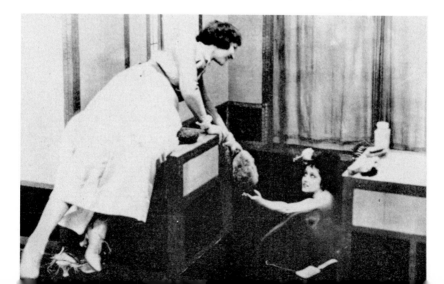

MABEL NORMAND: One of the most gifted comediennes in movie history, it was her misfortune to be an intimate of William Desmond Taylor, handsome director of the silent era, when he was murdered in his Hollywood home. It was clear she was not responsible for the unsolved crime, but her future was destroyed through guilt by association. Headlines about this murder raised an outcry for movie censorship.

WALLACE REID: Adored film idol of the silent screen, who died trying to break dope habit. Hollywood has never been able, since then, to fight off insinuations that its stars carry hypodermic syringes in make-up kits.

Museum of Modern Art

THE GOLD RUSH: Chaplin's genius and international popularity were at stake while this film was being made. He had become involved in a sensational scandal with Lita Grey, whom he married hurriedly. Their divorce was as lurid as the marriage. But the movie made him a sort of public paradox. The character with Chaplin is Mack Swain.

JEAN HARLOW: Hollywood's sex queen of the early thirties was involved in sordid stories when her husband Paul Bern, an important Metro executive, was found dead. Officially it was suicide, but there were—and still remain—suspicions of murder that did not help Hollywood in its campaign to fight censorship.

HOLLYWOOD CATO: Geoffrey M. Shurlock, Hollywood's chief censor, is much more cultured than the vast majority of producers, directors and writers with whom he deals in the movie industry's most thankless job.

Richard Fish

4 | Aftermath of cowardice

It is one thing to mature in response to valid criticism, from either individuals or groups. It is another to sacrifice artistic freedom out of fear of criticism. Terror of what pressure groups may do at the box office has been one of the main reasons that Hollywood has failed artistically. The most shameful illustration of artistic cowardice is the blacklist, a creature of Hollywood's terror of pressure groups at their worst. With the blacklist has grown up something unknown in any democracy today—an underground in moviemaking that combines hyprocrisy, greed, fear and art. Fear of group criticism has become so ingrained in the movie industry mentality that it has led to a curious form of self-destruction that can be called pre-censorship. This is what prompts studio executives, producers, directors, writers to distort and water down the artistic merit of a script—not the industry's censorship code but fear that the original idea may somehow cause trouble, either with the code or with a pressure group. Coupled with this is that other manifestation of pre-censorship, the conviction that quality is inimical to box office.

1. *The Hollywood Blacklist*

The most vicious form of censorship in the movie industry has been the result of cowardice. For it was fear, the offspring of greed, that produced the Hollywood blacklist, a form of censorship inherent in dictatorship but anathema to democracy. What the blacklist means, in effect, is that any actor, writer or director considered too radical politically shall not be employed. Every major movie studio in Hollywood keeps a blacklist. The movie companies insist that they do not conspire to maintain the same list. But no one familiar with the chicanery of the movie business believes this. Regardless of what courts may rule, the facts indicate, very strongly, that the blacklists maintained by each studio are sufficiently similar to have been produced on a single mimeograph machine, with a few names dropped from one or added to another.

The power of the blacklist was demonstrated when Frank Sinatra, in many ways the most courageous man in Hollywood, tried to fight it, for he is a tolerant man. In 1960, Sinatra, then at the peak of his power as a movie star, producer, recording artist, television notable and close friend of the then Senator John F. Kennedy, who was to become President later that year, took on the forces of the blacklist. He had acquired the movie rights to *The Execution of Private Slovik*, the nonfiction book, by William Bradford Huie, about the only American to be shot for desertion since the Civil War. He then revealed he had hired Albert Maltz, one of the best known of the blacklisted writers, to do the script.

The attacks came, as Sinatra had expected, first by the Hearst press and then by the American Legion. Pressure was brought on disk jockeys not to play his records, and the smear campaign went so far as to question the patriotism of Senator Kennedy, then trying to win the Democratic nomination for President. Producers, directors and stars who had often paraded their liberal beliefs for safer causes, remained silent, though privately they had often expressed a loathing of the blacklist. But Sinatra insisted he had the right to hire anyone he pleased to write the script. Days passed, the attacks mounted, and no support came for Sinatra from his friends and associates. Curiously, Sinatra was not even supported by Otto Preminger, the producer-director who earlier that year had hired Dalton Trumbo, the most famous of the blacklisted writers, to write the screenplay of *Exodus*. Just as silent was Stanley Kramer, another producer-director who had flouted the blacklist by hiring Nedrick Young, another well-known blacklisted writer, under the widely publicized pseudonym of Nathan E. Douglas. Sinatra capitulated. He fired Maltz and sold his movie rights to the book to George Stevens, Jr.

When the blacklist has been discarded—as it must, inevitably—it may seem strange that there ever was such a thing in our democratic nation. How did it happen, in a country where men and women cast secret ballots and do not hesitate to criticize their most important officials, that this instrument of dictatorship prevailed? How did a blacklist arrogate such power in a field that likes to think of itself as artistic?

The blacklist was an outgrowth of what was subsequently known as "The Battle of the Unfriendly Ten." Briefly, between 1947 and 1953, a series of investigations—Congressional, state and private—zeroed in on Hollywood. The avowed object was to expose Communists in the movie industry. Ten men—eight writers, a writer-producer and a director—were sent to jail for contempt of Congress when they refused to tell the Congressional Committee on Un-American Activities whether they were Communists or answer questions on communism in the movie field. Trumbo and Maltz were among the ten. Ironically, the chairman of this Congressional committee, Representative J. Parnell Thomas, later became a jail mate of some of these unfriendly ten, when he was convicted of payroll padding.

When the investigations began, the industry was at first eloquently indignant over the invasion of private rights. But the resistance soon crumpled and, late in 1947, Hollywood's leaders pledged publicly that the industry would not hire anyone considered politically dangerous. This pledge became known as the Waldorf Declaration because it was adopted at a meeting of fifty movie tycoons at the Waldorf-Astoria Hotel in New York. That the industry was fearful of what it had done was made clear by its then official spokesman, Eric Johnston, who said: "We are frank to recognize that such a policy involves dangers and risks. There is the danger of hurting innocent people. There is the risk of creating an atmosphere of fear. Creative work at its best cannot be carried on in an atmosphere of fear." The conservative *Los Angeles Times* quickly noted the inconsistency of the movie industry's position by saying: "First the [Congressional] committee was wrong in questioning; then the witnesses were wrong in not answering the question."

The timorous policy of the movie industry created the blacklist. And with it the dangers and risks that Johnston had feared materialized. How many innocent men and women were destroyed professionally by the innuendoes of unidentified accusers will never be known. The blacklist extended well beyond the 212 persons named in one fashion or another before the Congressional investigation. In an excellent study of blacklisting, published in 1956, The Fund for the Republic said: "It is apparent that studios now check the political record of their workers before placing them on the payroll." It was enough to have a name similar to that of a man named before an investigating committee to be blacklisted. One of the most vicious aspects of the blacklist was that the victim sometimes did not know his name had been placed on it.

Among the most pathetic cases is that of Louis Pollock, a writer who was condemned without ever knowing he had been tried. Louis Pollock's trouble was that a man named Louis Pollack, a California clothier, refused to answer questions before the House Committee on Un-American Activities on April 21, 1954. Until that day Louis Pollock, the writer, was doing well in the writing career for which he had forsaken newspaper work and then a $25,000-a-year advertising job.

"I was never a top price writer," he said. "But with each picture my price was going up and the best agents were interested in handling me. I was coming to where I was beginning to mean something. All of a sudden I could not sell anything. Fellows used to kid me. They would say: 'You must be on the list.' If I could only have believed this, I might have saved myself a lot of heartaches. How could I? I never belonged to any organization in my

life except the Authors League and the Writers Guild and no committee had ever asked me for information."

The months and years passed—five years—and Pollock's scripts
kept coming back. He had his only successes in magazine features, some of which he ghosted for famous Hollywood columnists. His house was mortgaged and then sold. A few times he and
his wife were on the verge of divorce. He began to believe he had
"lost the touch" and sometimes he thought "a clique was against
me." He might have wondered indefinitely.

Then, in the fall of 1959, he met an important executive he had
known when his fortunes were better. During a brief conversation he admitted to the executive that he could not understand why
everything he wrote was rejected. That afternoon the executive
phoned and asked him if he had been born in Hungary. No. The
executive asked a number of other questions that seemed irrelevant.
Finally the executive told him he was on the blacklist and that it
might have been a mistake. Pollock rushed to a public library and, in
a book on the hearings of the House Committee on Un-American
Activities, found the name of Louis Pollack. On the advice of the
Writers Guild he conferred with Martin Gang, one of the ablest
Hollywood lawyers. Gang checked the story and then wrote to a
local investigator for the Congressional committee. On December
3, 1959, the writer received a letter from Washington on the sta-
tionery of the Congressional committee. It was signed by Richard
Ahrens, staff director of the committee. The last paragraph of the
letter said: "The reading of the testimony of Louis Pollack in-
dicates that he is not the same person as Louis Pollock and I very
gladly point this out for your benefit and use."

After he received this letter the writer said: "Now I feel numb.
But I can't help thinking that in those five years nobody ever asked
me once: 'Are you this man?' 'Could you be this man?' Nobody
ever asked me."

Though the ethical and legal aspects of the blacklist controversy
have touched off moving essays and orations, the crux of the argument has become economics. The blacklist was not fashioned out
of patriotism, but out of fear of boycotts and other forms of
economic reprisal. And when the blacklist is finally abandoned it
will be for profit.

Who frightened Hollywood into accepting the blacklist it hated? Most important was the American Legion. It was, for a number of years, enough for the legion to say that a man was suspect for a studio to refuse to hire him. The legion was relentless in its determination to impose its will on the industry. It organized boycotts and threatened to mobilize opinion against any movies written or directed by those it considered politically unsavory. Because of its dread of the legion, the movie industry sent one of its top executives to the legion's national convention in 1960 to head off a resolution accusing the industry of permitting reinfiltration by Communists and their allies. Neither the legion nor any of the investigating committees has produced evidence that any movie written or directed in Hollywood contained Communist propaganda. Throughout the turmoil about these allegedly dangerous radicals, their former movies were shown repeatedly on television —with screen credit given—without arousing the public.

Nevertheless, Hollywood remained afraid. It was concerned that the legion, through allies in Congress, could touch off an embarrassing Congressional investigation; that it might persuade the Hearst press and assorted gossip columnists to attack certain movies or studios. And at all times the movie industry feared the anti-Communist position of the Catholic Church favored a blacklist.

But as the years passed and some legion attacks—its boycott of *Exodus*, for instance—had little effect on the box office, movie companies became braver. But more important, the jungle competition of the industry tended to undermine the blacklist. Television had cut movie attendance in half. Every studio began living for the smash hit that would make up for the bulk of movies that did not make money. The quest for the cinematic gold mine compelled studio executives and producers to cast covetous eyes on the blacklist. As a top producer at one of the biggest studios put it: "There are not many first-rate writers, so why should we let the independent companies and the foreign companies grab off the cream of the blacklisted writers? Apart from the ethics, it's just stupid business. I want a good script and I don't care who writes it."

One of the most important forces in undermining the blacklist was United Artists, a company without a studio but with an idea.

Its plan was to try to get the most creative talent in Hollywood by offering absolute freedom in making a movie. It was inevitable that the first breakthroughs would be achieved by independent producers making movies for United Artists release.

From the very beginning of its use of a blacklist, the movie industry found itself in a terribly embarrassing position. If it did not use a blacklist, it would be subjected to pressures ranging from snide allusions through vilification to boycott. If it did use a blacklist it might be sued for conspiracy in restraint of trade (as it was eventually anyhow). The solution was to have a blacklist but not call it a blacklist. How this was done was unwittingly spelled out by the late Benjamin B. Kahane, at the time vice president of Columbia Pictures. Kahane, incidentally, served on occasion as the liaison between the movie industry and the American Legion. In a letter to Paul V. Coates, a Los Angeles columnist and television commentator, Kahane wrote in 1959: "First, let me state emphatically and definitely that so far as Columbia is concerned, there is no so-called 'blacklist'.

"We at Columbia check on writers, actors and others before employing them. We started doing so in 1947 when the 'Unfriendly Ten' appeared before the House Un-American Activities Committee and shocked the country with the attitude they took and the intemperate statements they made which resulted in prison sentences for contempt of Congress. . . .

"With a desire to protect our large financial investment in films and yet to avoid doing anyone an injustice, we decided to engage a reputable firm of public relations men who could investigate cases that arose and report to us all facts and available information. . . .

"If we checked on a writer or actor, the report we received was not that he was on a blacklist or any kind of list, but a report setting forth the facts and information our public relations firm was able to collate. Such a report, for example, would state that there was no information that was found which linked him with the Communist party or any 'front organization' designated by the U.S. Attorney General as subversive.

"In other instances, the report would state that the person was identified as a member of the party or was involved in some way with suspect organizations. They would specify full details on the report. We would then examine the reports.

"In most instances we would discuss the report with the person's agent, who would in turn discuss the matter with his client. In the majority of cases, we would receive a letter or affidavit negativing or explaining the alleged connection with the party or party front organizations. We have kept a file of all reports. If that can be considered a 'blacklist' we are guilty."

Kahane's letter raised questions that showed how thoroughly the industry's conscience had been warped by fear. Why, for instance, was not the accused questioned directly? Why was there rarely any indication of the source of the accusation? Why, with an F.B.I., an Attorney General's office, numerous criminal enforcement groups, was it necessary to hire a "public relations" agency for this sort of work? How did it happen, if there was no collusion among the studios, that Louis Pollock was blacklisted throughout the industry? Or did all studios use the same "public relations" agency?

The fact is that the key to the answers to these questions was missing—the role played by Roy M. Brewer of the International Association of Theatrical Stage Employees and Motion Picture Machine Operators of the United States. This is the most powerful union in the movie industry. It attained nation-wide notoriety when its president, George E. Browne, and his personal representative, Willie Bioff, were sent to jail for extortion and conspiracy. Brewer was sent to Hollywood to lead his union in a fight against a rival union that claimed jurisdiction. Brewer told the House Un-American Activities Committee in 1947 that the rival union was Communist and called upon the Congressional committee to "destroy the Communist menace in the motion picture industry." Brewer, who had come to Hollywood in 1945, was to become the most important union official in Hollywood for nearly ten years. But more important, so far as the blacklist goes, he became known as "strawboss of the purge."

His labor power and anti-Communist campaign gave him influence with the House Un-American Activities Committee and the American Legion. With an ex-Communist as an assistant, Brewer set up a sort of "rehabilitation" technique for radicals who wished to recant and give names. Through friends in the movie industry,

Brewer helped find work for admitted ex-Communists who admitted guilt and supplied names. Men who somehow became unemployable for political reasons were advised that if they could placate Brewer they would be cleared. Eventually Brewer's price for clearance was a letter of repentance that he virtually dictated. It is by following this technique in the case of Marsha Hunt, the actress, that one is led directly to Kahane's office at Columbia Pictures and to the meaning of his "public relations" agency.

There was never any question that Miss Hunt, a talented and very successful actress, was not a Communist. However, she was an outspoken critic of blacklisting. Soon Miss Hunt found work difficult to find. In 1952, after she was signed for a Columbia movie, *The Happy Time*, to be made by Stanley Kramer, she was asked to sign a loyalty oath. She refused, but offered to write a statement saying she had never been a member of the Communist party. Whereupon Sam Katz, chairman of the board of Kramer's company, expressed dissatisfaction with her statement and told her to sign another statement prepared by Columbia's legal department, in which she apologized for certain political activities. She refused. Katz told her: "You don't have to sign to make this picture, but you'll never work again in films if you don't." Miss Hunt offered a sentence that satisfied Katz. It was: "If any of these activities have furthered the cause of communism, I regret having done them." During shooting, Miss Hunt was badgered to crawl publicly. Again she refused. Suddenly no more movie parts were available. In 1954 Miss Hunt consulted John L. Dales, executive secretary of the Screen Actors Guild. In response to his question she told him she was not a Communist. He advised her to meet Brewer. After two long meetings Brewer told her: "If you want to, I will send your statement out to my people, but I can tell you now it won't do any good."

The investigation of Brewer's activities by The Fund for the Republic concludes: "Brewer denies that he kept people from working. But when he was not satisfied he would not help people find work, and many studio executives were loath to hire anyone who did not have his positive approval."

Gradually, the Hollywood climate for blacklisted writers changed, and 1960 was the key year. It was the year that Kramer disagreed openly with the head of the American Legion. It was the year that Dalton Trumbo's name reappeared on a movie screen as writer of *Exodus*, produced and directed for United Artists by Otto Preminger. It was the year that Sinatra, though defeated, showed it was possible to demand the end of the blacklist and still remain a great box office favorite, produce his own movies, put out his own records, stage television shows—all without retaliation from the forces that terrified Hollywood.

How much the Hollywood attitude had changed in 1960 was demonstrated when Jules Dassin, blacklisted writer-director, was guest of honor at a gathering of the Screen Directors Guild. There, after a showing of his *Never on Sunday* (also a United Artists release), he was the subject of admiration and congratulation by many of Hollywood's top stars, producers and directors. The homage was not a form of apology for his blacklist status in Hollywood. It was a tribute to the fact that Dassin had written, directed and produced *Never on Sunday* for about $150,000 and would gross some $6,000,000 from the film. Dassin, a wiry, gray-haired man with sharp eyes and wry humor, was struck by the irony of these accolades to one blacklistee when so many others were still unemployable in Hollywood—even himself.

After the festivities had subsided Dassin described his feelings to an acquaintance. "About a year and a half ago," he said, "before the opening of my picture *He Who Must Die*, invitations went out to all the fine gentlemen of Hollywood for the same sort of screening—exactly the same. That movie, too, by the way, was made in Greece. As a member of the blacklist I could not have made a movie in Hollywood. I was amazed, therefore, to see that the R.S.V.P.'s showed that nearly everyone was coming. And then came the day of the preview. It was as though a secret button had been pushed. Hordes of men suddenly discovered unavoidable dinner engagements. There was this inexplicable epidemic of grippe and high fever. Of all my director friends—and I have friends—one came. Just one.

"Now things are different. The fact is that Hollywood has invested some $20,000,000 in blacklisted writers. The blacklist is unnatural to the American character. It was bad casting to begin with, and now it is in the throes of its last agonies. Most people in

Hollywood are ashamed of the blacklist. I am talking about studio executives. Many of them now say: 'You know I am against the blacklist. I hate it.' Then comes the long series of 'buts'. It used to be difficult for me to persuade any American star to work for me. Now I get telephone calls from leading actors offering to work in my pictures.

"I do not believe that the American public ever created a blacklist. The blacklist was always a fraud, an extraordinary fraud."

In 1956, Dassin recalled, when his French movie *Rififi* won a Cannes Festival award, the French flag was presented at the ceremony. The picture was of course a French entry, and afterward someone said to him: "*Quelle belle revanche.*" Dassin felt no sense of revenge. "The truth is, it made me sad."

But the blacklist, though weakened, is very much alive in 1964 and its advocates have no intention of letting it die. Consider a letter sent to Preminger on December 11, 1962, by the American Legion after Preminger had announced the employment of Ring Lardner, Jr., a blacklisted writer, to do the screenplay of *The Genius*, a novel by Patrick Dennis. This is not a political book. It deals with a flamboyant movie director determined to make a comeback in Mexico.

The letter from the legion's National Americanism Commission, written by its chairman, Daniel J. O'Connor, was not concerned with the subject of the book. O'Connor was interested solely in the fact that a man he considered politically radical was being employed to write a movie. His suggestion and the implied threat were very clear. "I believe," he wrote, "that it would best serve the interests of the theatre-going public if you would reconsider your decision to employ Ring Lardner, Jr., for the purposes indicated. There is extant an abundance of competent script writers whose loyalty, integrity, good taste and discretion have never been questioned."

Preminger, in his answer eleven days later, said he agreed with O'Connor in his opposition to communism, but not with his methods of fighting it. He urged strict adherence to legal methods and democratic principles. He opposed totalitarian means like boycott, blacklisting, usurpation of police or judicial powers. Then he stated his own case.

"Among the many writers I have employed are two who have been convicted for contempt of Congress, Mr. Dalton Trumbo and Mr. Ring Lardner, Jr. Both served their sentences and have, according to the Constitution, the right to work in their chosen profession. I believe that I have an obligation as an American citizen to respect this right without discrimination. If they should now, or in the future, violate the law again or if they should try to use their job for the slightest bit of subversive propaganda, I shall dismiss them at once.

"Until then I feel that I am serving the public by doing openly what other producers have done secretly for many years while giving hypocritical lip service to an illegal blacklist. Thus I make it possible for anybody who wants to discriminate against these writers to stay away from the films which list their names among the official credits."

In his short letter Preminger touched all bases. Blacklists do not belong in a democracy and certainly not in a field that is an art form and a mass medium. Once accepted, a blacklist will not just vanish by being ignored. It will not be eliminated by deals made in the shadows. The blacklist was born in cowardice and it can be destroyed only by courage.

2. The Hollywood Underground

Eeriest of the offshoots of the Hollywood blacklist is the Hollywood Underground. It is far more bizarre than any of the underground movements portrayed in the movies. The condition of its members ranges from poverty to affluence; from bitterness to compassion. Though the network of this underground extends to many parts of the world, it remains in effect an intellectual ghetto. Here live the men and women who were blacklisted by the movie industry solely for political reasons. Hollywood is not likely to make a movie out of them. Hollywood pretends that this underground, like the blacklist itself, does not exist. It is all part of the Big Lie that Hollywood has spun over its mansions, swimming pools, Rolls Royces and Impressionist paintings with its spidery blacklist.

With aliases, false fronts and a strict code, the members of the Hollywood Underground—they dislike thinking of themselves in this fashion—have created a world as carefully concealed and as labyrinthine as the accusations that forced them into this way of life. In a business where distrust of man for man is axiomatic, they trust one another. No matter where they are—New York, London, Paris, Rome, Mexico City, Ceylon—they keep in touch. They do not forget either those who informed against them or those who befriended them. They are alert for any harm that may threaten one of their number. For they have learned that for them the bell that tolls for one tolls for all. They never completely lose their suspicion of the outsider, nor the feeling that at any moment those blacklistees who are living in comfort, even luxury, could lose everything. In the wondrous history of show business there is nothing like this coterie of the Hollywood Underground.

Consider how they get work. First there is the use of the "front." A blacklisted writer does a script. He knows it will not be produced with his name on it. He approaches a "clean writer"—one who is not on the blacklist—and suggests that the latter's name be used on the script. For this the front usually gets a fee, sometimes running as high as 50 per cent of the sale price. The front generally does nothing more than lend his name to the script. There are some nonblacklisted writers who have refused to accept payment for this service, an admittedly risky undertaking in the timorous environment of Hollywood. Then there are fronts who do some of the writing with the blacklisted writer. If the blacklisted writer has a reputation, his agent may book the fronts for him.

The producer nearly always knows who the real writer is and often discusses rewrites with him in person. Sometimes stars, whose parts need changing, confer with the blacklisted writer. In the vast majority of cases, the studio that finances and releases the movie knows the identity of the writer behind the front. Nevertheless, a studio maintains, over and over again, the pretense that it is ignorant of the real writer. This requires a special kind of logic. The studio, since it claims there is no blacklist, cannot admit it is refusing to use certain writers. That would be an admission that there is a blacklist. At the same time it dare not admit it is using writers who are on the "nonexistent" blacklist. That would antagonize powerful groups.

What happens in this world of the Big Lie is shown clearly by just a portion of the record of Hollywood hypocrisy.

One of the most ludicrous situations involved *Spartacus*. Dalton Trumbo, the best known of the blacklisted writers, worked on the script for many months. Kirk Douglas knew he was doing the writing, because the star's insistence was one of the main reasons Trumbo was hired. Nearly all the other stars in the movie discussed their roles with Trumbo. The top executives at Universal, the company that distributed the picture, knew he was doing the script. So did executives at the studio. Douglas wanted to say so openly but, though a courageous man, he encountered resistance among Universal executives who feared criticism and boycott of this $12,000,000 picture. Even after *The New York Times* said flatly that Trumbo had written the script, no one of importance connected with the movie would admit it. Then Preminger reaped enormous publicity by announcing he would give screen credit to Trumbo for *Exodus*, thus becoming the first producer to defy the blacklist. Only then did Universal, after much cogitation, decide to put Trumbo's name on the movie of *Spartacus*.

Others never were admitted. The name of Paul Jarrico, a blacklisted writer, never appeared on the movie *Jovanka*, released by Paramount. Michael Wilson, who left the country to escape the purge, has never been listed by Columbia as one of the writers of *Bridge on the River Kwai*, one of the biggest money-makers in movie history. Fox made many millions from *The Robe*. But it has yet to admit that one of the reasons for the success of this 1953 movie was that Albert Maltz, one of the "Unfriendly Ten," was one of the writers. Nor did the name of Ian McLellan Hunter, another blacklisted writer, ever appear on the screen of the enormously successful *Roman Holiday*.

As of 1964 there is only one unclaimed Oscar statuette at the Motion Picture Academy of Arts and Sciences. It was awarded to "Robert Rich" in 1957 for writing *The Brave One*. But no one ever appeared to claim this Oscar. That is because the script was written by Trumbo. Robert Rich was a relative of one of the three King brothers, who produced the movie. He was not a writer and had nothing to do with the script.

The use of fronts has produced other situations, none as extraordinary as the "Robert Rich" incident, but extremely interesting to those who seek skeletons in the Hollywood blacklist closet. One writer, whose output was neither substantial nor particularly good before the blacklist, has become an enormously prolific and successful producer-writer since the blacklist. Blacklisted writers say he has built his reputation and wealth by becoming a front for a "stable" of blacklisted writers.

There have been amusing aspects of the fronting business. The front for *Cowboy* was Hugo Butler. He was himself blacklisted for alleged radicalism shortly before the movie was released. Whereupon the studio removed the name of Butler from the credits. When Butler told Trumbo about this the latter said angrily: "They can't do this to you." Butler, who was not accepting a fee as a front, was astonished at this strange outburst. "Why, you damned fool," he exclaimed, "you wrote the script." Trumbo had forgotten that this script had come from his mill.

Then there was the rather inept writer who suggested a rewrite to the much more talented blacklisted writer for whom he was fronting. The blacklisted writer turned it down brusquely. The foolish front protested. "After all," he said, "my name is on this script and I have to consider my reputation as a writer." On the other hand, there were young writers of ability who fronted for blacklisted writers and thus received recognition on their own.

By an irony that Congressional investigators never anticipated, some blacklisted writers have profited from their stigma. There has grown up a widespread belief in the movie industry that all blacklisted writers are excellent. The top blacklisted writers say readily that just as there are good writers who are not blacklisted, so there are mediocre writers who are blacklisted. Yet, some producers, if they cannot get the services of the best of the blacklisted writers, will hire a blacklisted writer who is probably not as competent as some "clean" writer.

"It is a sort of mystique," said one blacklisted writer. "I, for example, am really nothing better than a competent hack. But because I am blacklisted I am now entrusted with enormous assignments that I might never have got if I were not blacklisted."

The most remarkable production record in the black market was established by Trumbo and Wilson. For eighteen months they turned out a script every five weeks. Their method was extraordinary. Wilson did the screen treatments in sections. This means he arranged plot, scenes, presented characters. As Wilson finished each section of treatment he sent it to Trumbo who supplied dialogue. Trumbo, while doing dialogue for one section, did not know what Wilson was preparing in the way of scenes for the next section. And Wilson, while writing ahead in his section, did not know what dialogue Trumbo had inserted in the preceding portion. In the end, of course, they would meet to unravel the knots.

In addition to the front there is the pseudonym. The best known of these is Nedrick Young's nom de plume, Nathan E. Douglas. Young's secret became known when the New York Film Critics chose *The Defiant Ones*, by Young and Harold J. Smith, for a writing award. The two writers—Smith is not blacklisted—received Oscars for this script. So idiotic are the blacklist pretenses that even after the Oscar award, when everyone in show business knew the true identity of "Nathan E. Douglas," that name turned up on the script of *Inherit the Wind*.

One of the sleaziest methods by which movie companies obtain the services of blacklisted writers without risking criticism has been to purchase pictures after they have been made abroad by independent companies.

Take the case of Warner Brothers, the company headed by Jack L. Warner, who never tires of making speeches about patriotism. This company bought a movie called *Moment of Danger* when it was made in England. When Warners distributed the picture in the United States it was called *Malaga*. When the movie was bought its credits included the name of Donald Ogden Stewart, a very talented blacklisted writer, who has been living abroad since the blacklist. When the movie was shown in the United States the name of Donald Ogden Stewart was missing.

To make life easier for Hollywood studios, some foreign independent companies make contracts with blacklisted writers that include an unusual clause. It says that the writer will receive screen credit in the Eastern Hemisphere, but in the Western Hemisphere the distributor has the right to remove the credit.

In some cases the Hollywood studio does not have this right. It must then distribute the picture with the names of blacklistees who are unemployable under their own names in Hollywood. Thus, Metro-Goldwyn-Mayer purchased the distribution rights to the French film *Le Loi*—The Law. This movie was directed by Jules Dassin, the writer-director who, as we have seen, is unemployable in Hollywood despite his success with *Rififi*, *He Who Must Die*, and *Never on Sunday*.

Then there was the English movie *Blind Date*. It was written by Ben Barzman and Millard Lampeil, and directed by Joseph Losey. All three are on the Hollywood blacklist. Nevertheless, Paramount bought the movie and changed the name to *Chance Meeting*.

As in any underground, an unwritten code is followed. It is a cardinal rule in the world of the blacklisted that a writer must not reveal he wrote a script unless the producer first agrees. Thus, after *The New York Times* printed the story that Trumbo had done *Spartacus*, another writer disparaged Trumbo's contribution to the movie. Trumbo could not, because of the blacklist code, defend himself. Another example occurred after it became known that Nathan E. Douglas was the pseudonym for Nedrick Young. The writer told reporters, falsely, that Stanley Kramer had not known it was his pseudonym when he signed him for *The Defiant Ones*.

Another rule of the blacklist underground is to try to help others on the blacklist. If one blacklisted writer is too busy to take on a project he will recommend another. If one blacklisted writer hears about a movie that is being considered abroad he will notify black-listees abroad about this approaching venture. When blacklisted writers become directors abroad they try to hire blacklisted actors. London has become a refuge for the Hollywood blacklisted.

The fate of the blacklisted actors has been more grievous than that of the writers. When a face is, literally, a man's fortune it does him no good to change his name. Gale Sondergaard, an Oscar winner for her supporting performance in *Anthony Adverse*, never received another job after she was blacklisted. Other gifted performers, such as Ann Revere and Morris Carnovsky, returned to

Broadway. Some, such as Sam Wanamaker, became part of the English colony. Others managed to keep alive in their own field by directing community dramatic groups, giving readings or teaching.

Jeff Corey was making about $30,000 a year, with a good future, when he was blacklisted. Studios refused to hire him in Hollywood, though they invited him to study screen tests and paid him for his advice. Leading stars were sent to him, or went voluntarily, for coaching for special movie roles.

In its manner of life, as well as in its working habits, the Hollywood Underground is unique. In the financially stratified life of Hollywood, the community of the blacklisted is unexampled in its indifference to the income of its members. Prosperous ones share with those less fortunate. For example, one blacklisted writer who was doing well in Europe learned that a Hollywood blacklisted writer was hoping to write, direct and produce his own movie abroad. Without being asked, he sent to his Hollywood colleague his bank books, with power of attorney, and told him to use what he needed.

At a gathering of the blacklisted it is impossible not to sense the special kind of friendship that exists among them, though they argue about all sorts of things, sometimes with considerable heat. They rarely cry in each other's beer. Alvah Bessie, a writer who before the blacklist found no difficulty getting more than $1,500 a week, was handling the spotlight in a San Francisco night club in 1963. Others have worked as junkmen, bartenders, repair men. An ironic twist was that of the blacklisted writer who opened a television repair store. An employee of his, not knowing the boss's background, when applying for a civil service job that required security clearance, gave the blacklisted writer as a reference. The writer does not know if the young man got the job.

The underground was born in the early days of the blacklist. It became common, for instance, for a man dodging a subpoena to hide out for weeks. Friends helped the children of those seeking refuge. Children were told to lie about the whereabouts of their parents. One child, knowing his father was lying flat in the bottom of a car parked in the neighborhood, would tell any stranger that daddy was out of town.

One blacklisted writer says: "We had a terrible sense of isolation for a long time. Even in the late fifties it was considered an act of courage by many in Hollywood to say hello to a blacklisted writer in a public place."

The common bond among the blacklisted is most noticeable in their dealings with those who co-operated with Congressional committees. One day a blacklisted writer and his young son entered a Hollywood restaurant. They almost collided with a man who had given names several years earlier to a Congressional committee. Before that the blacklisted writer and the witness had been good friends. The witness held out his hand to the blacklisted writer. The writer turned to his son and said: "This is a stool pigeon." Not all of the blacklisted are so bitter. There are some who simply hope they never have to meet a "co-operative" witness, but who say that if they do they hope they will not be too cruel.

The writers who went to jail had the most vivid experiences. One writer sent a series of made-up stories from his cell to his seven-year-old boy. As heroes, he invented an Indian and a cowboy who served as confidential spies for Lincoln and sneaked behind Confederate lines. One day the warden of the southern jail summoned the writer to his office. The warden was furious. He waved a letter he had intercepted. It was the latest episode the writer had done for his son. The warden considered this glorification of Lincoln proof that the writer was a Communist. He ordered the writer to desist from any more such subversion. The writer refused and threatened to make a public issue of it. The warden surrendered and the Indian and cowboy continued to work for Lincoln for the rest of his jail term.

While Trumbo was in jail for contempt of Congress his daughter won and accepted a citizenship award at school for grades, leadership and co-operation. The prize was awarded by the American Legion. The legion knew she was the daughter of the man it had helped to send to jail.

Another writer recalled the reaction of other prisoners to the writers. "At first," he said, "we were regarded as weird. Then, when it became known that we had earned $2,000 a week in Hollywood, we acquired prestige. Then we acquired popularity because we wrote letters for uneducated prisoners to their wives, children or sweethearts."

But for all its pathos, personal tragedy, hypocrisy, the Hollywood blacklist and the Hollywood Underground represented the worst kinds of censorship because of what they did to the movie industry as an art form. If, in spite of the blacklist, Hollywood had grown artistically, it could be argued that the blacklist served the same healthful purpose as weeding out a garden; that without the strangulating influence of radicals in the industry, Hollywood's more beautiful plants had a chance to flourish.

This did not happen. Quite the contrary. For as the reign of terror spread through Hollywood with the growth of McCarthyism, even the most innocuous liberals became worried that their mild opinions would be construed as radicalism fit for blacklist purgatory. No job was considered too unimportant for judgment by the House Un-American Activities Committee, the American Legion and Brewer. Schary, who was boss of the Metro-Goldwyn-Mayer studio during much of this period, is convinced that one of the reasons he lost this job was that he was very enthusiastic in campaigning for the Democratic party.

None of the investigations into communism in Hollywood showed any evidence that Communist propaganda had been worked into films by radical writers—how actors could have done it has always been an unexplained mystery. Still the word passed like an epidemic through the movie industry that movies with serious themes were to be avoided.

Controversy was to be avoided at all costs. In 1947, Hollywood had filmed the delightful satire on national politics called *The Senator Was Indiscreet*. But after the blacklist atmosphere set in, such spoofs of politicians, a traditional form of American humor, were taboo in Hollywood. In 1947 the movie industry attacked anti-Semitism by making *Gentlemen's Agreement*. No more of that was wanted by Hollywood in the blacklist era.

Dorothy B. Jones, who made a study of the relationship between the investigations of Hollywood and the content of films, concluded that a decline began in serious themes in 1947, the first year of the blacklist, and continued to fall steadily into 1949, though "some social theme movies continued to be made." The years 1950-52, when the blacklist epidemic became most virulent, Mrs. Jones said, "can be described as a period when the industry radically reduced the number of social theme movies and devoted itself to escapist fare of all kinds."

Admittedly, it is difficult to say what is a "social theme." But a more explicit explanation of the kinds of pictures that Hollywood wanted was made during the blacklist heyday by Eric Johnston, as liaison between Hollywood and Washington and the official spokesman for the American movie industry. He made his point in a talk to movie writers. As one writer recalled it, Johnston said: "We'll have no more *Grapes of Wrath*. We'll have no more *Tobacco Roads*. We'll have no more films that show the seamy side of American life. We'll have no pictures that deal with labor strikes. We'll have no more pictures that show the banker as a villain." The memory of the writer could have been at fault, but the results have conformed to that talk. Hollywood was scared stiff.

In April of 1961 a movie star, known to favor freedom of speech and the United Nations, was asked to participate in a Hollywood rally to espouse both causes. It was not a meeting of radicals. Among the speakers were two United States Senators—Clifford P. Case of New Jersey, a Republican, and Eugene J. McCarthy of Minnesota, a Democrat. Important educators and clergymen in the Los Angeles area were behind it because it was a response to the bombing of the homes of two ministers who had praised the United Nations and criticized right-wing extremists.

Knowing this background, the star replied: "I don't want to get involved in anything more controversial than a charity for crippled children." This comment was typical of the answers of other Hollywood celebrities who declined to be at the rally.

What was true of the effect of the blacklist on the personal behavior of Hollywood was even more true of its artistic life. The blacklist paralyzed artistic growth. From this affliction, despite the worrisome competition of the serious movies made abroad, Hollywood had still not recovered in the early sixties. It was devoting the bulk of its money to such "safe" films as *Cleopatra, El Cid, Lawrence of Arabia.*

There is no doubt that Hollywood can bloom artistically without ever using a blacklisted writer, director or actor. But it is very unlikely that as long as Hollywood continues to tolerate a blacklist it will mature. Artistic integrity requires the sort of courage that is the natural enemy of a blacklist. Without integrity there can be no art in Hollywood. The atmosphere that produces a blacklist and has maintained it is the most terrible of censors precisely because it is a censor that hides in the mind, that cannot be refuted or changed like the written word of a censorship code or law. As long as there is a blacklist in Hollywood, there will be little stature to its art.

3. *Pre-censor First—Think Later*

Hollywood's terror of pressure groups, plus its tendency to assume that artistic values make poor box office, have created another form of censorship that is much more characteristic of a brutal dictatorship than of an entrenched democracy. This is pre-censorship, a form of self-destruction that its practitioners look upon as the key to survival. Pre-censorship is what prompts studio heads, producers, directors, stars and writers to distort and water down scripts, not because of objections from Hollywood censors, but because of preconceived ideas that the original script may rouse pressure group antagonism or hurt the box office because it is "too good." Pre-censorship is what makes even intelligent and sensitive persons in the movie industry destroy what they want most without being ordered to do so—or even being asked. Pre-censorship is the infantile paralysis of Hollywood.

Pre-censorship, despite what its advocates say or how they rationalize it, is not the same thing as making changes to improve the entertainment or cultural values of a script. Pre-censorship tends to reduce these values. It stems entirely from fear, stupidity or both.

Indicative of this kind of thinking on the top echelon of the movie industry was a remark attributed to Spyros P. Skouras, then president of Twentieth Century-Fox: "Abraham Lincoln is box office poison." It is true that the movie version of *Abe Lincoln in Illinois* was disappointing at the box office. That there may have been artistic reasons for its poor showing is not explored. The taboo against movies about Lincoln will continue until someone makes a successful one. There was just as strong a prejudice against Civil War movies. No one wanted to make a picture of *Gone With the Wind* until David O. Selznick decided it was nonsense to refuse to make a movie because of an unproved superstition. The picture was an Oscar winner in 1939 and had earned, through 1963, more than $67,000,000, to be one of the greatest hits in movie history.

The main reason that the films of foreign producers and directors have dominated American art houses is not that the directors are more brilliant than the best of Hollywood. It is because they do not suffer from pre-censorship. They are willing to carry through to the end an idea that sparked their enthusiasm. They are not frightened by the unusual or intimidated by the possibility of failure. This is why a *Rashomon* comes from Japan; an *Open City* from Italy; a *Wild Strawberries* from Sweden; a *400 Blows* from France. It is nonsense to blame Hollywood's shortcomings on its censorship code. Most of the top foreign movies could have obtained a seal of approval in Hollywood with little or no change. It is the movie-makers themselves who, too often, censor themselves. In their dreams of "box office" they underestimate their audiences. It is pre-censorship that prevents Hollywood from realizing its artistic potential—and its commercial potential as well.

The best way—perhaps the only way—to explain pre-censorship is to show how it works. Some examples may seem so ludicrous as to be exceptional. But there is nothing so ridiculous as the distortion of a book or play to placate the whims of pre-censorship. It has happened so often in Hollywood that it may be categorized.

First there is the pre-censorship to maintain the "upbeat" ending. An upbeat ending is not necessarily a happy ending, though it used to mean that. As Hollywood has matured it has come to accept a hopeful ending as upbeat.

One of the best examples was Tennessee Williams' *Sweet Bird of Youth*. In Williams' Broadway play, purchased by Metro-Goldwyn-Mayer, the chief male character is a handsome young gigolo who attaches himself to a fading actress in the hope that she can help him to a career. He is castrated in his home town, permitting Williams to draw once more the moral of man's bestiality.

In the movie, the man, instead of being castrated, is beaten up, but he gets the girl he has loved since boyhood, thus permitting virtue to triumph over evil. Williams himself, it should be noted, rewrote the play after it closed on Broadway to eliminate the castration. But the gigolo remained a gigolo, trailing his middle-aged actress.

The upbeat ending was not devised to avoid censorship. The picture would have had no trouble getting a seal of approval with the original ending minus the castration. The hero could simply have been beaten to death. For example, in *The Fugitive Kind*, the movie version of Williams' *Orpheus Descending*, the hero, instead of being devoured by dogs—another quaint Williams finale—was virtually forced by the police to be burned to death. And it is particularly interesting that the two best adaptations of Williams to the screen—*A Streetcar Named Desire* and *The Rose Tattoo*—adhered to the play as much as possible within the limitations of the production code. They were both financial as well as artistic successes. They both received a seal of approval.

The need for an upbeat ending has often forced the most drastic kind of pre-censorship on films. If it seems impossible to leave the audience smiling, a book or play will rarely be bought. Thus it is generally agreed among top writers in Hollywood that John O'Hara's novel *Appointment in Samara* is the best suited of all his books for movie adaptation. Yet, though O'Hara books have been made into movies, *Appointment in Samara* has been ignored by studio heads and producers. Its downbeat suicide ending has discouraged Hollywood purchasers.

Then there is the terror of destroying a star's public image. Sometimes the star is just as culpable as the movie company. Consider the case of the engaging Truman Capote novelette, *Breakfast at Tiffany's*. The heroine, Holly Golightly, was an amusing hoyden with very few moral inhibitions. Part of her humor was her indifference to promiscuity. But when Audrey Hepburn was cast in the role it was considered improper to let her public see her depicted in this fashion. In the words of Blake Edwards, who directed the movie, the following changes were made: "In the movie we don't say exactly what Holly's morals are. In a sense she can be considered an escort service for men. . . . Risqué dialogue was deleted and she no longer discusses her affairs with men. Holly is now a patroness of the arts."

There was no regulation at the Hollywood censorship office that prevented Holly from being promiscuous, any more than the censorship office demanded that *Sweet Bird of Youth* have a happy ending. *Butterfield 8* had a nymphomaniac for a heroine. She remained so in the movie by the simple expedient of *not* being shown in bed with a man. Holly was just a victim of Hollywood pre-censorship.

Pre-censorship really blooms when it deals with the subject of love. And in *Gulliver's Travels*, Swift failed to realize that two centuries later, when Columbia was making his satire into a movie, it would need romance. But the movie company arranged for a strong dose of love. Arthur Rose, who did the adaptation, gave Lemuel Gulliver a sweetheart instead of a wife. More romantic. He even created a pair of lovers among the Lilliputians. "I wanted," he explained, "to personalize the life of Gulliver in Lilliput. It may be a shopworn cliché, but it is uncontestably valid that a love story gives Gulliver more identification for the audience. Love gives dramatic application to the struggles of individuals against destiny."

Perhaps the weirdest kind of pre-censorship crops up when Hollywood goes to work on the Bible. The Old Testament, in particular, has strong appeal for producers because, apart from being in the public domain, it has some interesting characters, strong conflicts and some excellent opportunities for sex in exotic costumes. It is no accident that, in the trade, a Bible story is called "lust-in-the-dust."

Since the adventures of Ruth, Naomi and Boaz are among the most touching romances in literature, it was inevitable that they would become a movie. But the film called for quite a few pre-censored improvements before it was ready for the movie houses under the title *The Story of Ruth.* Samuel Engel, who produced the film, knows the original Hebrew of: "Whither thou goest I will go; and where thou lodgest, I will lodge: thy people shall be my people and thy God my God." For years, writers dating back to Maxwell Anderson had done treatments on the subject for

Twentieth Century-Fox. Finally came a treatment from Norman Corwin and Engel decided, from Corwin's skeleton of the screenplay, that he had a movie.

"We decided," said the producer, "that the Bible version was weak because the story was not about Ruth but about her mother-in-law. The part of Ruth was fattened. A Moabite civilization was created. Complications were worked out for the love story." Self-censorship to placate the imagined taste of the public caused this film disaster.

Those who suffered through the movie may wonder how the producer was able to say: "It is all treated with the greatest respect, of course . . . After all, you must remember that Ruth was the great-grandmother of David and an ancestor of Jesus."

Life can become particularly gruesome when novelists and playwrights adapting their own works for the screen are caught in the toils of Hollywood pre-censorship. Leon Uris, for instance, before he had become famous with his novel *Exodus*, was fired while adapting an earlier book, *The Angry Hills*. The reason: "I was told I did not understand the characters." Uris was to exact a peculiar sort of revenge after *Exodus* made him a writer of power in Hollywood. He formed his own company and called it Dagon, the Hebrew name for the Philistine god that was half man and half fish. "It reminds me of the men with whom I have done business here at one time or another."

More painful was the tale of Robert Anderson, who adapted his hit play, *Tea and Sympathy*, for the movies. In the play the heroine makes it clear to her husband that their marriage is finished. At the climax of the play she is about to sleep with the youth, Tom, to prove to him that he must not consider himself a homosexual because he was unable to have intercourse with a whore. But in the movie her adultery with the youth had to be the cause of the breakup of her marriage.

"What they made me do for the movies," said Anderson, "was more immoral than what happened in my play. It is far more immoral that a woman who had not broken with her husband should sleep with this youth than if she had already broken with her husband. Always we seemed to be quibbling. I had to cut too many corners. They persuade you to give in on so many things by saying: 'We'll let you keep the core of the story.' You become convinced you're saving the story. But you're not. I will never again give in as I did on *Tea and Sympathy*. Robert Frost once told me: 'Don't be first to be second.' "

A weird sort of pre-censorship mongrelization took place when a movie was made of William Faulkner's *Sanctuary*. James Poe, who did the screenplay, and is an ardent admirer of the author, had to combine *Sanctuary* with the Nobel Prize winner's *Requiem for a Nun*. Richard Zanuck, producer of the film, had the whole idea worked out on the back of an envelope for Poe. "We wanted very much to talk to Mr. Faulkner," said Zanuck. "But we could never get to him. From what I understand, Mr. Faulkner does his best to avoid Hollywood." Faulkner, who had once worked briefly in Hollywood, had probably heard the comment another Nobel Prize winner, Ernest Hemingway, made about Richard Zanuck's father, Darryl F. The elder Zanuck made a Hemingway potpourri called *The Snows of Kilimanjaro*. Hemingway called it *The Snows of Zanuck*.

These—and many other—foolish cases of pre-censorship have planted the idea in the minds of many sensitive moviegoers that it is impossible for Hollywood to adapt a play or novel without mangling it. Each time a particularly ridiculous adaptation comes to the screen, the public forgets the tasteful movies that have adhered to the original novel. Thus it is forgotten that George Stevens did not follow the usual movie custom of making a happy ending when he adapted Theodore Dreiser's *An American Tragedy* to the screen under the title *A Place in the Sun*. In the movie, as in the book, the ambitious young man (Montgomery Clift) allows the poor young woman (Shelley Winters) he has made pregnant to drown in order to be free to marry a wealthy girl (Elizabeth Taylor). He is still arrested and condemned to the electric chair. According to Ivan Moffat, who did the script, Stevens, from the very beginning, knew the movie had to be tragic, regardless of dour prophecies in Hollywood that this was box office suicide. His indifference to Hollywood's love of the happy ending brought him an Oscar for the best direction of 1951 and a substantial hit.

Curiously, it was Moffat who was eventually to be criticized by

The New Yorker magazine for being too faithful to a book when he adapted F. Scott Fitzgerald's *Tender Is the Night.* "You can't win, it seems," he said. "The heart of the matter—and I think this is often forgotten—is that a film should be a continuous assault on the emotions. A book can be absorbed intellectually as well as emotionally. But the intellectual reaction to a movie comes after one has left the theater."

Movies have sometimes profited from changes made during the adaptation process. One case was Walter Tevis's novel *The Hustler.* Drastic plot changes made the movie, directed by Robert Rossen, one of the major American artistic successes of 1961.

Please Don't Eat the Daisies was an amusing collection of anecdote-strewn essays written by Jean Kerr. It seemed unsuited for films. But a screen writer, Isobel Lennart, gave it a plot, built up characters, created dialogue and conflict that made it possible to convert the book into a successful movie.

Why does Hollywood pay huge prices for best-selling novels and hit plays when, after brief consideration, it realizes it does not intend to retain the literary and dramatic values that made the book and play successful? The answer is contained in three words that comprise a mystique as important to the movie industry as were the utterances of the oracles to the ancients. The words are: penetration, chemistry and insurance.

By penetration Hollywood means the extent to which a book or play has embedded itself favorably in the American public's mind. A best seller that has been serialized in a magazine with a multimillion circulation is presumed to have penetrated so deeply that the American public will be unable to resist that classic Hollywood appeal: "You read the book, now see the movie." That an average of three years passes from the time a book is bought for a movie until it becomes film in a theater does not upset the penetration theory. Behind the theory of penetration seems to be the belief that the moviegoing audience reads very few books in three years. In recent years paperbacks have narrowed the span between book publication and movie release. In a number of cases the paperbacks have been issued as a sort of advance publicity for the movie or to capitalize on the film's publicity.

Then there is chemistry. This means, to a movie executive, the formula that brings together the perfect blending of story, stars and director for the multimillion-dollar, Oscar-winning smash. To producers, though they talk about the need for a "good story," the basic ingredient of the chemistry is the star. For with stars they can obtain loans from bankers. The bankers care little about the script. They look at the names of the stars. To get a star many producers feel they must have a best seller or a hit play. Stars want the prestige and "protection" of a successful book or play—and they are strong believers in penetration and chemistry.

Insurance is a development of chemistry. It is, in the eyes of Hollywood, the philosopher's stone of movie-making. The best seller is important to "insure" the success of the picture. Just as the chemists like to ignore the vastly successful *High Noon*, which was adapted from a short story, so the insurers prefer to forget about Edna Ferber's best-selling *Ice Palace*, bought for $400,000 by Warner Brothers and a commercial flop.

Unmentioned by producers and movie executives in all their glib talk about penetration, chemistry and insurance are the two words that have created this arid formula as well as pre-censorship. The words are: stupidity and fear. Rare is the movie executive or producer who can appraise a novel in cinematic terms. And even among those movie-makers with taste and judgment there is a strong desire to have an advance alibi if the movie fails. Which movie president or board of directors will blame a man for buying a best seller? Obviously, if the movie fails it is someone else's fault. The fear and stupidity that have produced thoughtless pre-censorship are the main causes for the sense of guilt Hollywood writers have about their occupation. The gibes of novelists and playwrights have given them spiritual calluses. But yet, why should the Hollywood writer have to wear the badge of shame for the mistakes of his employers? Some of the top writers have rebelled. Wilder, Diamond and Brooks have become writer-director-producers. Stanley Shapiro and Abbe Mann formed their own producing companies.

The resentment writers have for the blanket blame that is not theirs was summed up by Ernest Lehman, one of the most successful Hollywood writers, in a hypothetical question. "A producer acquires the rights to a novel. He contacts a writer to do the adaptation. They discuss financial terms and agree. The writer takes the book into his office, puts paper in his typewriter and writes a dramatic script. The producer likes it. A director agrees to do it. The director and producer assemble the best cast they can find. The entertainment venture that results is acclaimed by the critics and the public. Perhaps it even wins a few prizes. Now, from what I have just said, can you tell whether this was a movie or a play?"

The answer is that when there is no interference from stupid pre-censors, it is difficult to tell whether Lehman is discussing a movie or play. For example, Tad Mosel won a Pulitzer Prize for the play *All the Way Home*, which was a dramatization of James Agee's *A Death in the Family*. And Broadway musicals which have won Pulitzer Prizes are, by their very nature, the work of many hands. However, the playwright, by his contract, can refuse to submit to pre-censorship. He need not change a word of his script. The movie writer has no such protection.

The pre-censorship situation was stated dramatically by another writer, Edmund Hartmann, a former national chairman of the Writers Guild of America. He said: "The writer has never held the throne. The writer is too many steps removed from the moment of decision before the cameras. The script has always been a tool used by the struggling mammoths. Movie-making is essentially the telling of a story. But the simple function of the story-teller has been obscured by a complex machinery of manufacture. Each step of the assembly line has become a madhouse of distortion to press the story in the image of the producer, the director, the star. The movie script too often has been a chunk of meat thrown to the lions. The producer tears off a chunk. The director claws what he can get. The star roars and snarls for the largest bleeding bits."

This is pre-censorship. Art does not emerge readily from a jungle.

THE OUTLAW: Cause of the most celebrated censorship fight in movie history, it pitted industrialist Howard Hughes, as producer-director of the film, against virtually the entire movie industry, countless religious, civic organizations. This advertisement of the heroine (Jane Russell) became the most celebrated in Hollywood annals and demonstrates why the movie, among other things, touched off the long era of mammary madness.

BOCCACCIO '70: Italian-style décolletage considered unfair competition by Hollywood. The not very secret weapon is Anita Ekberg.

Charles Feldman

A STREETCAR NAMED DESIRE: This movie made Hollywood censors expand their horizons to consider taste and quality, as well as the subject. In this scene, Stella (Kim Stanley) vainly tries to prevent her husband (Marlon Brando) from destroying the radio in their home, after it had been turned on by her visiting sister, Blanche (Vivian Leigh). Blanche's tentative suitor (Karl Malden) is bystander.

United Artists

THE MAN WITH THE GOLDEN ARM: Movie forced change in censorship code to permit depiction of dope addiction. Frank Sinatra was Hollywood's pioneer cokey.

THE MOON IS BLUE: Prize boner of Hollywood censors was their refusal to give seal of approval to this innocent comedy. Several years later, censors, in unprecedented action, reversed themselves. Urbane wolves here are William Holden and David Niven, with Maggie McNamara quite safe between them.

United Artists

FROM HERE TO ETERNITY: Adultery became permissible without terrible punishment in this Oscar-winner. Famous love scene depicts Burt Lancaster with Deborah Kerr. Censors tried to force director Fred Zinnemann to throw robes around them.

Warner Brothers

BABY DOLL: Study of immorality in the South so infuriated Cardinal Spellman that he attacked the picture from the pulpit of St. Patrick's Cathedral. In this shot, the husband (Karl Malden) realizes his wife (Carroll Baker) has committed adultery with owner of cotton gin (Eli Wallach).

INHERIT THE WIND: Fundamentalist churches of the South fought against showing this argument for evolution based on the Scopes Trial, in which Clarence Darrow (Spencer Tracy) defended Darwinism against William Jennings Bryan (Fredric March).

FREUD: Example of Jewish pressure on movie. Dialogue in which neurotic makes anti-Semitic remarks about Freud was deleted at request of Jewish groups. Here are Freud (Montgomery Clift) and patient (Susannah York). After film was in distribution, Universal, in attempt to boost appeal, changed title to *Secret Passion*. At some theaters the marquees used *Secret Passions of Freud*.

GONE WITH THE WIND: Loudest of teapot tempests in movie censorship was when censor tried to ban use of "damn" by Rhett Butler (Clark Gable) to Scarlett O'Hara (Vivian Leigh). "Damn" was finally allowed.

MGM

4. *The Devil in Hollywood*

On September 19, 1960, the blacklist made Hollywood the laughingstock of the world in a situation more fit for a Voltaire than for the scores of reporters and photographers from many nations who recorded the event, most of them unaware that they were tasting the cream of a magnificent, bitter jest. On that day a short, moon-faced man arrived in Hollywood with greater fanfare than any star had ever received. He had motorcycle escorts before, State Department and Los Angeles officials behind. The most important stars awaited him impatiently at the Twentieth Century-Fox studio. In the Hollywood that had often played host to Presidents, kings and queens, nothing like this day had ever been known. But the cause of all the commotion seemed unimpressive when he appeared at the studio. His clothes, at least twenty years out of date and ill-fitting, gave his short broad figure a slightly simian look. When his moon face broke into a smile, he revealed spaces between his teeth that would have been intolerable to a Hollywood actor. As he headed for the studio commissary he looked more like a bit player hired for the role of a tenement house janitor than a man for whom the mightiest of Hollywood had gathered to pay homage. He was Nikita S. Khrushchev, Premier of the Soviet Union, the most powerful man in the Communist world.

Escorting him was a tall handsome man in smartly tailored suit. His white hair, erect carriage, poised manner, gave him the aplomb that Hollywood expects of its symbols. He was Eric Johnston, spokesman for Hollywood throughout the world. This smiling companion, nodding affably each time Khrushchev spoke to him, was the same man who had said in 1947: "We will not knowingly employ a Communist or a member of any party or group which advocates the overthrow of the government of the United States by force or by any illegal or unconstitutional methods."

In all the speeches that were made that day and night, as Khrushchev toured Hollywood and Los Angeles, no one mentioned the fact that among the guests at the luncheon in his honor was Edward Dmytryk, a director who had been sent to jail for contempt of Congress in refusing to "co-operate" with the House Un-American Activities Committee, and who was present only because after serving a jail term he had recanted and given names of men and women in Hollywood that were to be added to the blacklist or were already there. In none of the speeches was there any allusion to the fact that Hollywood was the last major stronghold of that symbol of McCarthyism, the blacklist. No one mentioned slave labor in Russia and no one mentioned blacklisting in Hollywood. For the first day in thirteen years it was permissible to speak openly about communism; to shake hands with the devil.

But behind the scenes for more than two weeks the story had been very different in Hollywood. Status had vied with fear. Movie notables had become more concerned with where they would sit than what they stood for. There was more concern with what Communists would like to eat than with what they would like to say. Khrushchev and his wife probably never noticed it, but at the moment they entered the vast commissary at Fox— about the size of a couple of basketball courts—men were still scuttling about trying to placate stars who did not like their seats, deftly swiping and rearranging seating cards.

Early in September, when Johnston notified Hollywood that "as desired by our government, a luncheon will be held . . . so he [Khrushchev] can meet a limited number of individual motion-picture leaders and creators" the subsurface uproar began. At once, some columnists wrote that the luncheon would be poorly attended, almost boycotted. Hedda Hopper vowed she would not attend a luncheon honoring a Communist. She was the only one who avoided it. Hollywood executives' fear of what columnists might say was reflected at the first meeting of planners of the luncheon in the executive dining room at Fox.

One veteran producer declared he could not attend a luncheon to honor a Communist. As he talked it became evident that he was wondering if some years hence the blacklist might be expanded from the list of guests at the Khrushchev luncheon just as the current blacklist had been recruited in part from lists of names on petitions for the Spanish Loyalists prepared during the thirties. In the silence that followed his remarks it was obvious that his thoughts were not unique.

But wiser voices counseled that this could not be since the heads of all movie companies had agreed to be present or be represented by top assistants—in which case the whole industry would have to be blacklisted. This argument prevailed and then the discussion swept to the opposite extreme. How would they be able to limit the number of guests at the luncheon with the minimum of anguish and cries of revenge from those excluded?

It was suggested that wives be excluded. Or, if the guest was a female star, her husband was not to be invited. This immediately brought forth gasps of protest. One executive, famous throughout Hollywood for his toughness and uncouthness as a negotiator, shouted: "I can't do that. My wife will say: 'What kind of boss are you? Can't even get an invitation for his wife to lunch. You must be all washed up at the studio.' " He yielded, however, when it was pointed out that everyone else would be in the same position and it could always be indicated that the decision was made by the State Department.

Then an executive suggested that all talent agents be excluded. This brought forth cries of rejoicing. A wonderful opportunity to show superiority to the talent agencies that had become increasingly powerful in Hollywood, in some respects more so than the studios. "We'll fix the flesh peddlers," said one. Another added: "They're not really part of the industry. They're just parasites." This was easily the most popular ruling of the day. But by the day of the luncheon it was not only reversed, but there were denials that it had even been considered. Agents were among the 400-odd at the luncheon.

Just before the session adjourned, there was amused speculation about the furious reaction of the wife of one important movie mogul when she learned she could not be present at the luncheon. She would never force her way into this party, they vowed. She did! Her family owned stock in an important newspaper. She appeared as an accredited correspondent.

Within a few days after the end of the first meeting it became apparent that the lust for status was far greater in Hollywood than suspicion of harboring radical feelings. From all outposts of the American movie industry machinations were started to finagle invitations to the luncheon. When blocked in Hollywood, applicants turned to superior movie officials in New York, to members of boards of directors, even to officials in Washington. No debutante ever tried harder to get an invite to the ball of the season.

As the list of those invited became public the clamor of those not yet invited became more strident. For the list of those invited included Marilyn Monroe, Frank Sinatra, Marlon Brando, Elizabeth Taylor, Dean Martin, Tony Curtis, Gary Cooper, Audrey Hepburn, Gregory Peck, Shirley MacLaine, Bob Hope, Debbie Reynolds. This list was the Who's Who of Hollywood and anyone not invited obviously could never again say that in September of 1960 he was among the most important men or women in the movie business. Wives, who had seemed resigned to exclusion, suddenly leaped back into the fray. They pointed out that Khrushchev was bringing his wife and so was Spyros P. Skouras, then president of Fox. That the luncheon was a tribute to a Communist was not an issue. It was now certain the luncheon would be the status symbol of 1960. By this time the sniping of columnists had subsided. When Sinatra was asked if he was worried that the luncheon he was attending was for a Communist he replied: "If President Eisenhower is not worried, why should I be?"

As pressure mounted for invitations, it was decided to spread the blame of refusal in self-defense. So whenever an importuning executive called the committee on arrangements, he was told to get in touch with his own studio; that each studio had received the same quota. This touched off a bitter rejoinder that Fox was padding the list with its own people by naming them to various jobs at the luncheon. Union officials were referred to the heads of their unions. All important movie unions were represented.

The seating arrangements were as knotty as anything ever handled at the White House or State Department. For in Hollywood there are no rules of protocol. Status varies with the latest contract, with the box office returns of a star's last movie. A mistake might cost a studio the chance to get a star in the next movie. Or, at the very least, a stiff increase in the fee paid to the star. In short, everything but a slide rule was used by Harry Brand, then in charge of Fox publicity, to make sure that no one's prestige was slighted. But even so, when guests arrived for the luncheon, a delicate situation arose that for a while threatened to become a public explosion. It involved Elizabeth Taylor and Debbie Reynolds. At that time Miss Taylor had taken from Miss Reynolds the latter's husband, Eddie Fisher. Miss Reynolds arrived to learn that Miss Taylor was closer to the dais than she was. Seating cards were hastily rearranged and Miss Reynolds received a more satisfactory vantage point.

One shrewd device was used to hold down complaints about seating. Men in charge of seating appealed to important guests to take seats at unfavorable locations. Anyone near these important personages could hardly complain about the demeaning seating position. Nevertheless, when the luncheon began it was obvious that prestige and table position went pretty much together.

Indicative of the sort of silliness contributed by the State Department to this luncheon was the story of the army chorus. This idea was conceived by Frank McCarthy, who was in charge of most arrangements for the luncheon. McCarthy, then a Fox executive, was particularly well qualified. As secretary to General George C. Marshall during World War II he had worked with the general at the conferences at Casablanca, Potsdam, Yalta, Teheran and Cairo. He had met Stalin, Churchill and Roosevelt. After the war he was an assistant secretary of state for the administration. None of these attributes helped him, however, when he wanted the army chorus.

McCarthy, then a reserve brigadier general, was well informed about the activities at Fort Ord in California. He knew that its language school had trained many soldiers to speak Russian and had even organized a chorus that could sing Russian songs. He thought it might be a good idea to have the soldiers serenade Khrushchev in Russian at the luncheon. The army agreed, providing Fox would see to it that the soldiers did not go hungry. Fox made provision for this. Suddenly the State Department vetoed the entire project. State claimed that the fact that there were Russian-speaking American soldiers might implant the idea in Khrushchev's mind that the United States was preparing for an invasion of the Soviet Union.

Then there was the problem of the vodka. Should vodka be

served at the luncheon or not? The pro-vodka group urged it as a matter of simple hospitality. The anti-vodka school contended it was dangerous. Many of the guests were known to be high-spirited even without bottled assistance. A few shots of vodka might encourage one of the exhibitionists at the gathering to heckle Khrushchev, Skouras, or both. The solution was as follows: vodka would be served. But only to those seated on the dais.

The menu became an excuse for a parochial gesture. Everything in food, it was ruled, should be from California—shrimp, squab, wild rice, marble-sized potatoes, half canteloupe with chilled fruits. And the wine too. The wine was a subject of warm discussion. But the final choice, after a consultation with Mike Romanoff, the Hollywood restaurateur, was a California white wine, Pinot Chardonnay, served chilled. This menu received approval from the State Department after it rejected two other menus.

Mike Romanoff himself became a subject that taxed the minds of the luncheon arrangers. He explained that he had never before asked to be invited to any Hollywood affair. But this one he wanted to attend. Romanoff, the committee appreciated, had been helpful. He had been a good friend in the past. But how could it be done? He was not a movie executive. Not a star. Not a director. Not a writer. Not a reporter. Not a member of the State Department. He could hardly be pressed into service as a waiter. At that, someone had the idea. He was named "technical adviser" and was in the commissary when the luncheon began.

Zsa Zsa Gabor created a flurry. An invitation had been sent to her. No reply. Finally McCarthy called her home to learn if she planned to attend. The maid told her that Miss Gabor was in Las Vegas. She was finally tracked down and accepted the invitation. A day or so later, one of the gossip columns ran an item questioning how a Hungarian could attend a luncheon to the head of a state that was holding Hungary in captivity and had thwarted Hungary's struggle for freedom with bloodshed. A short time later Miss Gabor decided not to attend. "How could I go to that luncheon," she demanded, "being a Hungarian!"

The State Department became a nuisance in allotting seats. The first agreement—in which State participated—had 100 seats set aside for itself and the Russians; 100 for press; 150 for the entire movie industry. But State began vacillating. It cut its own allotment to seventy, then to fifty, presumably to increase the seats available for stars. Then, at the last moment, it asked for an additional thirty, thereby creating a near panic among those handling the invitations.

In the midst of this turmoil McCarthy was told there was a phone call from Mitzi Gaynor—one of 132 that day. There were three calls ahead of hers that moment. One of them was the refusal of Sol Siegel, then studio head of Metro, to attend the luncheon because his wife was not invited. (She finally was and he came.) Miss Gaynor had a different problem. McCarthy was bewildered about Miss Gaynor's call. She had been invited and had accepted. If she reversed herself that would make another badly needed seat available. But Miss Gaynor was not shunning the invitation.

"Should I," she asked McCarthy plaintively, "wear a hat?"

He retorted: "I can't think of anything less important!"

Next came the question of the chauffeurs. Would guests be permitted to arrive in chauffeur-driven cars? After careful discussion this was allowed, with two provisions. The chauffeurs, after unloading their employers, were to drive the limousines to a special parking area and remain by the cars. And employers were to supply their drivers with box lunches.

The committee was advised to be sure that Negroes were represented at the luncheon, lest the Russians make a point of their absence to illustrate American racial prejudice. Among the Negroes at the luncheon were Nat (King) Cole, Sammy Davis, Jr., and Louise Beavers.

Flags created a touchy situation. There were long and earnest meetings about which flags were to be displayed. Washington was as deeply concerned as Hollywood. The decision was that only Russian and United States flags were to be at the luncheon. Even the United Nations flag was rejected to avoid giving offense to the Russians.

The exact cost of this Hollywood clambake will never be known. But some charges are certain. Fox paid $7,600 and the rest of the movie industry chipped in an equal amount. A sequence of *Can-Can*, filmed for the pleasure of the Russians, cost $25,000. The footage was useless and all of it had to be reshot. Insurance for the day was increased from the usual two million dollars to five million dollars. Security forces were so elaborate they included a helicopter that buzzed low over the studio to make certain no one climbed fences.

The windup of the occasion was perfect for this study in hypocrisy. No sooner had Khrushchev left Los Angeles than he attacked his host. He said Fox's most elaborate entertainment, the sequence from *Can-Can* staged for him, was vulgar and obviously indicative of American taste in art. Yet while watching it he had beamed like a habitué of baldhead row at the burlesque as the shapely dancers pranced about in an exciting display of leg work.

This was Khrushchev's thanks to Hollywood. It was little more than Hollywood deserved for groveling to a blacklist and to the world leader of communism at the same time.

5 | Boudoirs and blood

The two insoluble conflicts Hollywood faces are: how to be romantic without sex; how to create physical conflict without violence. Since romance without sex is as undramatic as a fist fight without bloodshed, the major points of the censorship controversy never change. They are sex and violence, just as they were early in the century. Sex can range from the contour of clothes to tolerance of homosexuality. Violence can be the number of corpses, the close-ups of death agonies, the volume of blood. Particularly intriguing are the changes in what the public considers sinful, carnal, brutal. For these changes are wondrous barometers of changes in national mores, the weakening of one tribal custom and the tightening of another. What was violent controversy in the days of Clara Bow became innocent merriment in the days of Marilyn Monroe. The biology of sex may not change, but the symbols and accouterments of sex certainly do. To regulate morality in a world that has gone from carriage to space rocket in half a century is more difficult for Hollywood in the 1960's than it has been at any time in its history.

1. *Sex*

Sex is in an agony of growing pains on the Hollywood screen and the nation is having tantrums. After decades of creating travesties on sex, the American movie industry is trying to deal maturely with this explosive subject. For Hollywood, this break with tradition is outright revolution and it has created confusion among movie-makers and censors alike. Producers have learned that the old sex patterns have lost audience appeal. Censors have realized that the mere words of the code are inadequate for judging the "adult" approach that seeks out themes of adultery, rape, homosexuality, abortion, prostitution, sadism and masochism. Costumes are for bosom and hip. Dances and songs are for bump and grind. All on the biggest of multicolored screens in history—screens ideal for Rabelais or Hieronymous Bosch.

The new version of Hollywood sex is a weird mongrel of authenticity and opportunism; of art and hypocrisy; of experiment and sensationalism. The result is that it is almost impossible to predict what sort of sensual goulash will come up next. Hollywood, in trying for maturity, has often come up with vulgarity. Abnormality has often become just another kind of lurid appeal. Ribaldry has frequently turned to dirt. The extremes of the tawdry and artistic are immeasurable.

One of the most controversial issues in the new Hollywood concept of sex is homosexuality. At first there were just flirtations with the subject, as in *Cat on a Hot Tin Roof*. Then, as pressure increased to permit treatment of this subject that was exploited in the daily newspapers and national magazines, the censorship code was changed. The ban on homosexuality was dropped. Perversion made the Hollywood big time as a prime inducement for anyone in the market as movie material. *Suddenly Last Summer*, *The Best Man*, *Advise and Consent* were hardly considered handicapped because they dealt with homosexuality. Another form of degeneracy became the subject of a delightful comedy, *Lolita*, which dealt with the infatuation of a man approaching middle age with a fourteen-year-old. In the novel by Vladimir Nabokov she was twelve.

For unadulterated hypocrisy in sex all prizes are won by Hollywood's Bible movies—excepting such a rarity as George Stevens' *The Greatest Story Ever Told.* To American movie-makers the Bible is the best excuse for sex on an orgiastic scale. Sunday school stories become perfect pastures for men who want a maximum of lust with a minimum of interference from the code and civic and religious organizations. There is very little of the beauty of the Bible in *David and Bathsheba, Solomon and Sheba, Samson and Delilah.* One of the most touching love stories ever written became dreary vulgarity in *The Story of Ruth.*

There are also many non-Biblical examples of hypocrisy in dealing with sex in the movies. For example, no movie tycoon of the 1950's and early 1960's extolled the wholesome "family" picture more frequently than did Spyros Skouras, when he was president of Twentieth Century-Fox. Before conventions of theater owners and to press conferences he coupled "family movies" with patriotism. They were his antidote for adultery, rape, lewdness and degeneracy.

It was therefore understandable that Elia Kazan was nervous while waiting to learn whether the movie industry's censors would give him a seal of approval for *Wild River.* Kazan had directed the movie for Skouras's company. During its filming he had encountered censorship problems because of illicit sex adventures between the heroine and hero of the film—Lee Remick and Montgomery Clift. When Kazan was informed that the seal was his he was jubilant. He rushed to a phone and broke the news to Skouras. The executive was silent for a few seconds, then he said: "Too bad," and hung up.

Skouras is hardly unique. Jack L. Warner, head of Warner Brothers, bought from Twentieth Century-Fox the movie rights to *The Chapman Report,* which was so heavy with sex that even Skouras became worried about it.

Or take *The World of Suzie Wong.* Here prostitution was depicted in a sentimental haze, but without missing the opportunity to emphasize the sexy side of a whore's life—more as fun than as sordidness. *The Chapman Report* dangled nymphomania before the public and *All Fall Down* combined sex with sadism.

Much has been said about the influence of Plutarch on the latest version of *Cleopatra*, starring Elizabeth Taylor. Still it was sex that made the picture a matter of public interest—not history or literature.

But Hollywood has also been making strides in presenting sex honestly. This was true of *The Sundowners* in which the director, Fred Zinnemann, showed a man and wife, Robert Mitchum and Deborah Kerr, sharing a love that was, without any vulgarity, physical as well as spiritual. Then there was *The Apartment* in which Wilder and Diamond made it clear that a good deal of illicit sex was in progress. However, the movie was amusing, not dirty. In Richard Brooks's version of *Elmer Gantry*, Gantry was still the lecherous minister of the Sinclair Lewis novel. But sex was an important part of the drama, rather than an excuse for it. *The Hustler* could easily have been a vulgar movie. It dealt with the life of a poolroom hustler, Paul Newman, and his unsanctified sex life with Piper Laurie. However, as directed by Robert Rossen it was a fascinating, sympathetic, adult study in human relationships.

Too often, because of the many examples of bad taste in the handling of sex, there has been a tendency to overlook the fundamental causes of Hollywood's radical change. It was more a result of inexorable outside forces than of insidious Hollywood scheming.

At the end of World War II, Hollywood found itself faced with two major national developments—both of them threatening. First there was television, which cut its audience in half. Second, there was a postwar reaction similar to that which followed World War I. Moral values changed. Though churches boasted of increasing attendance, divorce, adultery, illegitimacy all increased at a staggering rate. The moral tone of earlier Hollywood movies was outmoded, lagging badly behind reality. Consequently, Hollywood, in its need to find material that was not available on television and that would be closer to American thought and behavior, drifted toward its old reliable solution—more sex and in more stimulating form.

But the code was the same. Either the code had to be changed or its interpretation had to become more flexible. As we have seen, the truth is that the main provisions of the code that apply to sex and allied fields are not as restrictive as many persons claim.

The code provides that the "sanctity of marriage and the home shall be upheld" and that "no film shall infer that casual or promiscuous sex relationships are the accepted or common thing." It also says that while adultery and illicit sex are sometimes necessary for plot, they "shall not be explicitly treated, nor shall they be justified or made to seem right and permissible."

Scenes of passion are intended for plot, not mere titillation, and must be "treated in such a manner as not to stimulate the baser emotions." As for rape, this should "never be made to seem right and permissible" and "never be more than suggested, and then only when essential to the plot."

The code also contains prohibitions against dances that suggest or represent sexual actions or emphasize indecent movements; against obscene words, gestures, references, songs or jokes; and against vulgar dialogue.

Probably the majority of Americans, regardless of intellectual levels, have no serious objection to the terms of such a code. For it has become apparent that the interpretation of the code is more important than the words today. The Hollywood censors have followed the trend of literature, theater and the public in taking a broader view of scripts and films. These censors are also much more keenly aware of constitutional rulings on censorship than are most Americans. They know that the Supreme Court has ruled that art must be judged by the taste and over-all content of the material, not just by an isolated word or action. The censors have changed decidedly.

In 1949 a seal was denied to the artistic Italian movie *Bicycle Thief*. The reason was that the father, hunting desperately with his young son for a bicycle stolen from him, wanders into a brothel. But by 1962 censors had given a seal to *A Walk on the Wild Side*, which dealt with a whore house and a madam who was a lesbian.

The change in attitude of the censors is clearly illustrated by the incident involving the movie version of O'Neill's *Anna Christie*. When it was first made, in 1932, as Garbo's first talking movie, she was a whore, as in the play. (Pre-seal of approval.) Then, in 1940, and again in 1946, Metro-Goldwyn-Mayer, which owned the movie rights, wanted to remake the movie. The censors ruled that if this were done she could not be a prostitute. Metro shelved the project. But in 1962, when Metro wanted to reissue its original Garbo movie, the censors gave it a seal at once. "Times have changed," said chief censor Shurlock. There was no public complaint about the reissued movie.

The censors are in the middle. If they are too tolerant about sex they are blamed by the public. If they are too strict Hollywood protests that they are stifling creativity by applying the past to the present.

A good illustration of the tightrope the censors walk these days on sex themes is *Butterfield 8*. When the first version of the John O'Hara novel was presented the censors rejected it at once. Shurlock reported in a memo: "We have the feeling that the characters in this story are preoccupied almost exclusively with sex . . . appear to talk about nothing but fornication . . . shown indulging in sex on numerous occasions." After months of negotiations nymphomania had been reduced to promiscuity that was more hinted than stated.

Of particular importance in movie censorship is an over-all principle underlying the code—"moral compensation." In other words, against sin must be balanced punishment or contrition. This is the point that has probably subjected the code and its censors to more ridicule over the years than any prohibition.

A classic case of how "moral compensation" can work occurred in the making of *Forever Amber*, after the Kathleen Winsor novel about the lusty life and times of Amber St. Clair, a prostitute of the Restoration who became a mistress of royalty. In trying to outwit the censors Darryl F. Zanuck, then head of the Twentieth Century-Fox studio, agreed that Amber would not be glorified, but that the film would be handled as tragedy for her. However, he shot the movie not from the script cleared by the censors but from one they never saw. When the film was made the censors realized that Amber was having her sin and a pretty happy ending as well. Zanuck was blocked by protests from the Legion of Decency and two cardinals. Fox became terrified. To restore the idea of "moral compensation" Fox added prologue and epilogue. The prologue reduced an already mediocre film to soap opera. It said: "This is the tragic story of Amber St. Clair . . . slave to ambition . . . stranger to virtue . . . fated to find the wealth and power she ruthlessly gained wither to ashes in the fires lit by passion and fed by defiance of the eternal command . . . the wages of sin is death."

The issue of the validity of "moral compensation" was raised in much more intelligent fashion by Max E. Youngstein, then vice president of United Artists. He protested that *Butterfield 8* received a seal of approval, but not *Never on Sunday*. He claimed this was because in *Butterfield 8* the sinning heroine (Elizabeth Taylor) dies and in *Never on Sunday* the prostitute who refuses to work on Sundays (Melina Mercouri) does not die. Shurlock retorted that the heroine's death was not the reason the film had been accorded a seal. In *Butterfield 8* he pointed out the prostitute had expressed deep remorse. But in *Never on Sunday* she saw nothing wrong or sinful in her occupation.

The censors are badgered occasionally because there has been no remorse or punishment for two unmarried adults who indulge in sex. Shurlock says there is little he can do about it. "It is difficult to prove that damage was done to either party. Then how can we impose punishment? Occasionally those involved have pangs of conscience. And that's about all."

For all the ridiculing of "moral compensation" in the Hollywood censorship code, is the principle so far from the standards of great literature? Tolstoy lost no stature because Anna Karenina's adultery led to her death by suicide. Stendhal is not laughed at because Julien Sorel's sinfulness in *The Red and the Black* brought him death. Does anyone find the punishment of Oedipus for incest too silly? Are the fates of Hamlet, his mother and uncle, of Richard III, of Macbeth and his lady dismissed as sentimentality? Yet all are examples of "moral compensation."

Where the code seems to go astray is in its occasional failure to distinguish between serious drama and comedy in weighing the necessity for "moral compensation." Aristophanes, Molière, the Restoration dramatists are not too concerned with "moral compensation" for adultery when they turn to satire and comedy. Laughter is entitled to different ground rules for "moral compensation."

Even in the most maudlin periods of movie-making special allowances were made for comedy. Mae West, for instance, was a walking spoof of movie morality, using her generous curves, ample breasts, to caricature Hollywood sex. With the exaggeration of insinuating speech and appraising eyes, she delivered such lines as: "Come up and see me sometime"; "Give a man a free hand and he'll try to put it all over you"; "Between two evils I always pick the one I never tried before." Moral compensation was not demanded of her any more than it was of the Marx brothers.

Those who claim censors are too restrictive tend to forget how far the censors have traveled since the introduction of the code; how vast is the change between movies today and the treatment of sex from the mid-thirties until after World War II.

The old kind of Hollywood sensuality was simple. Romance was for good boys and girls and was climaxed, usually to the swoon of fiddles, with a kiss. Sex was sometimes sinister—for men and women of weak character. Romance was seen through rose-colored glasses. Sex was seen through the eyes of a peeping Tom. The late Herman Mankiewicz summarized the old style of Hollywood sex. "The hero, as well as the heroine," he said, "has to be a virgin. The villain can lay anybody he wants, have as much fun as he wants cheating and stealing, getting rich and whipping the servants. But you have to shoot him in the end. When he falls with a bullet in his forehead, it is advisable that he clutch at the Gobelin tapestry on the library wall and bring it down over his head like a symbolic shroud."

Then there was the happy sex—no sins, only temptations. Sometimes they were considered "sophisticated." Here one found Myrna Loy, Anne Sothern, June Allyson, Ginger Rogers. The great wizard of sophisticated sex was Ernst Lubitsch, who directed *Ninotchka*. He sought the champagne taste of Molnar, but knew that by movie rules chastity limited boudoir comedy and marriage was the only course of love.

The closest the censors came to worrying about nudity in the thirties and forties was in the leggy—but innocent—musicals. The Sam Goldwyn Girls showed long bare legs and shapely figures on lavish, polished stages. Eleanor Powell tap-danced, Sonja Henie skated, Esther Williams swam. Betty Grable and Rita Hayworth pranced about in musicals, and the mail for pin-up photos mounted. Music might be by that genuine sophisticate, Cole Porter; but when transferred to the screen for Fred Astaire films, sex became innocent to the point of quaintness for Ginger Rogers. Sex received less attention in the musicals than the huge staircases, mirrored under bright lights.

Until *A Streetcar Named Desire* the code was able to cope with nearly anything in the way of Hollywood sex. Consider the highlights of Hollywood sex in the thirties and forties. There were the love triangles that brought long lines to the box office to see Joan Crawford, Hedy Lamarr, Bette Davis, Susan Hayward, Barbara Stanwyck. Virtue was tampered with, but never conquered. That sin would have its wages was certain. The only doubts were as to how much and how they would be paid. Would the sinning woman renounce the husband of the other woman, although she truly loved him? Would the apparently timid wife throw away her manners and pound hell out of the hussy? Would a child bring the errant man—or woman—back to the realities of eternal morality? These were the laws of the Hollywood of a *Mildred Pierce* or a *Gone With the Wind*. These were wonderful days for a Shirley Temple, a Deanna Durbin. It was an era for *Andy Hardy* and *Lassie*. Patterns of sex were so tremulous and so unvarying that in 1947 I. A. L. Diamond pleaded in *Screen Writer* for a story about a secretary "who does not become a raving beauty by sweeping back her hair and discarding her horn-rimmed spectacles."

Only the untalented, the tasteless, the unscrupulous and the timid are unable to make creative movies with sex. There is little wrong with sex in Hollywood movies that cannot be cured by imagination, taste, sensitivity and a sense of humor.

What cannot be pushed past the censors with words is often tried with costume. Marilyn Monroe was an expert at this—often to the despair of designers. Miss Monroe refused to wear underclothes. She felt they inhibited the rotary motion of her hips, dulled the color of her skin and, in general, reduced her sex appeal. Even in a high-necked gown with long sleeves she managed to be so revealing that on one occasion beads had to be added as a sop to the censors.

Miss Monroe's favorite comment about the concern of censors

with her cleavage was: "The trouble with censors is that they worry whether a girl has cleavage. They ought to worry if she hasn't any." To make sure her cleavage was shown to best advantage, she would slyly pull down the décolletage before camera time. This infuriated some of her designers.

There have been many apocryphal reports to the effect that censors have worked out a mathematical chart for costumes; that they appear on sets with tape measures to see how low is the décolletage, how high the crotch. Actually, it is all a matter of the individual censor's judgment when he sees the film. Sometimes censors in the Production Code Administration disagree among themselves. Important to the censor in his appraisal is how the costume compares with what the average intelligent American woman either wears today or does not consider objectionable. This was what made the Bikini bathing suit, previously rejected, acceptable in *Town Without Pity*. The censors also consider the situation in which the costume is worn. If a woman is supposed to be alone in her bedroom she may be permitted to wear less than if she is accompanied by a man. If she is doing comedy her costume may be more abbreviated than if she is in a serious movie. The over-all taste with which the picture is made also is weighed by the censor.

There was a time when décolletages were much lower than they are today—and caused no complaint. This was during the late twenties and early thirties. The fashion in those days was the flat chest. A décolletage then, according to Edith Head, one of the top movie costume designers, could be cut almost to the navel without revealing anything. Jean Harlow and Carole Lombard, two sirens of the thirties, wore no bras. "Our only rule in those days," she recalls, "was will it stay on? If dresses fell off, we just shot again."

The great to-do about the latest Cleopatra movie with Elizabeth Taylor is not the first of its kind. In an earlier *Cleopatra* version an actress appeared on screen wearing only jewels on the nipples of her breasts and a long gauzy skirt. The complaint of the censors was that her navel was revealed. Showing the female navel was vetoed by censors until the early 1960's. So a make-up man was ordered to plug up her navel. This looked ghastly. Whereupon a jewel was placed there and she appeared with a diamond-studded navel.

It is generally believed that realism in movies automatically increases salaciousness. This is not so. Quite often it works the other way. Thus, when Clara Bow, one of the most famous of Hollywood sex symbols, played tennis in one movie her leg line was considered so important that she played in high heels. Realism would not have permitted this.

Mere exposure of skin is not in itself a criterion for censoring costumes. When Lana Turner, as "The Sweater Girl," became one of the Hollywood sex queens in the forties, she caused considerable commotion without any décolletage. Her specialty was the bosom-revealing sweater that was so tight it impelled the censors to issue a warning against suggestive knitwear. Marlene Dietrich excited audiences merely by crossing her legs.

Falsies, which have attracted a great deal of attention in print, are very often used, not so much to expand the size of the bust as to improve the fit of the costume. Make-up artisans try to enhance sex appeal by darkening the cleavage to make it look deeper, or whitening expanses of breast to make them seem fuller. Some actresses put pads of Kleenex or rolled up stockings under their breasts to elevate them.

Much of the silliness has been taken out of the costume interpretations of movies. There is nothing comparable, for example, to the day the Hays Office killed a shot in a musical that showed a group of attractive girls in bathing suits. The censors had no objection to the bathing suits. But the shot had been taken in a public park. In the background was a statue of a nude woman. It had been on display before countless thousands for decades. But it was considered erotic for a movie.

"Nowadays," said Adolph Zukor, "you can see sexier clothes in a supermarket than on the screen. I don't think we could get away with such tight-fitting Capri pants or such sexy shorts on film as you see on the streets today."

Nevertheless, there is a strong drive to make costumes more revealing, partly to meet foreign competition, partly to cope with realism, but mainly to build up attendance.

The dance, once just incompetent in movies, has often become an excuse for salaciousness. This is mainly because stars who knew little about dancing—such as Marilyn Monroe, Debbie Reynolds and Natalie Wood—were permitted to try roles that required trained dancers. Whereas a professional dancer in a jazz ballet makes her performance artistic, the loose-fleshed imitation dancers make these same steps—the few they can do—seem like salacious bumps and grinds. A Gwen Verdon can do a number like the devil's star seductress in "What Lola Wants, Lola Gets," in *Damn Yankees*, and offer laughter, not lewdness. Also, the professional dancer, though she wears skin-colored tights, wears more undergarments beneath tights than will a star who thinks she can dance.

Regardless of the denunciations of sex and degeneracy in Hollywood movies today, it is likely that the new themes will be absorbed and that the result, eventually, will be an improvement in American films. In Hollywood's favor this time is a factor that did not exist in previous public uproars. The public is more sophisticated. Hollywood also has a reservoir of young, creative talent that has been largely blocked by stupidity, crassness and short-sightedness among many studio officials. In self-preservation Hollywood will have to either deprive executives of power over creative movie-makers, or else find executives who know how to make the best use of talented men and women. It is becoming evident, in 1964, that Hollywood has learned that talent, not bookkeepers, will make the movies that can meet the challenges of this generation.

2. *Mayhem for the Masses*

The battle by the movie industry's own censors to restrain lurid crime and violence has been a story of retreat, with occasional advances when bolstered by an aroused public. This has been inevitable ever since Hollywood discovered long ago that crime, contrary to the police and the movie industry's censorship code, does pay—and, with uninhibited brutality, pays very well indeed. Hollywood producers have made more loot from crime than any gang of criminals. They have mined more gold from sadism and masochism than any cult of psychoanalysts. Sex is the life blood of Hollywood, but crime and violence are its adrenalin.

Patterns of movie crime and violence have varied because, like all dramatic art forms, the films have vogues that sometimes follow life. Thus Hollywood's private world of mayhem for the masses has reflected the gangsterism of the Prohibition era and the hood-lumism of juvenile delinquency. In the field of fantasy it has drawn blood from the ghoulishness of the monsters of mad scientists, the black superstition of primitive folklore, the realm of science-fiction and bloodthirsty versions of Biblical and ancient historical tales.

Sound and color have made crime and violence the number one target of public indignation, replacing sex. There have always been lawlessness and brutality in movies. For, as in all drama, movies must have conflict and this often requires a bit of pummeling, swordplay or gunfighting. Throughout the silent film era of the westerns, the manliness of the hero resided in the power of his fists and the accuracy of his gun. There were dastardly villains galore to tie heroines to railroad tracks or truss heroes to fuse-burning casks of dynamite. In 1912 D. W. Griffith did a "gangster" movie, *The Musketeers of Pig Alley*. Griffith told Herb Stern, a veteran Hollywood publicist and an authority on silent movies, that this was the first gangster movie ever made. Though it had gang killings, set in Manhattan's Lower East Side, it did not indulge in the sadism that was to become characteristic of gangster pictures.

It took sound and color to surround gruesomeness and gore with box office halos. Now came the crunch of breaking bones, the groans and screams of the afflicted, the crack and whine of bullets. Blood was no longer a dark smudge. It was rich, flowing red. And with the huge screen and close-up, torture was scrutinized under a miscroscope and horror was brought forth to the last gasp of breath and the final beam of light in the bulging eyeball.

It has become impossible for the cold words of a censorship code to cope with this new technology of portraying crime and violence. A code can warn against "brutal" killings, but with these new weapons of color, sound and a large screen, a producer can squeeze out more horror with a piercing scream and a harrowing close-up than the silent movies were able to do with a dozen killings. And how can a code, written before the atomic bomb, have the same validity afterward? In a world that has lived through genocide and faces the possibility of annihilation it is difficult for a censor to enforce the code regulation holding that "the taking of human life is to be held to the minimum." Precautions against "excessive flaunting of weapons by criminals" seems childish in a nation where the bomb shelter is commonplace. In a civilization that has come to learn a great deal about mental agonies it has become increasingly difficult for a censor to argue against suicide.

All of these problems, however, could be solved under the heading of good taste except for one thing. Taste, in movies about violence and crime, is considered the enemy of profit by too many Hollywood producers.

Hollywood's censorship troubles with crime and violence, for all the frenzy, can be sorted into fairly clear categories: gangsterism, juvenile delinquency, Biblical and pseudo-historical "spectacles," and horrors.

Gangsters set the pace in the early thirties. Anyone who wants to understand the approach of American movie-makers to these movies can find the key in a terse telegram buried among the many thousands of documents that have accumulated over the years in the files of the Motion Picture Producers Association. The telegram says: "No picture on the life or exploits of John Dillinger will be produced, distributed or exhibited by any member. . . . This decision is based on the belief that the production, distribution or exhibition of such a picture could be detrimental to the best public interest. Advise all studio heads accordingly."

The year of this telegram is important. It was sent in 1934. This was the year that the movie industry's four-year-old censorship code finally got teeth. It was reinforced with the seal of approval, which could be withheld by the censor. Until then the Hollywood code had been almost a joke. Since the telegram was sent by Will H. Hays, the so-called czar of movie morals, to Joseph I. Breen, his chief censor in Hollywood, it was a matter of primary urgency.

Hays dispatched the telegram in a desperate attempt to stem the wrath of the nation's most powerful religious and civic organizations. Millions of American moviegoers were in turmoil about crime and violence in films. Hollywood, gloating over the profits from these movies despite a nation-wide depression, had ignored this rising outcry for four years, ground out such films as *Little Caesar* (1930), *Public Enemy* (1931), *Scarface* (1932). All of them reflected the most murderous aspects of the dying Prohibition era.

Actors concentrated on learning how to talk out of the side of the mouth and around a cigar. Gangster heroes were epitomized by Paul Muni, Edward G. Robinson and James Cagney. The most popular prop in the studio was the machine gun, and bullet-riddled bodies were as common in the movies as lipstick. As sordid violence increased in the early thirties, so did the spread of censorship in cities and states. Finally, in terror of expanding boycotts, the industry succumbed to the advice of Hays and he sent the telegram that was supposed to have ended Hollywood gangsterism.

Presumably Hollywood should have learned that wanton violence was dangerous. But the Bourbons of the movie industry neither learned nor forgot. They looked for a loophole—and found one. A wave of kidnapings had focused national attention on the Federal Bureau of Investigation. They now made the FBI agents the nominal heroes, but gave the same fat parts to the gangsters. As a sop, they had the gangster killed or punished at the end. It was in this phase of Hollywood gangsterism that Humphrey Bogart rose to movie stardom, starting with his gangster role in *The Petrified Forest*. This era of cinematic gangsterism also found new work for Robinson (*The Last Gangster*) and Cagney (*Angels With Dirty Faces*).

It took World War II to accomplish what public pressure and Hollywood's own censors could not—end the gangster movies. For wars offer more violence than gangsters. But hardly had the Allies conquered the Nazis when the three colorful King brothers —one of them an ex-Marine and another a paratrooper—brought gangsterism back to the movies. Ironically, they went to the censors with a project about Dillinger. Breen appealed to Hays. But the latter, apparently assuming the public no longer cared, granted permission for the movie.

Shortly after *Dillinger* was released in 1945, Frank Borzage, then one of the leading directors in Hollywood, sent a scorching letter to the Motion Picture Producers and Exhibitors of America. "I have viewed with growing alarm the trend towards another cycle of gangster and racketeer films. Nothing can do this country and the motion picture industry more harm at this time than to glamorize gangsters and their way of life."

Hollywood was back on another lucrative crime-and-violence kick. This one exceeded anything that had gone before both in its sensationalism and in the anguish of public reaction. Also in the money taken in.

The post-Dillinger era of gangster films was followed by one which employed a much better gimmick for crime and violence —juvenile delinquency. At first there were such tentative feelers as *Knock on Any Door* or *Bad Boy*. In 1948 came the pattern-setter, *City Across the River*. Based on the book *The Amboy Dukes*, by Irving Shulman, it was about juveniles who indulged in brutality that made gangsters look like boy scouts. The beauty of juvenile delinquency films was that they could be called sociological studies made to arouse the community to examine and cure its social ills. Since *City Across the River* was the pace setter of a new Hollywood era, its passage through the hands of the censors deserves attention.

The first reaction of the censors was blunt. The script was turned down "because of its treatment of illicit sex, rape, murder . . . It is our considered judgment that any story concerning juveniles mixed up with elements of raping twelve-year-old girls, consorting with whores, performing brutal sex acts, smoking 'reefers' and engaging in murder and vicious violence could in no wise be approved."

For six months RKO-Radio Pictures bartered with the censors about this sordid story of the Brooklyn slums. Rape became attempted rape. Crimes were reduced, both quantitatively and qualitatively. But the censors were still worried. One of the censors, Vizzard, showed a sense of the future when he wrote a warning to Breen. He said: "It is not at all necessary to stretch the imagination to conceive of violent public complaint . . . by the organized members of the teaching profession . . . little defense available for the makers of this picture." He was referring to the murder of a teacher by one of the delinquents. Nevertheless, in August of

1948, five months after the warning by Vizzard, the project was approved by Breen after the age of the juveniles was increased and assurances were received that no breasts would be shown. A foreword to the movie was delivered by Drew Pearson. The critics did not seem much concerned. A reviewer for *The New York Times* saw it as "a revealing, purposeful and dramatically exciting study of the contributing influence of environment as a breeder of delinquency."

Parent-teacher groups took a different position. The California Congress of Parents and Teachers was angry, not only at the movie, but because it had been released after previews at which representatives of many civic organizations had voiced strong objections. The Congress of Parents and Teachers pointed out that because of the movie, youngsters were making knives and guns. They pleaded for withdrawal of the movie and urged that no more such movies be made.

Breen challenged the Congress of Parents and Teachers to produce evidence that the movie had adversely affected youngsters. The state group replied with a list that exceeded the original charges. Bullets were being sold for the guns that high school boys had learned to make from seeing *City Across the River* and there was a noticeable increase in insolence toward teachers by students. In some cases the students chanted a song from *City Across the River*. A teacher at one high school asked pupils what they thought was the moral of the movie. The prevailing opinion was that squealing was dishonorable. The murderer had been caught because one youngster informed the police.

The basic complaint of civic organizations was not so much the quality of the movie, or even its subject. They contended that such films should not be made available to children.

But this was precisely the audience Hollywood wanted to reach. Television was booming and making savage cuts into movie attendance by youngsters. Showing crime and violence among teenagers was the way to woo the youngsters away from television back to movies.

Hollywood seemed to have run out of steam on its juvenile delinquency kick when, in the fall of 1954, a script was completed that was to become one of the most explosive movies about violence and crime in history. It was adapted from Evan Hunter's novel, *The Blackboard Jungle*, a story about juvenile delinquency in a vocational high school in an unnamed metropolis. To Hollywood censors the major problem in this script by Richard Brooks was that it was a serious, highly dramatic study of juvenile delinquency. By this time newspapers and magazines were devoting vast amounts of space to the subject. Still, the script did contain violence, brutality, coarse language. But there were sound dramatic reasons for the use of "dago," "nigger," "pope lover"; for an attempted rape of a teacher by a student in a darkened school library; for the merciless pummeling of two male teachers by a gang of students in an alley; for such remarks as "even a prostitute makes more money than we do" and "tell me about your stinkin' sister." All of this was exceeded by stories in the daily papers. Public officials in New York, Chicago and Philadelphia refused to allow the movie to be shown in their schools. They said these problems did not exist.

Geoffrey Shurlock had just taken on the job of chief censor and he was deeply concerned about this movie. "I was confronted with a situation that could make a joke of the censorship code sections on violence and brutality," he explained years after the furor had subsided. "If I tried to block the movie solely because it dealt with juvenile delinquency, I would be saying that movies must not deal with contemporary problems. And yet, juvenile delinquents act brutally and talk coarsely. So I asked that brutality be toned down and the language be made less offensive. That was all I could ask for."

Important executives of Metro ordered Brooks to make inserts. As director-writer he refused. When the film was finished the board of directors ordered it shelved for a while. Dore Schary, then head of M-G-M studio, refused. The day before the movie opened in New York a high school teacher was stabbed to death by a student in the Bronx. With this kind of advance coincidental publicity the movie was an instant success.

It touched off an outcry that swept the nation and found an echo in almost every civilized foreign country. In many countries substantial changes were ordered. It is likely that the United States was the only country in which the movie was shown to children.

In Italy, the movie was withdrawn from the Venice Film Festival when the U.S. ambassador, Mrs. Clare Boothe Luce, brought pressure.

The movie was released in March of 1955. By June of that year a Senate committee, headed by the late Senator Estes Kefauver of Tennessee, was gathered in Hollywood to probe crime and violence in movies and the effect on juvenile delinquency. *The Blackboard Jungle* was only one of the movies that received senatorial attention. Others were *The Wild One, Cell 2455—Death Row, Black Tuesday, Wicked Woman, Cry Vengeance, Big House, U.S.A., Kiss Me Deadly, Five Against the House, Violent Saturday, Hell's Island, Big Combo, New York Confidential, Crashout, Fort Yuma, City of Shadows, Chicago Syndicate, I Died a Thousand Times, Massacre.*

Black Tuesday, apart from excessive brutality and killings, showed a pattern for successful crime. This last is clearly forbidden by the code. *Big House, U.S.A.* had the kidnapping of a child, which is banned by the code. It even contained details of the commission of such a crime. *Five Against the House* was about crime by college youths for sheer excitement. This could easily be interpreted as calculated to inspire others with imitation, a violation of the code.

A few of the movies cited by the senators deserve more than summary treatment to show how they fared with the censors before they were approved.

When *Kiss Me Deadly* was first presented to the censors by Robert Aldrich, the director, it was rejected. The reasons were that it showed a private detective as a cold-blooded murderer and justified his many killings. It allowed him to take the law into his own hands and bring about "justice" by killing. These are clear violations of the code. But after about three months of haggling, Aldrich found the formula for getting Mickey Spillane's private eye, Mike Hammer, on the screen. He found a moral. He declared he was marrying "the commercial values of the Spillane properties with a morality that states justice is not to be found in a self-anointed, one-man vigilante."

Kiss Me Deadly received its seal of approval, but two days before it was due to go into release Aldrich learned that the Legion of Decency planned to give the movie a "Condemned" rating. In anguish, he wrote to Shurlock for help.

"This," he declared, "comes as a most rude and expensive surprise since it was my belief and understanding that there certainly could not be this wide divergence between the opinions of the legion and those of the Code Administration. The legion has even failed to recognize any voice of moral righteousness." Shurlock did nothing for Aldrich. Desperately Aldrich tried to cut down screams, reduce shots of a dead face, show less bashing of a head. But the film still contained murder, abduction, assault, and assorted lesser crimes. The legion relented slightly, giving it a "B" rating—morally objectionable in part for all.

Fort Yuma was also turned down cold by the censors when first offered in 1955—a few months before the senators convened in Hollywood. Shurlock said it contained sadism and excessive gruesomeness. The bargaining began. The producer agreed to reduce the number of killings from twenty-four to ten. Abolished was a man being spread-eagled and torn apart by horses; an arrow pinning a hand to wood; Indians' bodies, after hanging, swaying from tree limbs.

In *Black Tuesday* the censor whittled down a "wanton slaughter of law enforcement officers" to the killing of only two. Nevertheless, the final version showed a killer firing bullets into a hostage as he rolls down stairs.

One of the main threads of the Senate committee's investigation was the question whether simply to have a murderer die at the end lessens his stature in the eyes of moviegoers. Dr. Edmund Bergler of New York City, one of many experts who submitted opinions to the committee, declared: "Although all movies and television plays make the concession that the criminal is eventually punished, this climax has no effect on the real or potential criminal; he classifies such retribution as a bow to prevailing mores and dismisses it."

There was general agreement that movies of this sort adversely affect abnormal types. It was also suggested that normal persons would not be affected by them. But repeatedly there was concern among experts about childrens' being exposed to these films. It was conceded that if children were not permitted to see the movies there could be no serious objection to them.

Methods of advertising movies came in for considerable criticism. Among the most startling revelations were confessions by Hollywood moguls that they had little authority over advertising. Superiors in New York were to blame—so they insisted. Thus, Y. Frank Freeman, then vice president of Paramount, and one of the most important executives in the movie business, when questioned about an obnoxious advertising display for *Hell's Island*, replied: "I think it is very bad; no excuse for it." He blamed New York executives. Since advertising is subject to censorship by the movie industry censor in New York, the censor was asked about *Hell's Island*. He said he had objected and was summoned to the Paramount office to confer with the advertising manager, the director of advertising policy, who is a vice president, and the executive vice president of the company.

"I didn't like this," he said, "but they insisted upon using it, and I finally allowed myself, in this case, to be persuaded. . . . The executive vice president in New York thought it was wonderful."

Not even the Senate committee, however, was sufficient to deter Hollywood from the profits to be milked from the violence, crime and sensationalism of juvenile delinquency movies. Early in 1958, as the Hollywood censors scanned projects planned for that year, they were aghast. One producer alone was counting on doing twenty-eight movies on juvenile delinquency that year. There seemed to be no ceiling to either the number of movies or to the extremes to which producers would go to make each movie more sensational than competitors'. In desperation Shurlock turned to Johnston. He told him what was ahead—and about the furious mail he was receiving from organizations all over the nation. The word went out from Johnston that the heat was becoming too intense. The warning was heeded. Stories emerged from Hollywood which tried to blame everything on "quick buck" independent producers. But the major studios were just as much to blame. Quite often they financed and distributed the movies made by these independent producers. And the studios made quite a number on their own.

With juvenile delinquency ruled out, the studios still had a good outlet for violence, crime and bloodshed—the Bible and ancient or medieval history. Old Testament, New Testament and pagan mythology were used as excuses to wipe out humans by the horde or as individuals, in color and on the huge screen. It was good clean fun to toss Christians to lions or nail them to crosses; to have gladiators hack, carve, strangle and gouge one another. What gangster movie could show the bloodshed of *Spartacus?* What juvenile delinquency movie could compare with the arson, looting and torture of *Barabbas?* Then there were the spectacle films that were loosely tied to the Bible. *Ben-Hur*, in its post-mortem of the chariot race, showed as bloodied a body as has ever been seen outside a morgue.

The censors were trapped. They could not condemn the Bible or deny that periods in which barbarism flourished featured violence. Also, the companies that made most of these movies, whether American or foreign, did not care about a seal of approval. Actually, the Legion of Decency was more effective in curbing gratuitous bloodshed than the censors.

One Hollywood movie-maker, with juvenile delinquency throttled for the time being by public pressure, hit upon a new technique in the early 1960's to produce the same general results. He called it "quiet brutality." Samuel Fuller, who wrote, directed and produced *Underworld, U.S.A.*, explained his approach as follows: "What is quiet brutality? I'll tell you. We got a guy in this picture. He gets knocked out in a car. They pour gasoline over him. Toss in a match. Car in flames. All very quiet. We have a professional killer in my picture. He is no psychotic. He is no idiot. No strange chuckle before he kills. No twitch. A normal young man. He's just a professional executioner. When he gets a job to do there is no exchange of glances. It's a job and he does it. The only thing he does—and this is like the atavistic outcry of the warrior—immediately before the job he puts on his dark glasses. That separates him from the customer. If you are going to buck television you need an original idea."

At that time he was dreaming of making a movie to be called *Cain and Abel.* Here was the perfect opportunity to combine crime, violence and spectacle—all under the protection of the Bible. "Just think of it," he said. "The very first murder. The Bible is not too clear about the weapon. I think I'll have Cain use a club. Quiet brutality."

THE DEFIANT ONES: State Department did not like this movie about white and Negro (Tony Curtis and Sidney Poitier) chained together in jail break. It tried to keep film out of foreign film festivals because it might give bad impression of the United States. Movie became sensation in Mexico City Festival, where it was boycotted by American diplomats.

Warner Brothers

THE NUN'S STORY: Ended Hollywood myth that censors would not permit movie about nun who quits church. Legion of Decency tried vainly to force changes in one scene and quibbled about words, but eventually praised picture that starred Audrey Hepburn as nun.

top:

THE LONGEST DAY: Cause of private war between the Department of Defense and Darryl F. Zanuck, who made movie. Government cut allotment of American troops allowed in this picture despite protest by Zanuck that it would make role of U.S. on D-Day seem minor.

bottom:

FRANCIS GOES TO WEST POINT: The Academy thought it unseemly for a mule to be filmed there. It required Pentagon conferences and appointment of a general as technical adviser before the traditional U.S. Army mascot was permitted at the Point.

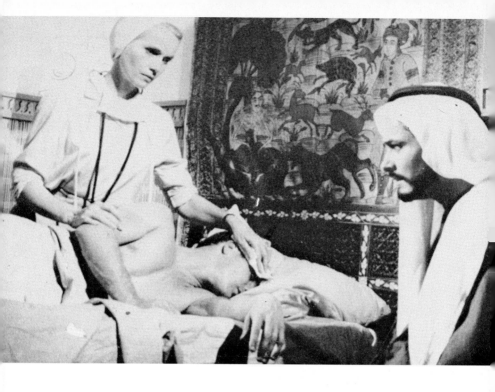

BRIDGE ON THE RIVER KWAI: Hand of the blacklist. This Oscar-winner never carried the names of two of its writers, Carl Foreman and Michael Wilson, because they were on the political blacklist. Man with knife is William Holden.

left:

EXODUS: In this movie about Israel's war for statehood, Otto Preminger became the first producer to give screen credit on an American film to a blacklisted writer, Dalton Trumbo. Haganah warrior (Paul Newman) is being doctored by adoring English widow (Eva Marie Saint). Friendly Arab is John Derek.

CAN-CAN: Movie industry's hypocrisy demonstrated by scene from musical put on for Khrushchev by Hollywood while it secretly enforced form of censorship known as blacklist against those it considered politically radical. Perfect ending was that although the Premier beamed with pleasure while watching dancers, he denounced film next day as vulgar.

20th Century-Fox

TEA AND SYMPATHY: Of this film, Robert Anderson, who adapted his Broadway hit for Hollywood, says: "They persuade you to give in on so many things by saying: 'We'll let you keep the core of the story.' You become convinced you're saving the story. I will never give in again as I did on *Tea and Sympathy*. Robert Frost once told me: 'Never be first to be second.'" Shown here are Deborah Kerr and John Kerr (not related), who starred in the movie as well as the play.

20th Century-Fox

SWEET BIRD OF YOUTH: Prime example of how movie is ruined in attempt to give it a happy, "box office" ending. This shot shows Geraldine Page as the actress who is terrified that middle age has ruined her career, and her gigolo (Paul Newman). Both are in a state of hashish-induced insensibility.

MGM

left:
SANCTUARY: Bastardized result of Hollywood approach to William Faulkner. Pre-censorship at work as Hollywood, without interference from censors, combines Faulkner's *Sanctuary* and *Requiem for a Nun* into film as rumpled as bed. Actress is Lee Remick.

A PLACE IN THE SUN: Director George Stevens refused to pre-censor himself and proved, with this film, that artistic fidelity can be box-office. He defied Hollywood custom by adhering to the unhappy ending in this movie version of Dreiser's *An American Tragedy*. As in the book, the pregnant poor girl (Shelley Winters) was drowned by her ambitious lover (Montgomery Clift), who wanted to be free to marry wealth. He was condemned to death. Stevens won the 1951 directing Oscar for this display of courage and taste.

GULLIVER: Hollywood decided Dean Swift needed help. Added romance to its version of *Gulliver's Travels*. Kerwin Mathews is the movie Gulliver kissing June Thorburn, the non-Swiftian love interest.

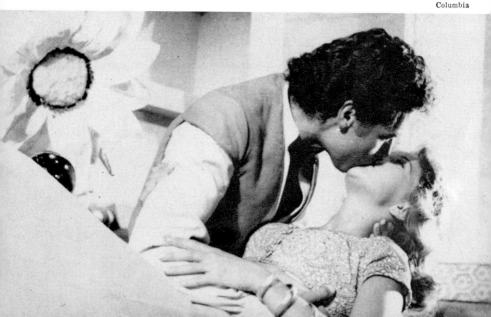

One cinematic formula for the most horrible and violent crimes has never disappeared from the screen since the early thirties. This is the horror film. Here revel the Frankenstein monsters, the Draculas and their apostles, the cat people, the werewolves, the skyscraper-tall gorillas and dinosaurs, the sea monsters and the creatures from other planets. Terror is the theme and brutal murder is commonplace. Jules Verne and Edgar Allen Poe have been ravished and served up to moviegoing youngsters with the popcorn. For a horror movie, entire nations were threatened.

Ironically, the master of instilling fear in movie audiences rarely has trouble with censors, churches, civic organizations. He is Alfred Hitchcock. His theory is simple. "You don't have to show the hero having his nails pulled out," says Hitchcock. "No need for violence and horrible scenes. And plot has become old-fashioned in theater and rather looked down upon—not by the public, but by creative people and by critics. Real suspense comes from fear on the part of the audience that something will happen to their characters on the screen. It is not a question of: will the bomb go off? But: whom will it injure? And in the background there should be a sense of levity. Suspense should be exhilarating and, as such, fairly superficial.

"The more a subject is colored, the more melodramatic it is, the greater the opportunity and the effectiveness of understatement. Consider the hangman, entering the cell of the condemned man, the day of the execution and saying: 'Good morning, old chap.' "

There is little evidence that Hollywood appreciates the wisdom of the Hitchcock approach. Even Hitchcock himself seemed to forget it in *The Birds*. So the nation may as well resign itself to more waves of crime, violence and brutality in Hollywood movies, each wave continuing until public pressure arrests it. Or until the public becomes so jaded the profits sag.

6 | By trial and error

Since 1952 the Supreme Court has been on an anticensorship spree that has knocked nearly all the legal props out from under the state and local movie censors. What little constitutional justification remains for them is under concentrated attack. The movie industry has been adjudged an art, entitled to the freedom enjoyed by books, newspapers and magazines. But draped in old and tattered statutes, the censors hand down edicts that have made them the elite among nincompoops. They are bureaucratic Canutes trying to stem the tides of public morals and mores with shibboleths compounded of ignorance, vanity and prejudice. Indifferent to Supreme Court opinions and the flexibility of a democratic society that makes yesterday's immorality tomorrow's custom, their utterances are the raw material for a modern Molière. Hollywood's own code and its administrators have escaped much of this opprobrium by changing its rules and interpretations. However, the increasing importance of the foreign market to American producers has complicated the entire censorship structure. It has become vital to pass alien as well as domestic censors. The result has been the creation of a weird, often amusing, Hollywood pastime of trying to outwit the censor.

1. *Censorship and the Courts*

Aloof from the greed, fears and sensationalism that inflame arguments about movie censorship is the United States Supreme Court, the ultimate arbiter of the clashes between movie-makers and censors; between pressure groups and creators; between the public and the government. In the serenity of its chambers in Washington this august group of nine men frames words that can change the entire censorship situation overnight. In the decisions of the Supreme Court are to be found more than the letters of laws. These opinions reflect the changing moral code of the nation. They can affect the cultural life of a country more than laws of Congress, states or municipalities.

From the apex of the Supreme Court movie censorship is not only a special problem of one industry but a part of the entire field of censorship. A censorship decision on books or newspapers, a ruling on antiwar demonstrations, can become a guiding principle for movie censorship. For in the Supreme Court censorship is a matter of human rights, not business or politics. The justices, regardless of differences of opinion, bring to their appraisals an awareness of the mosaic of American society and a probity that raises them far above the level of the market place or the convictions of pressure groups. Occasionally, lower federal judges of great vision and intellectual breadth have set censorship patterns before arguments reached the Supreme Court.

Individual decisions have been notable. But more important have been the trends that the major decisions have created during this century. They are as follows.

1. The movie industry, originally considered just another business by the Supreme Court, is now regarded as a communications medium entitled to most of the same rights the press enjoys.

2. Motion pictures, which once had no more status than vaudeville jugglers, are now regarded as an art form.

3. The concept of judging a movie by isolated words, bits of

dialogue or snips of film footage has been discarded in favor of judging a film in terms of its over-all taste and meaning.

4. Obscenity is considered cause for censorship and is not protected by free speech guarantees.

5. The courts have narrowed the area classified as obscenity.

6. Censorship for such vague reasons as vulgarity, sacrilege, indecency, immorality, tendency to create racial friction—has been thrown out.

Until well into this century Victorianism permeated the law of the land in regard to censorship. The American legal criterion was established in England in 1868 in the case of Regina v. Hicklin. Lord Chief Justice Cockburn ruled that a book could be censored if it "would suggest to the minds of the young of either sex, or even to persons of more advanced years, thoughts of a most impure and libidinous character."

This ruling was carried over into the United States in 1879 (United States v. Bennet). Finally, in 1913, Federal Judge Learned Hand (U.S. v. Kennerly) uttered a prophetic statement that was to become the position of the nation's courts twenty years later. "I question," said Judge Hand, "whether in the end men will regard that as obscene which is honestly relevant to the adequate expression of innocent ideas, and whether they will not believe that truth and beauty are too precious to society at large to be mutilated in the interests of those most likely to pervert them to base uses. Indeed, it seems hardly likely that we are even today so lukewarm in our interest in letters or serious discussion as to be content to reduce our treatment of sex to the standard of a child's library in the supposed interest of a salacious few or that shame will long prevent us from adequate portrayal of some of the most serious and beautiful sides of human nature."

The first of the key court cases that established the pattern of movie censorship for many years was decided by the Supreme Court in 1915 (Mutual Film Corporation v. Industrial Commission of Ohio). Here the court considered mainly whether Ohio movie censorship imposed a burden of interstate commerce. The court found no burden. But, what was more important for the future of movie censorship, was the court's view of movies. They were, the Court ruled, "a business pure and simple." They were a "spectacle or show and not such vehicles of thought as to bring them within the press of the country. . . . Their power of amusement and it may be, education, the audiences they assemble, not of women alone or men alone, but together, not of adults only, but of children, make them the more insidious in corruption by a pretense of worthy purpose. . . . They take their attraction from the general scene, eager and wholesome as it may be in their subjects, but a prurient interest may be excited and appealed to."

Four years later came a Supreme Court decision that seemed to have no bearing whatever on the movie business. This was Schenck v. U.S. It dealt with an effort to distribute antidraft leaflets during World War I on the grounds that this distribution was permissible under the freedom of speech and press guarantees. The opinion of Justice Oliver Wendell Holmes, one of the most famous of this century, pointed out that freedom of speech does not authorize a person to yell "Fire!" in a crowded theater. Justice Holmes introduced the concept of "clear and present danger" as applied to freedom of speech. "The question in every case," he declared, "is whether the words used are used in such circumstances and are of such a nature as to create a clear and present danger that they will bring about the substantive evils that Congress has a right to prevent."

Many movie censors, in banning movies, subsequently held that the exhibition of such films would constitute a "clear and present danger" to the community, undermining morality, promoting crime or provoking racial frictions.

In 1931 came a Supreme Court decision that was to have enormous impact on movie censorship, though it did not deal with movies. This was the case of Near v. Minnesota. A Minnesota law provided that any person in the business of publishing or distributing an "obscene, lewd or lascivious" or a "malicious, scandalous and defamatory" newspaper or periodical "is guilty of a nuisance." The state could then sue "to enjoin perpetually the persons committing or maintaining any such nuisance from further committing or maintaining it." Disobedience was punishable by a sentence up to a year in jail. The Supreme Court held the law unconstitutional by a vote of five to four.

The importance of this decision for movie censorship was that it struck a blow against prior restraint. By prior restraint is meant the right of a censor to ban something without first allowing it to be put before the public. Chief Justice Charles Evans Hughes did not flatly condemn all prior restraint. But he emphasized it was to be applied only in exceptional cases, such as preventing publication of the departure of troopships during war. Obscenity was another exception. So was incitement to violence. But the burden was shifted to the state to prove an extraordinary condition requiring an imposition of prior restraint.

"The exceptional nature of its limitations," said the Chief Justice, "places in a strong light the general conception that liberty of the press, historically considered and taken up by the Federal Constitution, has meant, principally although not exclusively, immunity from previous restraints or censorship."

Prior restraint was thus clearly labeled censorship and not to be used against the press. But since movies were still considered a business, and not entitled to the same freedom as the press, prior censorship could be applied against films.

The next major case was one of the most important rulings on censorship in this century. Though dealing with a book, it has been extended to movies. This was the famous *Ulysses* decision of 1933 in which Federal Judge John M. Woolsey lifted the customs ban on the James Joyce novel. Judge Woolsey carried forward the suggestion made in 1913 by Judge Hand that obscenity should not be based on the standards of children or the salacious. Judge Woolsey finished off the Victorian interpretation that had been laid down in England in the Hicklin ruling. The fair test, he said, was to judge by the standards of a mature person and on the basis of the entire work, not by isolated words or paragraphs.

"The meaning of the word 'obscene' as legally defined by the Courts is: tending to stir the sex impulses or to lead to sexually impure and lustful thoughts. . . . Whether a particular book would tend to excite such impulses and thoughts must be tested by the court's opinion as to its effect on a person with average sex instincts—what the French would call l'homme moyen sensuel.

". . . Reading 'Ulysses' in its entirety, as a book must be read on such a test as this, did not tend to excite sexual impulses or lustful thoughts but that its net effect on them was only that of a somewhat tragic and very powerful commentary on the inner lives of men and women. . . . It is only with the normal person that the law is concerned."

In 1952 came the Supreme Court decision that rocked movie censorship. This was the case of Burstyn v. Wilson, involving the movie *The Miracle.* New York State censors had banned the Italian film on the ground that it was "sacrilegious." The movie was about a simple-minded peasant woman who is seduced by a stranger she fancies is St. Joseph. She imagines her child is the result of miraculous conception.

The court, in a unanimous opinion, declared that movies were entitled to guaranties of free speech. It said that the fact that a movie entertained did not disqualify it as a source of information. This reversed the ruling that had stood since 1915, which asserted that the movie industry was only a business. The opinion, written by Justice Tom C. Clark, also declared that the word "sacrilegious" was too vague and indefinite to be a standard for censorship.

"It cannot be doubted," said the court, "that motion pictures are a significant medium for the communication of ideas. They may affect public attitudes and behavior in a variety of ways, ranging from direct espousal of a political or social doctrine to the subtle shaping of thought which characterizes all artistic expression. The importance of motion pictures as an organ of public opinion is not lessened by the fact that they are designed to entertain as well as inform.

". . . We conclude that expression by means of motion pictures is included within the free speech and free press guaranty of the First and Fourteenth Amendments. To the extent that language in the opinion in the Ohio case is out of harmony with the views here set forth, we no longer adhere to it."

The First Amendment says: "Congress shall make no law . . . abridging the freedom of speech or of the press."

The Fourteenth Amendment says: "No State shall make or enforce any law which shall abridge the privileges or immunities of citizens of the United States, nor shall any State deprive any person of life, liberty or property without due process of law. . . ."

The court, at one point, seemed on the verge of declaring prior restraint of the movies invalid, since movies were now entitled to the same freedom as the press. It said: "This court recognized many years ago that such a previous restraint is a form of infringement upon freedom of expression to be especially condemned. Near v. Minnesota, 283 U.S. 697 (1931) . . . In the light of the First Amendment's history and of the Near decision, the State has a heavy burden to demonstrate that the limitation challenged here presents such an exceptional case."

But then the court added that the guaranties for freedom of speech and a free press did not mean that the Constitution "requires absolute freedom to exhibit every motion picture of every kind at all times and all places."

Of the vagueness of the term "sacrilegious," the court said: "In seeking to apply the broad and all-inclusive definition of 'sacrilegious' given by the New York courts, the censor is set adrift upon a boundless sea amid a myriad of conflicting currents of religious views, with no charts but those provided by the most vocal and powerful orthodoxies." Furthermore, said the court, "the state has no legitimate interest in protecting any or all religions from views distasteful to them which is sufficient to justify prior restraints upon the expression of those views."

One point the court avoided in this case. Is obscenity to be included among those exceptions that justify prior restraint?

In the wake of the Burstyn case came a series of rulings by the court that tossed out reasons for censorship. Also in 1952, in Gelling v. Texas, the court reversed a ban on *Pinky*, a movie about a Negro girl who passed as white. When this ban was upheld by Texas courts, the Burstyn case had not yet been decided. But the Supreme Court decision reversing the Texas courts made it clear that it was improper to withhold a picture on the grounds it was "of such character as to be prejudicial to the best interests of the people."

In 1954 the area in which censors could operate was narrowed by three more Supreme Court rulings based on the *Miracle* case. In Superior Films v. the Department of Education of Ohio, the censors lost a double-header. It had banned *Native Son*, a movie dealing with racial frictions, on the grounds that it "contributes to racial misunderstanding, presenting situations undesirable to the mutual interests of both races; is against public interest in undermining confidence that justice can be carried out; presents racial frictions at a time when all groups should be united against everything that is subversive." The Ohio court had supported the censors, saying that despite the Supreme Court's ruling on *The Miracle*, there was a field in which "decency of morals may be protected from the impact of an offending motion picture film by prior restraint under proper criteria." The other movie, *M*, was about a madman who kills children. The censors ruled this movie was "harmful." The Supreme Court decided against the censors in both cases, citing its decision in the case of *The Miracle*.

At the same time the Supreme Court reversed the New York State Court of Appeals (Commercial Pictures v. Regents of the University of the State of New York), which had upheld the New York censors in connection with the French movie *La Ronde*. The New York State censors had refused to issue a license to *La Ronde*, charging it was "immoral" and would "tend to corrupt morals." The picture, based on the Arthur Schnitzler comedy *Reigen*, included promiscuity, adultery and seduction.

The Court of Appeals, in supporting the censors, said the movie "panders to base human emotions" and was a "breeding ground for sensuality, depravity, licentiousness and sexual immorality." The Court of Appeals then used this description to utilize the words of Justice Holmes in the case of Schenck v. U.S.: "That these vices represent a 'clear and present danger' to the body social seems manifestly clear." Once more the United States Supreme Court reversed the censors, citing only its *Miracle* ruling.

Justice William O. Douglas, in his own opinion—it was not, however, that of the court—refused to sidestep the issue of prior restraint. He insisted that all prior censorship in movies was unconstitutional. He denied that movies required more legal restraints than other mass media. "Motion pictures are of course a different medium of expression than the public speech, the radio, the stage, the novel or the magazine. But the First Amendment draws no distinction between the various methods of communicating ideas. On occasion one may be more powerful than another. The movie, like the public speech, the radio or television, is transitory—here now and gone in an instant. The novel, the short story, the poem and printed form are permanently at hand to re-enact the drama or re-tell the story over and over again. Which medium will give the most excitement and have the most enduring effect will vary with the theme and the actors. It is not for the censor to determine in any case."

In 1955 another excuse for censorship was ruled out by the Supreme Court in Holmby Productions Inc. v. Vaughn. The Kansas State Board of Review had banned the innocuous comedy *The Moon Is Blue* because of its "sex theme throughout; too frank bedroom dialogue; many sexy words; both dialogue and actions have sex as their theme." In a re-examination, the censors called it "obscene, indecent and immoral . . . tends to corrupt morals." The objection of the Hollywood censors to this film, noted in Chapter II, was that it made a joke of adultery, though none was committed. This time, in reversing the censors, the Supreme Court cited not only its ruling on *The Miracle* but also those for *Native Son* and *M*.

In 1957, the Supreme Court in an opinion covering two cases (Roth v. U.S. and Alberts v. U.S.) dug deeply into the question of obscenity. Samuel Roth, who published and sold books, photographs and magazines, solicited sales with circulars and advertising matter. He was convicted in lower courts of mailing obscene circulars and advertising matter, and an obscene book. David S. Alberts, who conducted a mail-order business, was charged with having obscene books and for publishing an obscene advertisement for them.

The majority opinion of the Supreme Court, affirming both convictions, was written by Justice William J. Brennan, and had an impact far beyond the subject at hand. For since the movies had, by this time, become entitled to freedom guaranties, they were affected by these obscenity rulings.

The court held in the Roth case that "obscenity is not protected by the freedoms of speech and press." It was noted that American history made it "apparent that the unconditional phrasing of the First Amendment was not intended to protect every utterance. . . ."

The First Amendment does not protect obscenity because it is "utterly without . . . social importance," said Justice Brennan. This was how he put it: "All ideas having even the slightest redeeming social importance—unorthodox ideas, controversial ideas, even ideas hateful to the prevailing climate of opinion—have the full protection of guaranties, unless excludable because they encroach upon the limited area of more important interests. But implicit in the history of the First Amendment is the rejection of obscenity as utterly without redeeming social importance. This rejection for that reason is mirrored in the universal judgment that obscenity should be restrained, reflected in the international agreement of over 50 nations, in the obscenity laws of all of the 48 states, and in the 20 obscenity laws enacted by Congress from 1842 to 1956."

At the same time, in the Alberts case, the court wanted it made clear that alleged obscenity could not be made an excuse for free-swinging censorship.

Justice Brennan declared that "clear and present danger" did not apply to obscene communications. He said that "sex and obscenity are not synonymous . . . Sex, a great and mysterious motive force in human life, has indisputably been a subject of absorbing interest to mankind through the ages; it is one of the vital problems of human interest and public concern. . . ."

The core of Justice Brennan's approach to obscenity and censorship was contained in the following: "The fundamental freedoms of speech and press have contributed greatly to the development and well-being of our free society and are indispensable to its continued growth. Ceaseless vigilance is the watchword to prevent their erosion by Congress or by the States. The door barring federal and state intrusion into this area cannot be left ajar; it must be kept tightly closed and opened only the slightest crack necessary to prevent encroachment upon more important interests. It is therefore vital that the standards for judging obscenity safeguard the protection of freedom of speech and press for material which does not treat sex in a manner appealing to prurient interest."

In a footnote "prurient" was defined as "material having a tendency to excite lustful thoughts."

Justice John Marshall Harlan, in dissent, feared that the majority opinion "paints with such a broad brush . . . it may result in a loosening of the tight reins which state and federal courts should hold upon the enforcement of obscenity statutes." He expressed strong reservations about generalized definitions of a term such as obscenity.

"Many juries might find," said Justice Harlan, "that Joyce's 'Ulysses' or Boccaccio's 'Decameron' was obscene, and yet the conviction of a defendant for selling either book would raise, for me, the gravest constitutional problems, for no such verdict could convince me, without more, that these books are 'utterly without redeeming social importance.' In short, I do not understand how the Court can resolve the constitutional problems now before it without making its own independent judgment upon the character of the material upon which these convictions were based. I am very much afraid that the broad manner in which the Court has decided these cases will tend to obscure the peculiar responsibilities resting on state and federal courts in this field and encourage them to rely on easy labeling and jury verdicts as a substitute for facing up to the tough individual problems of constitutional judgment involved in every obscenity case."

In another dissent, Justice Douglas, supported by Justice Hugo L. Black, said that before supporting censors, courts should consider if the result of the material being judged is "anti-social." To say it lacks social value is not enough. Nor is it enough to wonder about what sort of thought such material may instill in the mind of a reader.

"By these standards," he asserted, "punishment is inflicted for thoughts provoked, not for overt acts nor anti-social conduct. This test cannot be squared with our decisions under the First Amendment. . . . This issue cannot be avoided by saying that obscenity is not protected by the First Amendment. The question remains, what is the constitutional test of obscenity?

"The tests by which these convictions were obtained require only the arousing of sexual thoughts. Yet the arousing of sexual thoughts and desires happens every day in normal life in dozens of ways. Nearly 30 years ago a questionnaire sent to college and normal school women graduates asked what things were most stimulating sexually. Of 409 replies, 9 said 'music'; 18 said 'pictures'; 40 said 'drama'; 95 said 'books'; and 218 said 'man.' "

The same year (1957) the Supreme Court, in reversing Chicago censors and the Illinois Supreme Court (Times Film Corp. v.

Chicago), gave no opinion. But it was thus indicated that censors would find it difficult to prove a movie was obscene. The French movie in question, *Game of Love*, includes the seduction of a youth by a much older woman. As a result of this experience he has sexual relations with a girl his own age.

The Supreme Court struck at the censors again in its decision on the movie *Lady Chatterley's Lover* (Kingsley International Pictures Corp. v. Regents). This film, based on the famous D. H. Lawrence novel, dealt with an adulterous relationship between a married woman and her husband's gamekeeper. The New York State censors denied the film a license because it showed adultery as a "desirable, acceptable and proper pattern of behavior." The censors called it obscene.

The Supreme Court conceded that the movie "attractively portrays a relationship which is contrary to the moral standards, the religious precepts and the legal code of its citizenry." This, however, said Justice Potter Stewart, is not the important issue. He declared that the constitutional guaranty is "not confined to the expression of ideas that are conventional or shared by a majority. It protects advocacy of the opinion that adultery may sometimes be proper, no less than advocacy of socialism or the single tax. And in the realm of ideas it protects expression which is eloquent no less than that which is unconvincing."

As a result of such decisions, state courts began turning down obscenity cases. One of the most conspicuous examples was *Garden of Eden*, the film about a nudist group in a private camp. The New York State censors called the film "indecent." The New York Court of Appeals said the word "indecent" was too broad for censorship (Excelsior Pictures Corp. v. Regents). "Nudity in itself, and without lewdness or dirtiness is not obscenity in law or in common sense," said the appeals court, reflecting the position of the Supreme Court in the Roth case and subsequent opinions.

The crucial issue of prior restraint was faced by the Supreme Court in 1961 (Times Film Corp. v. City of Chicago, *et al.*). In a decision with heated dissents, the court ruled, by five to four, that cities and states have the right to demand that movies must obtain a censor's permit before they are shown. The Times Film Corp. to test this right had applied for a permit but had refused to produce the film, *Don Juan*, for inspection. The picture was merely a film version of the Mozart opera *Don Giovanni* and would have had no trouble getting a permit. But since the company refused to produce the movie for inspection the censors refused to issue the permit.

The majority opinion, written by Justice Clark, asked whether "constitutional protection includes complete and absolute freedom to exhibit, at least once, any and every kind of motion picture. It is that question alone which we decide. . . . Petitioner claims that the nature of the film is irrelevant, and that even if this film contains the basest type of pornography, or incitement to riot, or forceful overthrow of orderly government, it may nonetheless be shown without prior submission for examination. The challenge here is to the censor's basic authority. . . . Petitioner would have us hold that the public exhibition of motion pictures must be allowed under any circumstances. The State's old remedy, it says, is the invocation of criminal process under the Illinois pornography statute . . . and then only after a transgression."

Justice Clark said that such a "claim of absolute privilege against prior restraint under the First Amendment" was "without sanction." He cited the ruling of Chief Justice Hughes in Near v. Minnesota that "the primary requirements of decency" were among the exceptional causes for enforcing prior restraint against obscene publications. He quoted from Roth v. United States "that obscenity is not within the area of constitutionally protected speech of press." He noted that in Burstyn v. Wilson it had been recognized by the court that "capacity for evil . . . may be relevant in determining the permissible scope of community control" and that movies were not "necessarily subject to the precise rules governing any other particular method of expression."

"It is not for this Court," Justice Clark ruled, "to limit the State in its selection of the remedy it deems most effective to cope with such a problem, absent, of course, a showing of unreasonable strictures on individual liberty resulting from its application in particular circumstances. . . . We, of course, are not holding that city officials may be granted the power to prevent the showing of any motion picture they deem unworthy of a license."

Chief Justice Earl Warren, in dissent, asserted that "the Court's opinion comes perilously close to holding that not only may motion pictures be censored but that a licensing scheme may also be applied to newspapers, books, and periodicals, radio, television, public speeches and every other medium of expression. The Court in no way explains why moving pictures should be treated differently than any other form of expression."

He pointed out that prior restraint puts a special burden on the movie exhibitor by forcing him to fight the censors through the courts. He observed that the *Miracle* case was argued in the courts for five years before the Supreme Court decision and then the film was never shown in Chicago.

"This," he said, "is the delay occasioned by the censor. This is the injury done to the free communication of ideas. This damage is not inflicted by the ordinary criminal penalties." To avoid such delays, he said, producers cut portions of a film, or even decide not to show it.

"It would seem idle," said the Chief Justice, "to suppose the Court today is unaware of the evils of the censor's basic authority, of the mischief against which so many great men have waged stubborn and often precarious warfare for centuries . . . of the scheme that impedes all communication by hanging threateningly over creative thought."

He then cited examples of unreasonable movie censorship under prior restraint.

"This," he declared, "is the regimen to which the Court holds that all films must be submitted. It officially unleashes the censor and permits him to roam at will, limited only by an ordinance which contains some standards that, although concededly not before us in this case, are patently imprecise."

In another dissent, Justice Douglas declared: "If, however, government must proceed against an illegal publication in a prosecution, then the advantages are on the other side. All the protections of the Bill of Rights come into play. The presumption of innocence, the right to jury trial, proof of guilt beyond a reasonable doubt—these become barriers in the path of officials who want to impose their standard of morality on the author or producer. The advantage a censor enjoys while working as a supreme bureaucracy disappears. . . . The First Amendment was designed to enlarge, not to limit, freedom in literature and in arts as well as in politics, economics, law, and other fields. . . . Its aim was to unlock all ideas for argument, debate, and dissemination. No more potent force in defeat of that freedom could be designed than censorship. It is a weapon that no minority or majority group, acting through government, should be allowed to wield over any of us."

Prior restraint may not squeak through the Supreme Court many more times. State and local censors seem to be on the ropes. But they may persist a long time unless the movie industry shows the determination of such small movie companies as Times Film, or the dedication of such lawyers as Bilgrey, Ernst, Lindey, London, Nimmer. The fight against state and local censors is the best investment Hollywood can make. But it must be prepared to go all the way. It must be willing to go into the courts every time it thinks its freedom has been violated. That is the only way it will carry to a logical conclusion the beginnings that were made by *Ulysses* and *The Miracle*.

2. *Loony Bins of Censorship*

Supreme Court decisions seem to mean very little to state and local censors. These censors have, by the irresponsibility of their rulings, supplied excellent proof that government censorship of movies is a mistake. Nowhere in the field of American censorship in this century is there more overwhelming evidence of the danger of placing the power of public officials and law behind censorship. Silly, bigoted, uneducated persons are common among the men and women charged with this duty by state and local governments. The best that can be said for them is that they have forced indignant movie-makers and distributors to fight them in courts and thus win major victories in the field of movie censorship. These court decisions, combined with the rising level of American literacy, have brought about the steady decline of state censor boards from twenty-seven to four—those of New York, Maryland, Kansas and Virginia.

It is generally assumed that these state censorship bodies have the support of the majority within each state. This is open to question today. Not too long ago one of the leading authorities on movie censorship, in a private conversation with the governor of a state that had censorship, was surprised to learn that the governor was opposed to censorship of movies by his state group. He was asked why he did not express his opposition.

The governor explained that state censorship had become a matter of politics and state finance. He pointed out that the censorship board gives him an opportunity for patronage. And even when political censors work without salary or fee, they enjoy the authority. Thus, some political workers who do not need the money can be named censors, leaving salaried patronage jobs to other workers for a winning governor. Then, the governor added, a fee is charged for each film reviewed by the censors. This is a nice donation to the state treasury. During the year the movie industry pays more than $1,500,000 in censorship fees in the United States. Finally, though the governor did not discuss this, there is the fear that dissolution of a censorship board might offend some religious groups.

In at least one respect there has been considerable improvement in state censorship of movies. The newer censors are not nearly as arrogant as their predecessors used to be. There was a time when, if they wished, they gave no reason for banning a movie—and the more ridiculous the ruling, the more likely were the censors to refuse to explain their position.

Characteristic of this whimsical attitude was the ruling of Kansas censors in banning one of the amusing film shorts made by Robert Benchley. In this film the humorist gave a delightful portrayal of a bumbling professor droning along about the sex life of a polyp, which is about as close as animal life can come to a vegetable. Kansas censors refused to say why they would not allow this movie to be shown. Moreover, as astonishment mounted among literate persons in Kansas, the governor was forced to take cognizance of editorial ridicule. He reviewed the film but somehow reached the same conclusion as his censors. He too gave no reason. Eventually the ban was dropped quietly, without reason, and polyps became moral in Kansas.

Even more of a nuisance to movie-makers than the state censorship groups are the local censors. The last count by the Motion Picture Association of America showed there were censors in Chicago, Evanston, Spokane, Pasadena, Detroit, Providence, Little Rock, Memphis, Birmingham and Atlanta. There are other censor groups in smaller communities. It is in the cities and smaller localities that the worst examples of ridiculous censorship are to be found.

An expert in the Motion Picture Association who has had to deal with such groups says they often realize that they are on shaky legal ground when they demand changes in a film or even ban it. "But they bludgeon distributors into doing what they wish with veiled threats. The distributor, rather than engage in what may be a long and costly lawsuit, goes along with them. Still, I think there is a little hope. These decisions are not quite as screwy as they used to be." He was probably referring to the days when some of these local censors objected to a word such as "diapers."

At times the threat of these local censors has been of value to the movie industry's own censors. In cases where some producer has obviously used excessive violence or sex without taste or dramatic justification—but barely within the code regulations—the industry censors point out that a number of local censors will demand deletions or may ban the film. This argument sometimes persuades the most mercenary of producers to control their greed and curb their innate vulgarity.

Nor is it necessarily true that large cities have wiser censors than small ones. In 1962, for example, the censors of Detroit considered a documentary called *The Sky Above, the Mud Below*. The film, dealing with aborigines of New Guinea, had won acclaim by educational, civic and religious organizations. But in Detroit the censors were concerned about the fact that female savages in New Guinea had not been dressed up with brassieres by the film-makers. They struggled with this problem and reached an amazing conclusion. The picture could not be shown in neighborhood houses. But it was permissible to show it to adults in theaters considered "art" houses. As soon as this decision was challenged it was reversed, of course.

Ephraim London, a New York attorney who has fought movie

censorship on many fronts, has been dismayed by the wide variety of standards among political censors. For instance, he has noted, there is a difference in criteria in some southern states. One kind of censorship applies to theaters attended by white persons and another to theaters patronized by Negroes. In one Texas city there was no trouble with *And God Created Woman* in a "white" theater. The censors banned it, however, from a second-run house attended by Negroes, "presumably on the theory that Negroes have a lower boiling point."

In this connection there have been local censors who have ruled that it is permissible for the breasts of brown or black women to be shown in movies—but not the breasts of white women.

London, in his defense of movies against censorship, has learned that his opponents sometimes place themselves above the Supreme Court. After he had won the Supreme Court decision for the film version of *Lady Chatterley's Lover* the picture was banned in Little Rock, Arkansas. London telephoned the censor, who was also a local newspaper editor. "When I reminded him that the picture had been found not obscene by the Supreme Court he said, in effect, that if the Supreme Court was for it, Little Rock was against it."

Vivid in London's memory is Providence, Rhode Island, where movie censorship is, or was until fairly recently, dominated by a police lieutenant. During one court fight the lawyer was examining a censor on the witness stand. The censor admitted he had seen only one movie in thirteen years. That film was *Baby Doll*. He had been invited to the showing by some clergy. His custom, he admitted, was to bother only with movies that received a "Condemned" rating from the Legion of Decency.

London, and other lawyers who have dipped into censorship cases, have learned that when a word is at issue an effective way to fight censors is to cite the Bible. The censors of Kansas demanded the deletion of the word "whores" from *Boccaccio 70*. Mr. London persuaded them to withdraw this objection by reminding them that the Bible, in Ezekiel, has the same word thirty-three times to condemn homage to harlots.

The late Jerry Wald, one of the most experienced of movie

producers, became intrigued with the censors of Memphis, Tennessee, who have banned more Hollywood films than censors in any other city in the world. He observed that across the Mississippi River, in Arkansas, was West Memphis, which often shows the films banned in Memphis, thereby attracting considerable movie trade from Memphis. "We have no reports," he said, "to show that West Memphis has become a slough of immorality due to its exposure to Hollywood movies banned across the river. Actually, West Memphis is a highly respectable and highly respected community, made up of home-owners, shopkeepers, farmers, front-lawn gardeners and parents; in short, a cross section of any good American community."

One of the most extraordinary comments on censorship was made by a lady censor from Pasadena when she was asked to define her job. "We don't censor the movies," she said. "We are not censors. We just tell the exhibitors what pictures they can't show."

The late Senator Kefauver, when he headed the committee that investigated sex and violence in movies, may have been thinking of this kind of censor when he warned against censorship in an article in *P. T. A. Magazine:* "In our war on pornography we should be aware of threats from within as well as outside our ranks. Proponents of extensive censorship may seek to join our campaign in order to use it as a front for attacking basic liberties, such as freedom of expression and privacy of the mails. We must keep our ranks free of the suppressors of freedom, the hypocrites, the perverts, and the would-be censors. On the other hand, many will try to pin these very labels on any opponent of filth, however sincere and level-headed. We must not be misled or sidetracked by either group."

Otto Preminger's technique is simple. The producer-director hits back hard and fast. When the Chicago censors banned his film *Anatomy of a Murder* he headed for the federal court there. The censors had found the picture obscene because of the almost medical language used during testimony at a rape trial and the heroine's account of how she was raped. Words such as sperm, contraceptive, penetration, were part of the movie's trial language. These are words common to court cases involving sexual offenses. But they are rare in movie versions of such cases. To the censors the words were anathema. But to the courts, recognizing the validity of trial usage, they were unobjectionable. Preminger won.

Sometimes it is difficult to fight censors because they give no reason for a ban. In Atlanta, for instance, the censors rejected *The Blackboard Jungle* without saying why. The answer of the courts to such action has become merely to reverse the censors, simply citing the titles of earlier cases on movie censorship.

Adolph Zukor says that at least one state—and many communities—opposed a portion of every movie Mae West made for Paramount. In every case, he says, his company won a reversal of the censorship decrees.

One of the constant brow-knitting problems weighed by these censors is to figure out the point at which romance becomes lust. Some have decided that if a man bends a woman backward while they kiss the purity of his intentions have been sullied to the point requiring censorship. In the days when Boston used to have one set of rules for weekdays and another batch for Sunday the word "bawdy house" was permitted in *Henry V* on weekdays but not on Sundays. In an article for *The Saturday Review*, Arthur L. Mayer, a highly reputable film historian, cited the cross-examination of a Chicago police captain who was assisted as censor by the widows of four policemen:

Q. Have you taken any courses subsequent to your high school?
A. No, sir.
Q. How many literature courses did you have during high school?
A. I don't remember.
Q. How many books on an average do you read a year? . . . A dozen, two dozen?
A. No.
Q. It is less than that?
A. Yes.
Q. How many plays do you attend each year?
A. Very few.
Q. Would you say one or two?
A. No.
Q. Do you read the book review section of . . . any newspaper?
A. No, sir.

Q. Are the members of the board required to have any special qualifications?

A. No, sir.

Q. Are any of them writers or recognized in other forms of art?

A. I wouldn't know.

Q. In the course of events is the producer of the film ever called in to explain ambiguities in the film?

A. No, sir.

Q. Is the distributor ever called in?

A. No, sir.

Q. Are other people's views invited, such as drama critics or movie reviewers or artists? Or are they ever asked to comment on the film before the censor board makes its decision?

A. No, sir.

Mayer says that court reversals of this board's decisions have finally brought about an improvement. The board now has an appeals group of five persons who have "more impressive qualifications."

Chicago censors have had the questionable distinction of becoming the comic relief of a Supreme Court decision. Justice Clark noted that censors from the Windy City had ordered the deletion of a scene showing the birth of a buffalo in Walt Disney's *Vanishing Prairie*. They refused licenses to several movies criticizing life in Nazi Germany, presumably because such films might offend the large German population in Chicago. They banned Charlie Chaplin's *The Great Dictator*, the satire on Hitler, apparently for the same reason. From newspaper files of 1959 Justice Clark cited an extraordinary criterion employed by a police sergeant in charge of the city's censorship. The sergeant said: "Children should be allowed to see any movie that plays in Chicago. If a picture is objectionable for a child, it is objectionable period."

Chicago movie censors have been virtually at war with the courts since the Supreme Court's decision on *The Miracle*. From 1952, the year of that ruling, until January of 1961, when Justice Clark's opinion on *Don Juan* was handed down, the censors have been reversed by the state courts every time their judgment was challenged.

The absurdity of censorial logic was illustrated in the Supreme

Court by Felix J. Bilgrey, one of a band of lawyers virtually dedicated to fighting censorship. In arguing the case of *Don Juan*, he recalled the position of Chicago censors, who banned *The Game of Love* as obscene. The Illinois Supreme Court had decreed that to be ruled obscene material must arouse sexual desires of normal persons. The Chicago censors admitted that *The Game of Love* did not stir their lust. But since they considered it obscene, Mr. Bilgrey wondered, did this mean that they ignored the standard or did it reflect on their capacity to censor?

A few examples of Memphis movie censorship suffice to illustrate the attitude of that city's movie censors. They banned *The Southerner*, a film about poverty among southern tenant farmers, because it "reflects on the South." Also turned down was the comedy *Brewster's Millions* because the Negro comedian, Rochester, was considered "too familiar." *Curley* was banned in Memphis because it showed white and Negro children in the same school.

Other censors have made similar contributions to the collection of curious movie standards. Maryland deleted from *Joan of Arc* the famous cry at the stake: "Oh, God, why hast Thou forsaken me?" Ohio banned the Russian-made *Professor Mamlock*, an attack on Nazi anti-Semitism, on the grounds that it would "stir up hatred and ill will and gain nothing."

One of the most articulate of state censors, Hugh M. Flick, considered the subject in an article in *The New York Times*. Mr. Flick had been director of the state licensing agency in New York for six years and had licensed some 10,000 movies, from abroad as well as from Hollywood. He was convinced that "there will be some form of control by the state, the organized industry, special interest groups and the police, until such time as workable legal safeguards are established." He did not say what he meant by "workable legal safeguards," but called for a full-scale study of the over-all impact of mass media on society. He argued that the "most effective way of ending the 'evils' of official censorship is the insistence on the part of the industry that the best possible professionally trained personnel be charged with the responsibility of processing motion pictures." He did not say what, if anything, was wrong with the present personnel employed by the industry for this purpose.

When former Governor Michael Di Salle of Ohio vetoed a bill calling for state censorship of movies and magazines he came closer to stating the danger of political censorship. "It is easy for people in power to feel that they know what is good for everyone and to attempt to limit expression of conflicting views by others. But the guarantee of freedom of speech and freedom of the press was one of the early amendments sought by those who had so recently felt the limitations that could occur if this freedom was in any way restricted."

The campaigns in local and state legislative groups to establish censorship have brought strong warnings from leaders of the Republican as well as Democratic parties. Former President Dwight D. Eisenhower said: "As it is an ancient truth that freedom cannot be legislated into existence, so it is no less obvious that freedom cannot be censored into existence. And any who act as if freedom's defenses are to be found in suppression and suspicion and fear confess a doctrine that is alien to Americans."

This is the essential truth from which these censors cannot hide. They are revealed by the grotesque costumes of their statutes and by the moral gimcrackery of their utterances. They are anachronisms of Victorianism and belong in the museum of history.

3. Censorship Exotica

Worse—and more numerous—than our state and local censors are the foreign varieties. Ours are a bane. Theirs are a plague. Abroad there are dozens of movie strictures that make ours seem models of enlightenment. There are foreign censors who, for sheer arbitrariness, make our worst seem gentle philosophers. Most unfortunately for American producers, while our statutory censors are on the wane, the foreign species is multiplying.

Foreign censorship was responsible for the creation of a job at Metro-Goldwyn-Mayer that was strange even for Hollywood. The work was to check films that might be shown in India— which meant most Metro movies—and to make a note of all scenes in which alcoholic beverages were being consumed. Then one of two things happened. The drinking scene was cut. Or, if this sequence was too important to the picture, a most unexpected scene was inserted before the drinking began. The insert showed a hand pouring milk into the glasses. This was supposed to create the impression that any merriment that followed the lifting of glass to lip must be attributable to the innate good humor of the guests or to the milk. Presumably, any tipsiness was also to be blamed on the milk. The explanation was that India, having obtained her independence from Great Britain, showed it partly with a strong campaign against liquor. A symptom of this reaction to the land of Scotch and soda was to ban any movies that showed men and women drinking liquor. It can be argued that anyone familiar with India should have realized there was a strong religious feeling against alcoholic beverages and that political independence would liberate this antipathy. But movie-makers are neither seers nor anthropologists, though with so many different censorship codes around the world it is becoming necessary for film companies to become both.

However, no amount of erudition can protect American producers and directors against the vagaries of the multitudinous censorship regulations abroad. More important, it is not enough to commit censorship rules to memory. For at any time a rule can be interpreted in an unpredictable fashion.

Consider the ban on movie musicals that existed for a time in a Baltic country. No one could understand it. No offers to make changes in a film could win admission for it. No pleas or expensive dinners could budge the censors. The investigation took a long time. The reason for the ban on musicals was particularly disturbing since this type of show is notoriously moral, with a simple boy-meets-girl plot and virtue triumphant. Eventually the censors offered to admit the films, but with dancing scenes deleted, the equivalent of trying to teach Sunday school without referring to the Bible. Finally, the truth of the situation was admitted in confidence. One of the top government officials had a mistress with heavy legs. She did not like movies that displayed beautiful limbs in such profusion that it seemed she was the only one who did not have attractive legs.

When politics enters the censorship picture it is equally impossible to anticipate rulings. Thus, in 1946, when the Communists were making a strong bid to take over the government in Italy, the film *Ninotchka*, one of Greta Garbo's most successful movies, was used as a weapon against the Reds since it ridiculed the bureaucracy of the Soviet Union. Anti-Communists in Italy showed the movie in garages, halls, large rooms. They rushed the film all over the country as valuable political campaign material. Years later *Ninotchka* was converted into a Broadway musical called *Silk Stockings*. The show was made into a movie with the same name. The film was banned in Uruguay. The reason: movie deemed pro-Communistic.

The death scene of Messala in *Ben-Hur* was an excellent illustration of differences in foreign tastes. It was considered permissible in Australia, which is often strict on violence. In Brazil theaters were ordered to put signs in front saying the picture had some violent scenes. Incidentally, for the benefit of patrons with children, another sign had to say that the movie ran three hours and forty minutes. Germany insisted on a shortening of the Messala death scene.

One of the oddest tales in the history of foreign censorship is treasured by Robert Vogel, the Metro-Goldwyn-Mayer expert in the field. For many years the Laurel and Hardy movies had been the delight of the studio. They always made money and never caused censorship troubles. Suddenly, they were being banned in Finland. An investigation narrowed down to Laurel's comic gesture of showing confusion by forming a sort of pincer with his fingers and pulling up the hair at the back of his head. Groups of children had a teacher with long hair and an oddly shaped head. They began doing this gesture behind his back and bursting into laughter. He learned the reason for the laughter. The teacher was on the board of censors.

As apartheid swept across South Africa and became the main plank of the government platform, American movie-makers were unable to evaluate the extent of the bigotry. They learned from experience. In *Bells Are Ringing*, probably the funniest scene was the famous "Hialeah" number. This was the section in which bookmakers explain, in song, how they can take bets without being caught by the police simply by substituting names of composers for race tracks. That hilarious number was never seen in South Africa, for in it Negroes were commingled with white singers. To the censors of South Africa this constituted something as serious as miscegenation. The movie was banned. To have the ban lifted, the scene was eliminated. Those South Africans who owned the record of the original Broadway show probably considered the deletion from the movie just another example of Hollywood stupidity.

Arab countries have been a ticklish problem for Hollywood in recent years. Egypt banned *Ivanhoe* because it showed Rebecca, the Jewess, in the same favorable light as she had been originally portrayed by Sir Walter Scott. And when Marilyn Monroe decided to become a convert to Judaism when she married Arthur Miller, Egypt banned all her films. For a time Elizabeth Taylor's movies were banned. But the reason given was not that she had married Eddie Fisher, a Jew, but that she had contributed financially to Israeli bond drives.

What happened to *North by Northwest*, the Alfred Hitchcock spoof on violence, was a crazy quilt of foreign rulings. In Ireland love scenes were deleted because they were considered too sensual and the accompanying dialogue too outspoken. France approved. Greece banned the picture for those under fourteen. India demanded the deletion of a portion of a line. The original line was: "You look good to me in all the right places." Deleted was: "in all the right places." India also insisted on shorter kisses and embraces. It is odd how the youngest of the democracies are the most petty censors. It may be the insecurity of youth or an excess of nationalism. Morocco objected to a shot of flags massed in front of the United Nations. The reason: the flags included that of Israel. In South Africa natives were not allowed to see the movie. In Spain a line was deleted. It was: "Now what can a man do with his clothes off for twenty minutes?"

The game of beating the ban calls for ingenuity as well as glibness, backed by generous hospitality. But expensive gifts, for example, will not work with a British censor. What is one to do, then, with a movie like *Waterloo Bridge* that looked like a sure-fire money-maker for the English market since it had the famous

British star Vivien Leigh, teamed with Robert Taylor, then an important box-office attraction? The British had banned this movie because in it Miss Leigh becomes a prostitute while her husband is away. The British are tough on prostitution, at least in films. The whole problem was solved by changing only one line of dialogue. In the original version, when Miss Leigh's husband, Mr. Taylor, returns, she tells him: "I've been with other men." The line was changed to: "I've been with another man." Thus was prostitution reduced to simple adultery and a ban removed from *Waterloo Bridge*.

In *The Barefoot Contessa* the heroine has an affair with a guitar player because her husband is impotent. The husband finds out and kills her. This immorality, despite the punishment for sin, was too much for the Spanish censors. The lifting of their ban was effected with changes in subtitles. The husband became a brother. And the brother killed his sister because she was having an affair before marriage.

American movie-makers run into particular trouble on violence because the standards, apart from code regulations, are more tolerant in the United States than in most civilized nations. In *Liberty Valance* for instance, Lee Marvin holds up a stagecoach and then beats up James Stewart, a passenger. The beating is quite thorough, including a drubbing with a whip. Nevertheless, since he is a villainous creature to begin with, the movie received a seal of approval. But in the United Kingdom a large chunk of the beating had to be eliminated.

Indonesia, according to Ed Schellhorn, Paramount's authority on foreign censorship regulations, has become a problem child of Hollywood. Movie-makers have just about given up trying to anticipate the reactions of censors in Indonesia. They are tough on sex and violence. They are sensitive about nationalism, not only their own but that of any new nation. They worry, since they are trying to get along with Communist forces, if there is anything that could be considered anti-Communist. One dare not even show political unrest in any young country, lest it be interpreted by Indonesian censors as incitement to rebellion in Indonesia. "It's become almost impossible to have a villain," said Schellhorn. "The only way out is that if you show, say, a Lebanese as a villain, you have to show other Lebanese as good guys. If you show a poor section of a country, you have to show something in the country that is not poor."

In one movie, according to Eli Levy, foreign censorship expert for Columbia Pictures, a Mexican was shown riding a donkey. He was asleep. To appease the Mexican censors it was necessary to have the rider awake. Millions of Americans have seen barefooted Mexicans. But if American movie-makers want to do business in Mexico they had better put shoes on the Mexicans. They can be cheap shoes.

In any film dealing with a Latin American nation, says Levy, it must be remembered that, as a rule, a movie that gives affront to one Latin American country may be construed as an insult by the others. This is why one movie that showed Nazis in a Latin American country had to be changed. A bit was inserted showing a member of that nation's secret police rounding up the Nazis. Truth has nothing to do with censorship.

Some aspects of movies about the Arab countries that used to be clichés are now *verboten*. Hollywood no longer shows a harem in an Arab country. An Arab now has a large number of girl friends with whom he gets along very well.

With the multiplicity of foreign regulations there has developed in Hollywood a small but valuable group of experts that claim to have the ability to detect which bits of a movie may affect that most delicate of censorship fibers—national pride. Probably the best known of these free-lance consultants on censorship was the late William Gordon, who was particularly valuable, during the fifties, to independent companies that could not afford to keep an expert on the payroll on a permanent basis.

One of Gordon's favorite coups was in connection with *Six Bridges to Cross*. A scene in this film carries President Roosevelt's radio address describing the attack on Pearl Harbor as "a day which will live in infamy." Gordon suggested that such a line might offend the Japanese, a considerable market for movie-makers. So, for the Japanese market, the picture carried a sound track to the effect that war had broken out between Japan and the United States—without Roosevelt quotes.

Another Gordon illustration deals with *The Secret Beyond the*

ROMEO AND JULIET: When Norma Shearer played Juliet to Leslie Howard's Romeo, movie censorship ruling was that if there was any passion in bed, lover, no matter how star-crossed, must have feet on floor.

CLEOPATRA: Gone forever is Hollywood's taboo against showing an unmarried couple in bed. Elizabeth Taylor as Queen of the Nile and Richard Burton as Mark Anthony show that beds are not for sleeping.

left top:

ELMER GANTRY: Wide assortment of churches tried to interfere with the filming of Sinclair Lewis' novel about a lecherous clergyman (Burt Lancaster). The lady of obvious profession is Shirley Jones.

left bottom:

TOWN WITHOUT PITY: Behold a female navel. First time it was approved by movie industry's censors. Bikini and lady around the navel are Christine Kaufman.

below:

SAMSON AND DELILAH: The Bible has long been an excuse for cinematic sex and violence. This "lust-in-the-dust" epic made Hedy Lamarr the Old Testament siren and Victor Mature the strong man she seduced.

Paramount

MCA

left:

MAE WEST: She became the sex symbol of the thirties by making a joke of sex —and by proving that the hourglass figure was far from dead if handled properly.

right top:

BETTY GRABLE: Queen of the pin-ups of World War II as she appeared in *Diamond Horseshoe.* The scene shows why although her photographs were so popular with G.I.s, her movies remained models of wholesomeness.

right bottom left:

LANA TURNER: Clinging garments made Miss Turner's torso the concern of the movie industry's official censors during the pin-up era. They issued an edict to all studios, warning against excessively tight sweaters.

right bottom right:

AVA GARDNER: Turbulence of her personal life, as well as her appearance, made her one of the most exciting of the pin-up stars who managed to bring sex to the screen without riling censors.

below:

RITA HAYWORTH: One of Hollywood's major contributions to morale uplift of G.I.s during World War II, shown here in shot from *Miss Sadie Thompson,* a remake of Somerset Maugham's *Rain.*

Columbia

20th Century-Fox

MGM

THE BLACKBOARD JUNGLE: New era in violence: Gangsterism replaced by juvenile delinquency. Teacher is Glenn Ford and delinquent is Vic Morrow.

NOTORIOUS: Hitchcock formula for combining tension and romance without violence or nudity illustrated in this spy thriller that brought together government agent (Cary Grant) and refugee (Ingrid Bergman) in Brazilian locale.

RKO-RADIO

I AM A FUGITIVE FROM A CHAIN GANG: Realism and a sense of social justice raised this Hollywood movie of crime and violence to a sociological force in the early thirties. It created so much controversy that the director, Mervyn LeRoy, who had been one of the pioneers in gangster movies of the talkies (*Little Caesar*), was banned for a time from Georgia, home of the chain gang. Picture starred Paul Muni (swinging sledge), who had established a sort of pattern for gangster films in title role of *Scarface*.

Warner Brothers

United Artists

WEST SIDE STORY: Violence, handled artistically and dramatically, caused no censorship problems except with some song lyrics. Young man with knife is Richard Beymer. On the ground before him is George Chakiris.

Universal

BEN-HUR: That one censor's healthy excitement is another censor's excessive violence was demonstrated in this enormously successful remake of the silent film. German censors, for instance, insisted that the death of Messala (Stephen Boyd), after defeat in the chariot race by Ben-Hur (Charlton Heston), be shortened. In ancient Hollywood tradition, hero has white horses and villian the black.

SPARTACUS: There were much fewer crucifixions in this scene by the time the public saw it because of pressure by the Legion of Decency. Crucified in foreground is Kirk Douglas, with Jean Simmons and Peter Ustinov sorrowing at his feet.

MGM

Door, in which the opening sequence was set in Mexico. To establish what Hollywood likes to call "mood," or "atmosphere," two men fought to the death in the streets over a woman. The Mexican spectators reacted as though they were Americans at a baseball game. Gordon suggested that Mexicans might be offended at this unflattering picture of their people. Since the characters in the fight had no dialogue the solution was to adorn them with bandanas, spangles and earrings and call them gypsies.

There is another aspect of foreign censorship that movie executives do not like to discuss—and generally claim does not exist. This is the Hollywood procedure of livening up a love scene for foreign consumption. It is known, for instance, that in the Scandinavian countries, France, Italy and West Germany the censors, while squeamish about violence, are tolerant of sex and nudity.

This sort of situation is made to order for the less scrupulous of independent movie-makers. One such producer, for example, hires strippers, in addition to his regular cast. First a romantic scene is shot with the actresses and actors for the American market. Then the strippers are called in for a much more graphic version that allows the women to strip at least to the waist and sometimes much more. Then there are the dance routines. For the American market the dance number is hardly objectionable. But in the alternate sequence for the foreign market the strippers and ex-burlesque performers get rid of their costumes during the dance.

Somewhat milder, but along the same lines, are the special filming techniques of the reputable major studios. At Twentieth Century-Fox, for instance, two versions of *Sanctuary* were filmed. This film contained a love scene between Yves Montand and Lee Remick. Americans saw Miss Remick in an irreproachably high-necked dress; and Montand's love-making, while fulfilling the dramatic needs of the script, was fit for domestic movie display. In the foreign version, however, Miss Remick's dress developed a lower décolletage and Montand's hands wandered much more freely and firmly about her anatomy.

The explanation of the director, Tony Richardson, was that the American version was much too puritanical, but was being done to satisfy American censorship requirements. He insisted that the European version was an honest dramatic portrayal.

If foreign censorship continues to proliferate in this insane fashion, Hollywood may be forced to make one of four choices. First: give up foreign markets, or at least become less dependent upon them. This is financially unsound. Second: make several versions of many scenes. This is terribly costly, apart from the artistic damage that can be caused in the confusion. Third: limit movies to innocuous Westerns. Fourth: continue to compromise, hoping that somehow censorship will diminish.

There is one other possibility. Assume that eventually there will be so many restrictions that the censors will have attained perfection. They will have trapped art so tightly in their webs that it will die. No pictures, no censorship problems. This cure is no less logical than the disease.

4. *Moral Brinkmanship*

Scattered through the movie industry's verbose censorship code are little gray areas, sentences and paragraphs that give the censor discretionary power, but not the clear interdicts he needs. In this limbo the teapot tempests of censorship are brewed in ambiguity, interpretation and national mores. In the eternal conflict on the movie censorship front this kind of fighting can be likened to patrols or guerrilla warfare. These are not the heavy assaults of *A Streetcar Named Desire* or *From Here to Eternity* that shatter an entire code sector. Rather, this is where producers, writers and directors win a minor outpost, perhaps set up a beachhead for a subsequent assault. In the fluid gray areas edgy censors battle so tenaciously they sometimes seem ridiculous, somewhat like men turning a battery of artillery on a solitary soldier armed with a pistol.

This is the arena of moral brinkmanship, a favorite nonscandalous indoor sport of Hollywood. Only the best can play this game. It requires the prestige of success and the experience that lend self-confidence. Frolics with the censors are not for idealistic novices.

One of the most adroit feats of brinkmanship was exhibited by

Marilyn Monroe during the filming of *Let's Make Love*. One sequence had her rolling around a bed with Yves Montand. It was so suggestive that Frank McCarthy, then the expert on censorship for Twentieth Century-Fox, was called in by the studio to study the situation. He told George Cukor, the director, that it would not pass the censors. Cukor balked. It was agreed that Shurlock should be invited to watch the filming of this scene.

As soon as Shurlock arrived on the set Miss Monroe turned on the innocent charm for which she was famous. "So you're Shurlock," she cooed. "This is the first time I've ever met a censor." They chatted amiably for a little while and then the scene was shot. Shurlock said it would not do. Miss Monroe turned to him with wide-eyed surprise and asked what the trouble was. He explained that her wriggling and rolling was in a horizontal position.

"I don't understand," Miss Monroe pleaded. "I don't understand what's wrong."

Shurlock paused to pick his words. Then he said: "Well—it's horizontal. It's as though you were getting ready for the sex act."

Miss Monroe brightened. She smiled her best little-girl smile and said: "Oh that. You can do that standing up. So what."

Her charming pseudo innocence and an off-color joke won an argument where logic would have failed.

Profanity is one of the most frequent causes of disagreement in this area. A striptease in a convent could not have created much more furor than the attempt to use the word "damn" in *Gone With the Wind*. One reason was that the antagonists were both strong-willed and resourceful men—Breen and David O. Selznick, one of the most successful movie producers. In retrospect, Shurlock concedes that "rows like this are what make the code seem ridiculous and difficult to maintain." The code leaves it up to the discretion of the censor to decide whether "damn" or "hell" are justified in special instances.

In the case of *Gone With the Wind* the circumstances were unusual. The offending word was added by the producer as a long afterthought. At the end of the book Rhett Butler (Clark Gable), finally fed up with his wife, Scarlett O'Hara (Vivien Leigh), tells her he is leaving her. What will she do, she asks. And he responds:

"Frankly, my dear, I don't give a damn." In the movie script by the gifted playwright Sidney Howard, the line read: "Frankly, my dear, I don't care." The script was approved without the "damn." The picture was shown to the censor without the offending word and was even previewed a few times with the milder sentence. Suddenly, Selznick decided the original line from the novel was essential. Breen refused. Selznick went over Breen's head in an appeal to Hays. The censor, determined to fight to the end against the "damn," wrote to Hays, late in 1939, saying: "We have withheld this line as profanity. David seems to think that because this picture is a screen characterization of a really great American novel, it is a sort of classic and that, as such, he should be permitted to use this line from the book."

Selznick argued that "damn" had been used in a film short made by Warners, based on Edward Everett Hale's short story "The Man Without a Country." The picture retained the most famous lines of the story in which Philip Nolan exclaims: "Damn the United States! I wish I may never hear of the United States again!" Selznick pointed out to Hays that the "damn" had won approval from the censor after a screening of a film that did not have the word. Breen retorted that in the Warner movie the word was not profane. The row became a public controversy. Selznick was sustained.

What the public did not realize, however, was that Breen had many precedents for his position. The public never knew, for instance, that in this same film a deleted line never restored was from Rhett to Scarlett: "May your mean little soul burn in hell for eternity." In this bit the censor also eliminated the reaction of Scarlett in making the sign of the cross. When an obviously reverent Negro used "Lawd," it was changed to "Lawsy." For years producers, writers and directors had avoided "damn." One of the best examples of how ridiculous this situation was occurred during the filming of O'Neill's *Anna Christie*. In this movie Garbo's voice was heard for the first time on the screen in the title role of the prostitute. The script of the film became so genteel that a Metro executive protested in writing against the schoolmarm language created for the whore. "There comes a point," he wrote to Louis B. Mayer, then head of the Metro studio, "in which Anna is so mad she could eat nails. Yet she says: 'I don't give a darn.' If a thoroughly bad girl speaks like that, we have never met a bad girl."

One of the most famous curtain lines of the Broadway stage was in the Ben Hecht-Charles MacArthur play about newspapers, *The Front Page.* At the very end, when it seems that the reporter finally is breaking away from the paper for good, his tyrannical editor waits until the reporter has left the office and then suddenly grabs a phone, calls the police and demands the reporter be arrested. "The sonofabitch stole my watch," he lies. In the movie the censors were forbidden by the code from approving that line. And no one wanted to change it. The solution was to have "sonofabitch" drowned out by the sound of typewriters. Incidentally, in the movie the reporter had become a woman.

This attitude by censors prompted the growth of a movie vocabulary in which "damn" became "darn" or "durn"; "hell" became "heck"; girls moaned that they had been "spoiled for any other man" or boasted they had "learned the facts of life." A brothel was changed to a gambling house. Sin, to a visitor from another planet who knew life only by American movies, might have seemed to be kissing near a bed or in a prone position. As late as World War II the movie about the British Navy in the conflict —*In Which We Serve*—was stripped in the United States of "damns" attributed to British sailors under horrible tension.

Great care was taken to see that the Lord's name was not taken in vain. Blasphemy was forbidden by the code. But it was qualified by saying that "reference to the Deity, God, Lord, Jesus, Christ, shall not be irreverent." Common expressions such as "for God's sake" or "By God, I'll do it," were taboo.

"We reached the point where we were defeating our own purpose," said Shurlock. "We realized there were many cases outside church in which the Lord's name was used without blasphemy. A mother, whose daughter's life was saved could say, in all reverence: 'Thank God she didn't drown.' The way things were going a condition was being created where God no longer existed in the movie industry unless the scene was in church. The impression was being created that we were a nation of atheists."

Methods as silly as the synthetic vocabulary had to be devised to circumvent rules about sex in movies. In *Mata Hari*, with Garbo as the spying seductress, in order to convey to the audience that she had gone to bed with her victim, two cigarettes were shown at the bedside. In *Primrose Path*, the movie version of *February Hill*, prostitution was permitted because the business was shown as ugly and stupid. In *The Mad Miss Manton*, a screwball comedy in which Barbara Stanwyck inherited a haunted house, there was a scene showing an elderly married couple in bed when they hear strange noises. The studio printed the film so dark that the audience could hear the voices of the couple but not see they were in bed.

Billy Wilder thought up a prize gimmick for the movie version of *The Seven-Year Itch*. In the hit Broadway comedy the husband, grown restless of monogamy after seven years of marital fidelity, has a sexual adventure with another woman. During the rest of the play he worries that his wife will find out about his betrayal. In the movie version he does not go through with adultery, but broods that his wife, on the basis of overpowering circumstantial evidence, will accuse him of the indiscretion he nearly, but not quite, committed. This touch was outdone by Wilder and his collaborator, I. A. L. Diamond, in *Irma La Douce*. A few of the choice items were as follows:

The naïve Paris policeman (Jack Lemmon) is advising Irma, the streetwalker (Shirley MacLaine), how to keep from catching cold in the rain. He recalls he used to use an old newspaper under his coat to keep warm. She replies tartly: "Look, mister—I'm in a very competitive business." Then later in the movie, when this cop, discharged from the force, becomes Irma's *mec* (pimp) he falls in love with her and cannot endure the idea of her going to bed with other men. He confides his problem to the worldly restaurant owner Moustache, who replies: "You're like an impresario. You're handling Pavlova—and you want her to dance just for you? It's a God-given talent—it was meant to be shared with the public." Their most priceless gem eluded not only the censors but most of Hollywood even after the movie was released in 1963. The mecs of Paris decide they must form an association. They call themselves the Mecs Paris Protective Association and then refer to themselves by the initials MPPA. Those initials stand for the Motion Picture Producers Association, which is made up of the chief executives of Hollywood studios. It pays the salaries of the Hollywood censors.

Charles Lederer threw a curve past the censors in the remake of *Mutiny on the Bounty*. When the ship first arrived at Tahiti, Marlon Brando, as "Mr. Christian," was preparing for a lovely roll in the bushes with the chief's eager daughter. He was interrupted by the despotic skipper of the *Bounty*, thereby irritating the chief's daughter even more than Brando. The native chief sent word he would be deeply offended unless the romance was resumed. Whereupon the skipper orders Brando to make love to the young lady. "It's a very different thing," says Brando wryly, "from being asked to *fight* for one's country."

On the other hand, a few words Lederer considered innocuous were deleted from the movie version of *Gentlemen Prefer Blondes*, which starred Marilyn Monroe. In a drinking scene, as a man prepared to gulp his liquor, he declared: "Bottoms up." This was considered too suggestive by the censor. Instead the line became "Here's how."

Good writers, finding themselves forced to keep alive a vocabulary fit for poor Victorian novelists, became increasingly frustrated and determined to break through censorship restrictions they considered outdated. They left profanity and blasphemy to the producers and struck at what they considered prudishness.

Ernest Lehman scored a victory in *Somebody Up There Likes Me*, a movie about the fighter, Rocky Graziano. In this script he had a scene in which Paul Newman, as Rocky, wanders into Stillman's Gym, near Madison Square Garden, at the moment when a sparring partner is needed. Among the things Rocky notices is a fighter drinking water out of a wine bottle. When the clamor rises for a sparring partner Rocky volunteers. He has never had a professional fight but he lies about his experience. He is told to see a trainer and get trunks and gloves. As he turns to seek out the trainer, the manager of the fighter with whom he is to spar yells at him, "And tell him to give you some cups." The unknowing Rocky retorts: "Oh, that's okay, I can drink out of a bottle."

The censor demanded this line be stricken out. Lehman's producer, an ex-writer, the late Charles Schnee, appealed and lost. Lehman carried the fight to Dore Schary, then head of the Metro-

Goldwyn-Mayer studio. Schary explained Lehman was wasting his time. Lehman asked for and received permission "to waste my time," and resumed the controversy with Shurlock. The censor said: "You know exactly what will happen when the audience hears this line. Then men will laugh and the women will turn to the men and ask them what the laugh is about and the men will have to explain." The writer pointed out that sports pages of family newspapers have often reported that boxers wear aluminum cups to prevent injury below the waist. Shurlock relented.

One of Lehman's notable triumphs in making the suggestive acceptable was in the Hitchcock film *North by Northwest*. This had a scene in which Cary Grant and Eva Marie Saint were riding in a compartment on a train. As the porter prepared the space for the night it became apparent there was only one bed. The following dialogue ensued:

> Grant: Kind of a good omen—just one bed.
> Saint: Uh huh.
> Grant: You know what that means.
> Saint: Uh huh—it means you're going to sleep on the floor.

But even the best of writers lose. On four different scripts I. A. L. Diamond has sought to slip through one sentence. He has lost every time. The line is intended to describe the feelings of a young man rebuffed in an attempt to seduce his date. He says: "I got to first base, but I was thrown out trying to stretch it into a double."

At the other extreme is the sort of script in which the humor is so heavy it merely accentuates the crudity of the situation. A prime example of this approach was *Convention City*, which raised censorship hackles. A few samples of the dialogue the censor ordered killed show how often the censor is on the side of good taste: "No, but it won't be marriage. I'll guarantee you that. A traveling salesman needs a wife like a baby needs a box of matches." . . . "Now you take off that dress and I'll take off my toupee, huh!" . . . "Girl's voice: 'Listen, sister, if they tire you, you better leave town before the Hercules Tool Company gets here."

And in *The Miracle of Morgan's Creek*, the censor killed the following attempt at humor:

"I'm your daughter aren't I?"
"So your mother told me."

Deleted from another film was an equally labored bit, when im-
mediatley after a wedding the bride asks the groom: "What are
you going to do now?"

Wilder wanted to use the title *Not Tonight, Josephine* for a
movie. The censors ruled against it. Wilder asked for the basis
of the decision. He was told it was the tag line of a dirty joke.
With a straight face the pixy asked what the joke was. No one
knew it as anything more than an apocryphal quote attributed to
Napoleon in saying there would be no sex that night. Nevertheless, Wilder lost. The title he substituted was *Some Like It Hot*,
one of the most suggestive titles in recent years.

No one came closer to a brinkmanship coup than three writers
who did the script of *Destry Rides Again*, starring Marlene Dietrich as the diseuse of a western saloon and gambling joint. During
one hectic evening of gambling she makes deposits behind the low
neckline of her dress. She pats her bosom and says dryly: "There's
gold in them thar hills." This passed the censor and at sneak previews the audience howled. The line stirred up so much advance
attention that the censors ordered it killed before it was released
to the general public. "It was the best line in the picture," rue-
fully recalls the producer, Joe Pasternak.

There is always a special consideration in the minds of censors
when they turn down a strong word—even when it is justified by
the scene, characters and over-all good taste of a movie. Experience has taught them that whenever they rule in favor of such a
word it is considered a precedent by less scrupulous producers,
who then try to draw attention to a movie with strong language
that has no dramatic justification. This was the argument Gregory
Peck encountered when he contended "bitch" was exactly the
right word to describe a woman in *Beloved Infidel*. The censors
agreed, but added that if they permitted it the screen would soon
be littered with "bitch" as a synonym for any woman who asked
her husband to do the dishes.

Those who saw *The Captain's Paradise* in its original British
form missed something that was added to get a seal of approval

in the United States. The movie dealt with a man (Alec Guinness) who kept two marriages going for a long time. It was pure comedy. But to get the code seal a prologue and epilogue were added in which audiences were advised not to emulate that role.

Choice examples of brinkmanship that the censors spotted—and rejected—were in *Gone With the Wind*. One was Rhett's assertion: "I've never held fidelity to be a virtue." Another was his comment: "He can't be faithful to his wife with his mind, or unfaithful with his body." Another victim of the censor in this film was the innocent line of Dilcey, the Negress: "An' whut it takes to feed a hungry chil' ah got."

The irrepressible Howard Hughes came up with an extraordinary gibe on censorship morality in his film *Cock o' the Walk*. Here the heroine is in grave danger of being raped by the villain. The knave advances upon her, confident of his triumph. But the heroine saves herself. She leaps into a suit of armor.

If the game of brinkmanship is played adroitly it can make for considerable free advertising for a movie. Ray Stark, who is in charge of production for Seven Arts Productions, is one of the brinkmanship experts. He exploited this advantage in a movie called *The Main Attraction*, and used columnists, reporters and even the star of the movie in his gambit.

The star was Pat Boone, who is known by speeches and books to be a moral fellow. In this movie with Nancy Kwan he was persuaded to do a scene that he thought showed him refusing to go to bed with Miss Kwan, the girl he loved. However, without his knowledge some lines were dubbed into the movie that made it clear he had found pleasure in her bed. Though he married her in the movie there was nothing to indicate either remorse or retribution. And premarital intercourse without regret or punishment is, as Stark knew, a violation of the code. Since Stark was angling for publicity for the movie he told nothing to Boone. Inevitably, Shurlock refused to give a seal of approval to the movie. Boone, horrified that this might change his public image of rectitude, denounced Stark. The actor demanded the right to remake the scene or to have lines dubbed into the movie that would win a seal for the film. Stark refused. Boone became angrier and Stark pretended he too was furious and talked of suing Boone.

By this time the censorship tale of *The Main Attraction* had won considerable space in the press. Stark, however, had overlooked one point. The movie was being distributed through Metro-Goldwyn-Mayer and Metro has never handled a movie without a seal of approval. Metro, after getting approval from a Stark subordinate, offered to insert lines in the picture in which Boone expressed regret. Whereupon Shurlock told Metro he had no objections to the movie. Stark, however, was upset when he learned the movie had obtained a seal of approval. He figured he could get quite a bit more publicity for the movie by letting Boone berate him to the press. He therefore demanded that the lines added to the picture be withdrawn. It was done and the seal was withdrawn too. This renewed the controversy. Stark, once the publicity gimmick had been fully exploited, agreed to have the lines reinstated. The girl said: "What I did last night was wrong." The picture received a seal and Metro distributed it.

When put to music, words can be useful to exponents of brinkmanship. The song "Let's Put Out the Lights and Go to Sleep" has been used to plant sexual ideas. Even profanity has had a help from music. In *West Side Story* one of the hit songs was "Gee, Officer Krupke." In this amusing number the juvenile delinquents poke fun at the police, social workers, psychiatrists and themselves. The conclusion of this fast-paced song comes when the delinquents explode with "Krup you!"

The producers were so certain this ending would be killed that they filmed it two ways. One with the "Krup you!" and the other with just a Bronx cheer instead of the "Krup." The censor let the original version pass.

Just as interesting is an example from the same movie of how lyrics have to be changed to satisfy the code administrator. This was in the same "Officer Krupke" number. As sung on Broadway it went:

My father is a bastard
My ma's an S.O.B.
My grandpa's always plastered,
My grandma pushes tea.
My sister wears a mustache,

My brother wears a dress.
Goodness gracious, that's why I'm a mess.

As rewritten for the screen by the original lyricist, Stephen Sondheim, they went:

My daddy beats my mommy,
My mommy clobbers me,
My grandpa is a Commie,
My grandma pushes tea.

The rest was the same.

In so many respects, the game of brinkmanship in the movie industry is amusing. But there is a serious side to it that was summarized one day by William Fadiman, vice president of Seven Arts Productions and one of the few Phi Beta Kappa men holding Hollywood executive jobs. "Just as an onerous taxation program has forced otherwise honest businessmen into a sort of self-corruption in trying to find tax loopholes, so the need to try to get around the code has forced many in the movie industry to invent evasions that make a mockery of their own movies and of the code as well."

Taken collectively, multiplied infinitely, these little tricks of moral brinkmanship are the termites of the movie industry's censorship code. Eventually, in armies, they may nibble the code into tottering instability.

7 |Television censorship

In many respects the story of video censorship seems to be following the path of Hollywood. Video too has a code, which it accepted reluctantly and enforced sporadically to subdue public clamor. It also has its blacklist and its attendant shame and hypocrisy. Video is subject to pressure groups that are more numerous and more effective than any Hollywood ever knew. But video has censors that are particularly dangerous—sponsors and advertising agencies and their allies in the networks. Just as movies, because they reached a larger audience than theater, were more exposed to popular criticism, so television, which reaches just about everybody, has replaced movies as the major target of would-be arbiters of taste.

1. The Toothless Code

Hidden in video's censorship jungle of sponsor taboos, agency restrictions, network interpretations, is something called a television code. Its existence is scarcely known to the public. Yet it is the heart of many of video's moral and ethical standard rules. Only when one looks at this code does it become apparent that the television industry of the early sixties is similar to the movie industry of the early thirties.

The code cannot be enforced any more than was the movie code of thirty years earlier. The television industry pays it lip service. The networks subscribe to it. About two thirds of the individual stations do too. But the television code administration, relying mainly on persuasion, can only advise, guide and then hope attention will be paid. This situation is so muddled that on April 1, 1962, the president of the National Association of Broadcasters, Leroy Collins, decided to bring it into the open. He told 3,000 executives at the association's annual convention that all networks were violating the television code. He called for a closer liaison between networks and the men who administer the television code. Discussions were held between the code representatives and the networks for several months. The code authority asked to be permitted to preview programs. The National Broadcasting Company agreed, but the American Broadcasting Company and the Columbia Broadcasting System rejected the idea.

The television industry, like the movie industry thirty years earlier, having been forced to adopt a code, did so. But each network has its own interpreters of the code. And no network can be forced to abide by any code ruling. The code authority has the power to expel stations from the code. But except for the expulsion of about thirty stations for showing commercials about hemorrhoids that the code administration considered offensive, this power has not been used. Incidentally, all thirty of the expelled stations were readmitted when they agreed not to show the commercials again. Like the movie companies of the early thirties, the networks have much more authority than the code administrators.

The code for television, which was drafted in 1951 and went into effect the following year, has been revised repeatedly. But it is clearly derived from the movie industry's code. It even has a preamble rich with a sense of public obligation. It points out immediately that television goes into the home and reaches children as well as adults; all races and religions and all sorts of educational backgrounds. "It is the responsibility of television to bear constantly in mind that the audience is primarily a home audience, and consequently that television's relationship to the viewers is that between guest and host." The code stresses the need for "respect for the special needs of children, for community responsibility, for the advancement of education and culture, for the acceptability of the program materials chosen, for decency and decorum in production, and for propriety in advertising."

The code itself is broken down into sections. They are: Advancement of Education and Culture, Responsibility Toward Children, Community Responsibility, General Program Standards, Treatment of News and Public Events, Controversial Public Issues, Political Telecasts, Religious Programs, General Advertising Standards, Presentation of Advertising, Advertising of Medical Products, Contests, Premiums and Offers and Time Standards for Advertising.

Those who have grown weary of the monotony and artistic shortcomings of the glut of series may be surprised at the aspirations of television stressed under the education and culture section. No responsible person could ask for more. The need for cultural and educational programs requires that broadcasters take the initiative in seeking out individuals and groups and inviting their co-operation in developing better types of programs. The broadcaster should keep fully informed on the cultural needs of his community and try to serve them. And to help the broadcaster there is even a portion of this code section that states he should not be required to worry about his responsibility toward children in planning adult cultural and educational programs.

The sections on responsibility toward children and community are covered partly by the preamble, but mainly by the section of general program standards, the fattest portion of the code. This section has thirty-two provisions. They forbid profanity, obscenity and vulgarity. They ban words that deride any race, color, creed, nationality or national derivation, except when calculated to combat race prejudice. There must be no attacks on religion. Marriage must be treated with respect. Physical deformities are not a subject for humor and the excessive exploitation of others must not be shown as favorable. Cruelty, greed and selfishness are unworthy motivations.

Policemen, except where essential to plot, should be portrayed with dignity and respect. Crime must not be condoned or even treated with cynicism. Revenge is not to be presented as a justifiable motive for murder. Suicide as a solution for human problems is not acceptable. Neither are sex crimes. And illicit sex is not to be presented as commendable. No lewdness should be suggested by dancers, actors or other performers.

Drunkenness is never desirable and narcotic addiction can be shown only as a vicious habit. Restrictions are listed against programs that incite gambling or foster belief in fortunetelling, occultism, astrology, phrenology, palm reading. Horror for its own sake is taboo and costumes shall be "within the bounds of propriety" and must avoid "such exposure or such emphasis on anatomical detail as would embarrass or offend home viewers."

Censors do not interfere with news programs. But the code specifies that news coverage should be "adequate and well balanced." Commentary and analysis must be clearly identified and pictures must not distort the story. The code warns against "morbid, sensational or alarming details not essential to the factual report, especially in connection with stories of crime or sex." The section stipulates that broadcasters must be careful that the presentation of news will not stir "panic and unnecessary alarm."

But who will say what is morbid and where the invasion of privacy begins? In 1963, for instance, television cameras and interviewers covered three different kinds of stories. One was the marriage of Charlayne Hunter, Negro graduate of the University of Georgia, to her white classmate, Walter Stovall. When they pressed her to discuss details of the marriage she told them it was personal. But they continued to hound her until she finally broke away from her tormentors. Then there was the inquisition to which they subjected a girl whose two roommates had been murdered. Or there was the long close-up of a bleeding corpse where gunmen were ambushed as they tried to rob the Bronx Zoo.

Since video censors have, properly, tried not to interfere with news coverage, it is obviously up to the networks to impose standards that will obtain news without violating the private rights of citizens or displaying flagrant bad taste. In an article appraising this situation, Jack Gould, television critic of *The New York*

Times, placed the blame on the policy-makers of television networks and stations who apply the pressure on their newsmen to
indulge in such excesses. Gould advised "the discipline of self-
restraint."

One of the touchiest problems dealt with by the code is that of
controversial issues. Considering how long it took television to develop this phase of its activity, it may surprise the public that the
code urges broadcasters to "seek out and develop . . . programs
relating to controversial public issues of import." Such programs
should be clearly identified and be conducted by persons or
groups with knowledge and a sense of responsibility.

The twenty-five paragraphs of the code that deal with advertising are often so vague, or so subject to personal interpretation,
that they explain why the best intentions of the code have been
thwarted so constantly in television's commercials. For example, a
broadcaster should deny his facilities when he has "good reason to
doubt the integrity of the advertiser, the truth of the advertising re-
presentations." He should also refuse advertising scripts which he
has "good reason to believe would be objectionable to a substantial
and responsible segment of the community." Advertising should
be presented "with courtesy and good taste." The code says
that a broadcaster should refuse advertising material that "in his
opinion offensively describes or dramatizes distress or morbid situations involving ailments, by spoken word, sound or visual
effects."

The foundation of code administration is that all scripts, live
programs and advertising must be cleared by code personnel. The
code administrators monitor the networks and stations. If the code
authority feels some program has violated the code it will ask for
an explanation. Usually, the broadcaster is more careful in the future. But sometimes the station will insist it is right. Each station is
accountable, in the final analysis, to the Federal Communications
Commission, not to the code.

The code administration does not have the right of prior censorship. It gets synopses of scripts in advance. These synopses are
called Advance Program Information bulletins (known to the
trade as API's). The API's are rarely in the hands of the code personnel more than two weeks ahead of shooting time. Very often

the code judges do not see the API's until a few days before the script is shot. This is not so much because television producers want to evade the code, as it is the hectic nature of television, in which a new segment of a series is shot each week. On the basis of the synopsis, a code official can make inquiries through a network. As a rule, according to Frank Morris, who is in charge of code work in Hollywood—there is another branch in New York—"the result is generally a compromise."

"We try to give the producer as much as possible without letting him get away with things," says Morris. "We try to help him make his programs mature, sane and lawful. There are just about no areas that television can't touch thematically. They've had abortion, narcotics, prostitution, drunkenness. Homosexuality is still untouched on television. We have no outright pledge that a station will withhold a show if it does not get code authority approval."

The extent to which the code will make allowances for good intentions and artistic merit was illustrated by the video production of O'Neill's *The Iceman Cometh*. The producers argued, with considerable logic, that this play should be done without change. At the same time it was generally realized that the play was not intended for children. The producers ran the show in two segments late at night. They ran disclaimers before the show started, alerting the audience about the content of the play.

Quiz programs are examined meticulously by code administrators. They check for any trace of collusion, which is a federal offense as a result of the scandals about big-prize quiz programs. They make certain that prizes are not large and that the network or stations pay for the prizes. "If we could generate as much nervousness about government corruption as we have about television quiz programs," says Morris, "this would be a much better country."

The major headache for the code is the fact that a third of the stations are not signatories. This has raised the threat that the Federal Communications Commission might make the code part of its own regulations and therefore applicable to all stations. Curiously, although the code was written by television broadcasters, the industry is fearful of having the government take over the job of enforcing the code. Here too is a parallel to the movie industry's plight of the 1930's. The solution there was to put teeth into the code to avoid regulation by law. The industry must decide whether to enforce its own code or have it done by law. As *TV Guide* has succinctly pointed out about TV stations: "As long as nearly a third of them refuse to sign the Code . . . there will be pressure for someone to act in the public interest."

Who that someone is is fairly obvious—the government. The networks cannot expect to talk and lobby their way out of trouble forever.

2. *Madison Avenue's Blacklist Tremens*

Nothing has demonstrated more clearly that television is subservient to advertising than its policy of censorship by blacklist. For video, by groveling before the blacklist, has confessed it would ruin a human being to sell a can of beans. The story of the television blacklist has made it apparent that the desires of the public are of less consequence than the threat of a lost sale. Time after time the blacklist has forced television to choose between its talent and its merchandise. TV has preferred the sponsor's phantoms to the reality of artistic integrity and common decency. The television blacklist is the story of how a mass medium has degraded its artists to salesmen.

This factor of salesmanship has made the television blacklist more fearsome than that of the movie industry. Without the sales pitch implicit in video entertainment, the blacklist might be little more than a footnote to the movie blacklist pattern. But when the actor, singer or writer is regarded as a salesman, and his audience as potential customers buying something other than his art, then new pressures arise. The television blacklist has demonstrated the censorship menace implicit in allowing a mass medium to be dominated by persons and groups whose main desire is something other than entertaining or educating the public.

Censorship by blacklist made its entrance into television in 1951 and had begun to weaken by the early sixties. But by then a great deal of damage had been done to innocent men and women. And shame had been endured by many important executives in television networks, advertising agencies and the huge corporations which, as sponsors, were party to this conspiracy that disregarded the most elementary concepts of fair trial in a democracy.

Typical of the television blacklist pattern was the behavior of Ed Sullivan. He hired Paul Draper, the dancer, to perform on his show. After protests from some veterans' organizations that Mr. Draper was a radical, Mr. Sullivan apologized publicly. But a few years later, when blacklisters had lost much of their power, his show included the Soviet Union's Bolshoi Ballet, an organization obviously more sympathetic to communism than was Mr. Draper. Mr. Sullivan apparently saw no inconsistency and neither did the network, the advertising agencies or the sponsors.

Garry Moore, who tried to challenge the blacklist, said it was like "fighting six men in a closet with the lights out—you can't tell who's hitting you." At times when he asked for certain performers he was turned down without explanation. "I would submit names to the network, as I was required to do, and the word would come back that such-and-such a person was unacceptable. We were never told why."

It was inevitable that once the movie industry had bowed to a blacklist television would do the same. For the men who dominate television are even less concerned with artistic values than are the moguls of the movies. And the men who rule television are as worried about their "ratings" as movie producers are about the box office. The insecurity and lack of moral courage is even greater in television than in movies. This means that, given the same pressures in television and in the movies, television would show less resistance to the imposition of the blacklist. But in television the pressures were greater and from more directions. Finally, television had one more weakness. Movies are a private enterprise. But television's airwaves, the foundation of the industry, are owned by the people and therefore subject to control by the government. This perennial shadow of government jurisdiction tends to make television executives more inclined to compromise than are the heads of private businesses.

On the surface, the television blacklist operated pretty much as did the movie industry blacklist that preceded it by about three years. Men and women were denied the right to work because they were adjudged too far to the left politically. Their judges were men who reached their conclusions without holding a trial and frequently on the basis of little or no evidence. Lists appeared and names were mentioned in such publications as *Red Channels* or bulletins of *Aware*. The American Legion and other veterans' groups passed judgment.

One of the major differences between movies and television was that Hollywood had only one blacklist. Television had many. Each network had a list. The most important advertising agencies had lists. Some talent agencies had lists. A man could be on one list but not on another. He could work for one network but not for another. Very often the men and women on the blacklists did not realize they were among the secretly damned until they found it impossible to get jobs as actors, writers, directors, on a particular network.

In 1951 Elmer Rice, the playwright, became so incensed that he wrote: "Everybody has a private list. Anybody's career can be destroyed. Crass commercial cowardice has become more important than standing up for the principles of liberty."

The meticulous study on blacklisting in radio and television done by The Fund for the Republic, under the direction of John Cogley, stated: "There was no conspiratorial decision on the part of radio-television management—there was simply a Gentleman's Agreement to keep silence. The industry decided that the public debate must come to an end. It accepted blacklisting as a burden of its day-to-day existence, but, for good reasons, decided that this fact must be kept secret. Blacklisting was institutionalized behind closed doors."

Another important difference between movie and television blacklisting was in how this vicious process was controlled. The movie industry, though greatly influenced by the same groups that imposed a blacklist on television, retained final control of the use of the blacklist. Television abdicated even this limited authority. Networks, it is true, had their own "security" officers. Yet the actual decisions were dictated to them by outside groups. The same was true of large agencies. The proof was that on occasion, when it was quite certain that a blacklisted person was not a Communist sympathizer, he was still denied employment by the networks because outside pressure groups had placed his name on a list in one of their publications.

In the words of the study by The Fund for the Republic: "The networks, agencies and sponsors no longer trusted themselves to hire and fire. They turned over their authority to outsiders. They grumbled against these outsiders, they complained about them, they resented them, but they never failed to try to placate them."

The "outsiders" were the men who prepared *Red Channels* or *Aware*, in which, under the guise of protecting democracy against communism, they listed those they considered dangerous radicals. To them there seemed to be no such thing as a neutral. They argued that an American was either actively anti-Communist or was assumed to be pro-Communist. The liberal was suspect. The man who was a-political was suspect. But the blacklisters managed to make their patriotism pay rather handsomely. Tied in with them were organizations such as the American Legion and some of their publications.

Exactly how these blacklisters operated emerged in New York State Supreme Court in 1962, when John Henry Faulk brought a successful libel suit against his blacklisters. He accused *Aware*, Vincent W. Hartnett, one of its directors, and a Syracuse supermarket owner, Laurence A. Johnson, of responsibility for connecting him with Communist conspiracy in one of the bulletins of *Aware*. Hartnett was also one of the principal authors of *Red Channels*. As a result of the comment on him in *Aware*, Faulk was discharged by the Columbia Broadcasting System in 1957 and blacklisted throughout the broadcasting industry. Faulk pointed out that *Aware* had attacked him after he had spoken out against the policy of blacklisting.

The first major point that came out in the trial was the recklessness with which *Aware* libeled a man. In this case it boiled down to the fact that Faulk had entertained at a gathering that the defendants considered suspect. The fact that he had entertained before many more organizations that were not suspect was not considered important. Since, as a rule, one blacklisting publication accepted with little question the lists presented by a similar organization, to be attacked by just one of these publications was as effective as being attacked by all.

Not only were these blacklisting groups the prosecutors, they were also judges. For they were often paid to "check" on the loyalty of those recommended for work in television. Their verdicts created lists compiled by the networks and advertising agencies. The blacklisters were paid by the name. The Borden Company paid Hartnett twenty dollars for each name checked. But as the names became more numerous the fee was reduced to five dollars a name. He was also retained by Lever Brothers, the American Broadcasting Company, Young & Rubicam. Each of these clients paid him five dollars a name.

Sometimes the blacklisters submitted "advisory" reports. Thus, Hartnett sent a letter in 1953 to the general counsel of ABC in which he said: "In my opinion, finally, you would run a serious risk of adverse public opinion by featuring on your network James Thurber, Kim Hunter, Olive Deering."

Miss Hunter's experience with the blacklist was shocking. Throughout the early fifties she was blacklisted from television and radio. The star had made the "mistake" of contributing money for the circulation of a pamphlet that opposed blacklisting. The pamphlet consisted of articles in the *New York Post* attacking the Syracuse supermarket patriot. About the middle of 1955 Miss Hunter was told by Hartnett that she would have a chance "to show my good faith, that I was a truly loyal American and not pro-Communist." Hartnett told her that affidavits of loyalty were not sufficient.

She was advised to appear before a meeting of the American Federation of Television and Radio Artists that was preparing to vote on a resolution condemning *Aware*. She was told to defend *Aware*. Miss Hunter refused to attend the meeting, but agreed, at Hartnett's suggestion, to send a telegram to the meeting pointing out that the resolution would give the union a pro-Communist tinge.

She did not believe what she said in the telegram. But thereafter the actress received television work.

The blacklisters, in effect, set themselves up as a supergovernment, accountable to no one except themselves. In fact, they were somewhat contemptuous of the government they professed to defend. Hartnett, when cross-examined during the libel suit by Louis Nizer, was asked if court procedures might not be the way to judge a man's loyalty.

"No," said Mr. Hartnett. "I think they are entirely unrealistic. They don't conform to realities."

The amazing scope of the blacklisting procedure in television was indicated by David Susskind. He said that during 1955 he submitted some 5,000 names for his show, "Appointment with Adventure." The names were turned over to the advertising agency, Young & Rubicam, which represented the sponsor, Lorillard cigarettes. Hartnett was a consultant for Young & Rubicam. Of the 5,000 names submitted a third were rejected without explanation. Susskind was convinced the rejections were because of the blacklist. When he protested that this screening for nonartistic reasons hurt the quality of the shows, the agency said it did not like blacklisting but could do nothing about it. Susskind said he was ordered by the agency never to reveal to anyone rejected that the reason was a political blacklist.

This atmosphere of arrogance, opportunism, cowardice and guilt had to produce the same sort of behind-the-scenes operations that existed in the movie industry. Writers began working under pseudonyms and through fronts. The television underground was even more complex because of the differences between one list and another, and because a number of the writers blacklisted in movies were able to write, with pseudonyms and fronts, for television. It was not uncommon for a writer to have three or four Social Security cards. Since the number was the same on each this was not illegal. Television producers were almost eager to use blacklisted writers, particularly since they could hire good writers for small fees.

"The only thing the television producers wanted was scripts," said one of the most successful blacklisted writers. "As long as the advertising agency and the network didn't know, they weren't worried. I sometimes thought that the agencies and networks pretended not to know many things in order to get good scripts. And maybe they were ashamed."

Particularly unscrupulous agents used the blacklist to their advantage. When they had clients who were not blacklisted, they whispered to the producer that the client was really just a front for a very skillful blacklisted writer. One blacklisted writer, in discussing this dodge, said wryly: "If this continues, I may lose my good name."

Another blacklisted writer, through his front, received an award for good citizenship. And yet, throughout the fifties, television was using reruns of old movies by the best-known blacklisted writers, giving screen credits for these writers. Thus, almost any time one could see on television *Murder, My Sweet* or *Mr. Lucky,* by Adrian Scott; *A Guy Named Joe* or *Twenty Seconds Over Tokyo,* by Dalton Trumbo; *Pride of the Marines* or *Destination Tokyo,* by Albert Maltz; *Sahara,* by John Howard Lawson; *Objective Burma,* by Alvah Bessie; *Wreck of the Hesperus,* by Edward Hibbs; *Friendly Persuasion,* by Michael Wilson.

Yet in spite of this industry-wide blacklist, television has managed to keep one phase, one aspect of its work honorable—the presentation of news. How did this happen? News programs have sponsors, advertising agencies, networks, local stations. They are, if anything, exposed to greater pressures than dramatic or musical shows. For news programs bring before millions of watchers the most controversial issues of the day. No one can doubt that one of the main reasons Senator McCarthy, leader of the postwar red-baiting and witch-hunting campaigns, lost his power was that, when he was brought before a Senate inquiry, the public judged him on television and distrusted him. The uncrowned king of the blacklist could do little to warp television coverage of his work.

If anything, television, in its news coverage, has probably been more ethical than the bulk of the printed press, though generally less efficient. Television probably resists the pressures of advertisers in news presentation more effectively than do many daily and weekly papers.

Why was the blacklist unable to move into news programs, an area it coveted more than any other type of video show?

Television journalism came from newspapers, via radio. It therefore inherited the concept of freedom of the press and the tradition of resistance to pressure. Unlike the entertainment phase of television it was not a major merchandising gimmick. As this form of reportage developed it drew upon newspapers and news services for its staffs. Increasingly, television journalism requires men who can gather information, appraise it, as well as deliver it. It is no longer enough for a television reporter to make a good appearance on camera, have a well-trained voice and utilize a few tricks of showmanship. The new kind of television journalist wants high standards for his work.

And top executives of networks, either because they realize the importance of honest news coverage, or have been affected by the men who do the work, have shown far more courage in this field than in entertainment. Where television reporters have argued with networks it has been, as a rule, about serious matters such as the distinction between straight reporting and interpretation. Disagreements were not about the pressure of blacklisters.

A notable example of the courage of networks in the newsfield was the program on Richard M. Nixon in 1962, after he was defeated for the governorship of California. Howard K. Smith did an appraisal over ABC during which he gave time to a number of persons, both pro- and anti-Nixon. Among them was Alger Hiss, who was convicted of perjury after he denied, before the House Un-American Activities Committee, that he had participated in a Communist espionage ring in 1938. Nixon had played a leading role in the Congressional investigation. In the half-hour TV program Hiss said that "political motivations played a very real part" in Nixon's activities on the committee.

Even before the program went on hundreds of telegrams and phone calls were received at ABC, objecting to the idea of permitting Hiss to speak on the program. Some network stations refused to carry the program. The pressure became even greater after the program. The Schick Razor Company tried to cancel a million dollars' worth of advertising contracts on two shows. The Gemper Insurance Company also sought to withdraw from another show. The network refused to permit withdrawals. James C. Hagerty, then vice president in charge of news for ABC, defended the network's position in fighting terms. "The issue," he asserted, "deals with the basic American principle of freedom of the press, of exchange of ideas, free speech, free assent and dissent.

"Perfectly aware of the background of Hiss, we sought neither to glorify him nor give him a forum of debate. Representing a chapter in Mr. Nixon's history, it seemed natural to put him on the program in historical context . . . But pressure in advance to force cancellation of a program and pressure after it by economic means to punish or intimidate is another matter. It threatens not only the very existence of freedom of the press, but enterprise itself. It must be resisted."

This healthy attitude was made even more important when it was supported by the other major networks and by Newton N. Minow, then chairman of the Federal Communications Commission. Minow said he agreed "most emphatically" with Hagerty. Ironically, it was ABC that had received the worst criticism from Minow for the low quality of its entertainment series.

In short, if television had shown the same courage in its entertainment programs as it did in news, it could have resisted the blacklist. Television is still far from clear of the blacklist. The indications are that it will recover its integrity. But just so long as television networks and stations permit anyone to tell them what their employment policies shall be, just so long is there a danger that some day television may become the instrument of a single economic or political group that will make a mockery of freedom of the press. The man who produces even the lowliest soap opera or western has just as much right to choose his cast, directors and writers as an editor has to choose reporters. The blacklist in television is more dangerous than that of the movies for the television blacklist can be the beginning of the blackout of freedom.

3. *The Bland Leading the Bland*

George Bernard Shaw, in his *Simpleton of the Unexpected Isles*, anticipated the story of television. In that play a husband says to his wife of many years: "I know I began as a passion and ended as a habit." Those who were part of the "golden days" of television in New York, during the fifties, no matter how much they have prospered since in the theater and in Hollywood, still look back with nostalgia and pride on those months of burning creativity. Those fires were dampened and the hot embers turned to ashes by censorship. It was the tedious rite of multiple censorship that reduced video's passion to dreary habit.

Nowhere in art or show business in the United States has there been anything comparable to the censorship that afflicts television. It has the usual pressure groups ranging through the religious, civic groups, social organizations, professional associations. And then it has much more. It has the censorship of a network and of each station that carries a program. It has the censorship of the sponsor and the advertising agency, unto the fifth cousin. It has the censorship of the government. And finally, it is exposed to the censorship of viewers, who are simultaneously potential customers and feel justified in writing indignant letters to sponsors as critic-moralists. This attrition of originality by censorship has made television writers the most frustrated hacks since man first learned to chip cuneiform characters into stone.

It was allegedly a television comedy writer who pinned one of the most damning labels on television. He said: "Television is the bland leading the bland." In the Hollywood mills of television series, writers spread the tale of the new children's game that has grown from video, a version of cowboys and Indians, or of cops and robbers. Only in this game one boy says to another: "You be the good guy and I'll be the guy with the problem." Eric Ambler, who has created exciting novels of tension and melodrama, complained it was no longer possible to have a true villain in TV. "They must all be maladjusted."

Theoretically, the government should have been the major monster of censorship in television since television channels belong to the public and are licensed to private owners by grant of the Federal Communications Commission. Periodically, the FCC has the right to re-examine—and even revoke—a station owner's license if he does not live up to his public obligations. This alone should have made the FCC a tireless and limitless force of censorship. Actually, for the most part the FCC has avoided artistic interference with television programs. Not until 1961, during the regime of President Kennedy, did FCC head Minow make an issue of the poor quality of television shows. He called TV a "vast wasteland," thereby stirring up a public outcry about excessive violence and sensationalism on television.

"I invite you to sit down in front of your television set when your station goes on the air and stay there without a book, magazine, newspaper, profit-and-loss sheet or rating book to distract you and keep your eyes glued to that set until the station signs off," Minow suggested to the convention of the National Broadcasters Association. "I can assure you that you will observe a vast wasteland.

"You will see a procession of game shows, violence, audience participation shows, formula comedies about totally unbelievable families, blood and thunder, mayhem, violence, sadism, murder, Western badmen, Western goodmen, private eyes, gangsters, more violence and cartoons. And, endlessly, commercials—many screaming, cajoling and offending. And most of all, boredom. . . . For every hour that the people give you—you owe them something. I intend to see that your debt is paid with service."

Large segments of the public regarded this speech as proper. But to broadcasters it was governmental intimidation. Minow was accused of trying to "club" television owners into obedience; of censorship "by the raised eyebrow"; of interfering with the rights of private business. Early the following year, Robert W. Sarnoff, board chairman of the National Broadcasting Company, told the FCC it "had already reached the view that it should be empowered to regulate networks." It was for the public to decide what it wished to see, he asserted.

But as a result of the Minow speech there was, over ensuing months, a decrease in violence and murder to the point of the ridiculous. A policeman, if he killed a bandit in a television show, was not supposed to take more than one shot to polish off the villain. Life-and-death battles among gangsters began to adhere more closely to Marquis of Queensberry rules. In one sequence of a crime series called "Cain's 100," when hired killers were frisked by the law, the guns taken from them were not shown. The end result, whatever its aim, was pressure brought by the government against television to force it to make changes in its programs. Dr. Frank

Stanton, head of the Columbia Broadcasting System, called it "a drift toward indirect, but nevertheless effective program control by the Government."

In a more overt effort of censorship a government official tried —but failed—to suppress the showing in Great Britain of a documentary made by the Columbia Broadcasting System. The documentary, dealing with migrant labor in the United States, was called "Harvest of Shame." Murrow, as head of the United States Information Agency, phoned the head of the British Broadcasting Corporation, which had purchased the film, and asked that it be withheld. The British official said that could not be done. Ironically, this documentary had been narrated by Murrow before his appointment as head of the USIA. He insisted he had taken the action entirely on his own responsibility, lest it be construed that the documentary had governmental support. Later it became apparent that he had been encouraged in this by other government officials. "In terms of principle," wrote Gould in *The New York Times*, "this episode is . . . dismaying. But the record should show that Mr. Murrow obviously was not acting alone, despite his sportsmanship in taking the blame, and that there are others who should help him hold the bag."

Compared with censorship by the sponsors and advertising agencies, the government's interference, for all the attention it draws occasionally, is negligible. For whereas the government is trying to improve television quality, the censorship by sponsors and advertising agencies generally lowers the content of video shows. The fact that the literature on which the show is based may be internationally famous means little to these censors when they decide to force changes for reasons that are often idiotic.

For example, a show was planned on the Hemingway short story, "My Old Man," which deals with a crooked jockey. The sponsor insisted the jockey must be honest. This brought about such an impossible situation that the script had to be abandoned. Sponsors leave very little to chance in tampering with scripts. Thus, in the Alcoa Premiere shows, a synopsis of every script went to the sponsor. Approximately 10 per cent were canceled by the sponsor.

It was because of a sponsor that the name of Abraham Lincoln

Joseph Burstyn

THE MIRACLE: Film that induced Supreme Court to hand down revo-
lutionary decision stating that movie industry was an art, not just a business,
and entitled to freedom of press. Anna Magnani, as a demented shepherdess,
who imagines the bearded vagabond who seduces her is a saint.

above:

PINKY: One of the few movies to deal with miscegenation. Banned in Texas, reversed by Supreme Court. Ironically, many years later NAACP criticized picture because it used white actress, Jeanne Crain, to portray Negro girl who "passes." Mother played by Ethel Waters.

right top and bottom:

THE BICYCLE THIEF and OPEN CITY: Censors all over the country refused to allow these innocent shots.

SEVEN YEAR ITCH: What happens when Hollywood discovers New York subway while it has Marilyn Monroe under contract. No complaints from censors or public. Leering male is Tom Ewell.

IRMA LA DOUCE: Perfect sample of how censors become more generous about cleavage allowance if subject is comedy—with ads saying movie not
for children. Shirley MacLaine, as Irma the French prostitute, looking as natural
as a mechanic in coveralls.

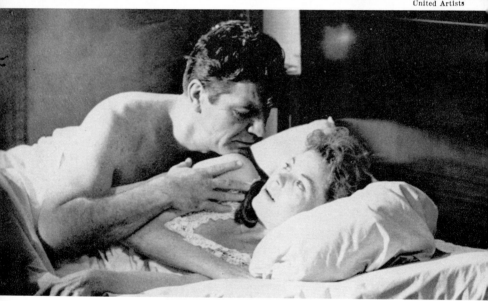

top:
NEVER ON SUNDAY: Prostitute (Melina Mercouri) enjoys her work and that was why movie could not get seal of approval from censor.

bottom:
THE DARK AT THE TOP OF THE STAIRS: Puritans, some of them important critics, squawked because Hollywood censors permitted this bedroom scene in which husband (Roger Preston) complains to wife (Dorothy McGuire) of her sexual coolness.

right:

ANNA CHRISTIE: First Garbo talkie and first Eugene O'Neill play to be filmed became prime example of changing censorship attitudes. When first made, in 1929, no seal of approval was required and Garbo was permitted to be a prostitute. But, in 1946, when Metro-Goldwyn-Mayer sought to remake its film, chief censor Joseph I. Breen said there could be no seal of approval for prostitution. Movie was not made. Finally, in 1962, when Metro reissued the original Garbo picture, it had no trouble getting seal. With Garbo in this scene is George Marion, who played her father.

below:

LOLITA: How censorship has changed over the years was illustrated by granting seal of approval to this sexual relationship between middle-aged man (James Mason) and a nymphet (Sue Lyon). Her age raised from 12 in book to 14 in movie.

MGM

LA DOLCE VITA: Roman orgy, directed by Fellini, goaded Hollywood into seeking ways of circumventing censorship code. Marcello Mastroianni is the jockey.

became "offensive" on one television show. The name was used in a show sponsored by the Chrysler Corporation. President Lincoln's name was deleted because the Lincoln automobile is made by a rival company. The show was one of the "Climax!" series over the Columbia Broadcasting System.

The producer of the show, Ralph Nelson, in reporting this incident at a hearing of the Federal Communications Commission, declared that for a sponsor to have any control over programming was "a basic corruption of the stated principles of broadcasting." He disagreed with another producer, Fred Coe, who contended that sponsors had the right to control programs. Sponsors, said Mr. Nelson, "want provocative dramas that don't provoke anybody." Perry Como, the crooner with the relaxed manner, was quite tolerant of the status quo. He said that any "so-called intellectuals" who did not like a program need only "flip the little dial, and it's all over."

Rather than be blamed for the sort of dramatic slop that is required of them by sponsors, some writers turned to writing daytime soap operas under assumed names. David Davidson, while national chairman of the Writers Guild of America—and himself author of many network television programs—was one of those who resorted to this practice. "One of the things that killed original drama," he said, "is the fear of the sponsor to deal with an unknown quantity—with the world around us today." He called sponsors "no, no men," and said the type was common throughout the television industry.

Ernest Kinoy, who won a Pulitzer Prize for the play *All the Way Home*, narrated an interesting story of the way in which noncreative elements in the industry shape programs. He told an FCC hearing that he was asked to write for a series to be called "The Breakdown," with two psychiatrists as central characters. They drove about in a sports car and were popular with women. They spent a good deal of time treating nymphomaniacs and others afflicted with "extreme and bizarre hallucinatory behavior."

Susskind said that a representative of Kent cigarettes once told him: "I want happy shows for happy people with happy problems."

A vivid description of the behavior of sponsors was narrated by Audrey Gellen, writer-producer. She was associate producer of the

"DuPont Show of the Month," for which one of the scripts was Horton Foote's drama, "The Night of the Storm."

"Getting it on was half the trouble," she said. "Then came the long letters: Could you put some jokes in it? Couldn't you brighten it up? There was the watchdog attitude. They came to rehearsals. They said: 'We're going to depress people with this.'" She said the "they" referred to representatives of the advertising agency, Batten, Barton, Durstine & Osborn. Nevertheless, she added, while these objections were raised they could be overcome by persistent argument.

One sponsor, Procter & Gamble, said it had its own censorship code that it applied to shows it sponsored. Morals of a show must be those of the large majority of the American public. This meant that all rape, perversion, profanity, morally suggestive scenes, excessive passion were taboo. Violence must be held to a minimum. Crime is evil. Members of the armed forces must not be cast as villains. If there is any attack on American custom, it must be rebutted completely on the same show.

Max Banshaf, advertising director of Armstrong Cork, said their show, "Armstrong Circle Theatre," would "deteriorate if we were denied the right to exercise programming control and we would then be unable to continue as sponsors." The advertising director of DuPont, J. Edward Dean, told the FCC that commercials embedded themselves better in the audience's mind during light entertainment than during serious drama. Another witness, Richard E. Forbes, head of advertising for Chrysler, reported that shows "may be so exciting as to completely remove normal approach to what advertising is trying to do."

General Electric made most of its rejections of scripts in the early stages. The main reason for turning down stories, according to David W. Burke, manager of institutional program operations for G.E., was on the grounds of their being "sad, downbeat, depressing." Allstate, which sponsored "Playhouse 90" for three years, turned down an adaptation of Conrad's *Heart of Darkness* because "evil seemed to be rewarded." It was done subsequently, but without Allstate's sponsorship.

Then there was C. Terance Clyne, senior vice president of Mc-Cann-Erickson, who said, in behalf of clients of his advertising agency, that sponsors are not involved in television to present shows that make an audience sad. Sponsors, he said, want the video viewer to have "a pleasant and favorable impression." Dan Seymour, vice president of J. Walter Thompson, declared that very frequently his advertising agency deletes any material it considers not in the sponsor's interest. His agency bans all political mentions and operates on the theory that "an advertiser cannot afford to lose any segment of society." Robert L. Foreman, executive vice president of Batten, Barton, Durstine & Osborn, declared his agency reviewed Theatre Guild scripts and participated in the revisions and even the casting. Sponsors, he said, avoid controversy on the theory that some viewers might then dislike the sponsor. He reported that even small amounts of mail worry sponsors and that the head of one large corporation read every letter from viewers.

Another advertising man, A. R. Pinkham, senior vice president of Ted Bates and Company, said that the manufacturer of nonfilter cigarettes wanted villains in his shows to be smoking filter cigarettes. The reverse is desired by the manufacturer of filter cigarettes. But perhaps the most serious point made by Mr. Pinkham was his remark that the creative men in television have come to know the whims and desires of sponsors and advertising men so well they can avoid offense without even being told. The brainwashing has taken effect.

Appraising the censorship power of sponsors and advertising agencies, Gould wrote: "Advertising agencies, which never solicit billing on the screen, in practice may be virtually the actual producers. . . . If the taboos, apprehensions and anxieties of sponsors and agency men may have application in the market place, it does not follow that such a set of mores should govern one of the country's major platforms for human expression."

Networks also use the claws of censorship on dramas. When the "Dick Van Dyke Show" did a light tale about a boy who had learned an unspecified word his parents considered objectionable, the Columbia Broadcasting System took offense at the title. Originally it was called "A Nasty Word." It was changed to "A Word a Day." The American Broadcasting Company killed a "Naked City" script called "The Execution," about a policeman ordered to watch an execution. The drama was considered too strong. A writer for a series reported that an executive of the series told him that one of the top officials of a network had ordered "no chinks or niggers" on the series.

Networks have their own censors checking every script and show. The severity of the censorship varies with the amount of public indignation about television violence or sensationalism. In the summer of 1961, for instance, the censors were being particularly watchful because of a Senate investigation into excessive homicide on television. Since Hollywood is the factory for the production of most television shows, the network censors there were alerted by New York executives. One of the West Coast censors was Robert A. Wood, manager of NBC's Western Division of Broadcast Standards. Here are some of the changes he arranged.

The original version of one series called for a man to fire a bullet into a load of dynamite. The resultant explosion killed him, but it also destroyed a band of thugs. The alterations were as follows. The valiant man fired a shot into one box of dynamite. The small blast knocked the bandits flat. He then warned them that unless they behaved he would fire another bullet into the entire pile of dynamite. They yielded peacefully.

There was the video tale in which a youngster boasted to admiring friends about the criminal past of his grandfather. In the altered version the boy's grandfather was made into a familiar of the great gunmen of the day because he mixed with the gangs as an undercover man for law enforcement agencies. "It did not make good moral sense in the first case," said Wood.

In fist fights, if one of the contestants was not evenly matched it was ruled he must not be hurt too much. Censors never could figure out what to do if the little man was drubbing the big one. "All fights have to be well motivated and not just for sheer audience excitement," said Wood. "And regardless of motivation there will be less breakage of furniture per brawl."

Judo and karati, such fun on private eye shows for a spell, were outlawed. Thereafter K.O. was to be by a hard left to the stomach, followed by the right to the chin. If the hero was established as a left-hander, he would be permitted to lead with a right. In any event, the loser was just left unconscious instead of dead.

The procedure for television censorship of this sort is methodical. The network censor deals directly with the producer. First the network receives a synopsis of the script to come. Then, if the network complains, the producer can head off his writer at the typewriter, thereby minimizing the anguish of rewrite. The network sees the rewritten version of the script and watches the rough cut of the film. The network has the right to refuse any show that declines to make required cuts or changes in a film.

Here are some comments from a network censor. The word "sweat" was too "graphic." Pointed out that cigars were being used in the show and this drama was sponsored by a cigarette company. "Spit" was also considered too "graphic." Suggested deletion of reference to coffee because one of the sponsors sold tea. Cigarette was dropped into a coffee cup. This was considered "distasteful use of sponsor's product." A warning that a scene showing models at work must cover them with utmost discretion.

One of the most amusing by-products of a Senate investigation of television concerned network definitions of sex. Walter D. Scott, executive vice president of NBC, told senators that when his network referred to sex it really meant "romantic interest," not lewdness. James T. Aubrey, Jr., president of the CBS network division, carried philology almost to philosophy. "Sex, as used among people who create films," he said, "is somewhat different than when it is used by those not in the business. I've heard it used in every connotation in the industry, from mother-and-child scenes to the way an actress walks."

But as senators dug into specifics, it developed that NBC officials had suggested that a certain show needed more sex. Aubrey was accused of trying to inject "prurient sex" into a show. The Senate came up with a memorandum saying that Aubrey had ordered "broads, bosoms and fun" for a show. The CBS executive said he did not think he had used such words, but added that someone in the business could easily have translated a request for wholesome pretty girls into "broads" and "attractive" into "bosoms." Ironically, the word broad, meaning woman, is a video taboo.

Individual stations affiliated with a network can also censor by refusing to show a segment of a series. If the complaints are strong enough the network may refuse to show the segment. This happened to a "Dobie Gillis" episode. The segment was about a baby-sitting business. Somehow the adolescent hero's father came to believe that his son was a father. Networks often show segments to affiliates in advance by closed-circuit television.

Unaffiliated stations also exercise censorship. In Chicago, quite a furor was raised when WGN-TV canceled a scheduled showing of the film *Martin Luther*. In Newark, WATV refused to show a commercially sponsored program prepared by the Emergency Civil Liberties Union. The program was a panel discussion called "Constitution-U.S.A." It would have included several schoolteachers dismissed after they declined to answer questions about their political affiliations. The president of the station, Irving R. Rosenhaus, said: "It is our policy not to allow commercial sponsorship—that is, where the sale of a product is involved—of a program about political or controversial matters."

After listening to a day of this kind of talk, Senator Thomas J. Dodd, Democrat, of Connecticut, said the explanations seemed to indicate "an unmistakable pattern" in network operations. "You all seem to use the same terminology—to think alike—and to jam this stuff down the people's throat. You all claim the writers and the producers are guilty—everybody but you."

Another form of censorship is the list of "Don'ts" supplied to writers by movie companies that make television series either directly or through subsidiaries. Writers for "Manhunt," for instance, were supplied with some "Don'ts" by Screen Gems, a subsidiary of Columbia Pictures. No show, they were informed, must show anyone smoking or using tobacco in any form. No matches or mechanical lighters were to be used. There must be no derogatory mention of any drugs, foods, automobiles. No shaving equipment. All of these were invoked to avoid offending any possible sponsor. Warner Brothers warned its television writers not to show children in danger; or blind or infirm persons as villains.

Religious groups are probably even more terrifying to television executives than is the government. The West Coast representative of the Film Commission of the National Council of Churches reported that the National Broadcasting Company had canceled plans to do a television play in which a Protestant minister commits adultery. Ed Sullivan deleted films of Sean O'Casey from his St. Patrick's Day show. He said he was yielding to the wishes of "nice" and "intelligent" persons. The famous Irish writer had often been accused by Roman Catholics of anticlerical writings. Jewish groups tried unsuccessfully to block a telecast of *The Merchant of Venice* that was being staged with a fine cast in New York's Central Park. They declared that the character of Shylock tended to stir up anti-Semitic feeling.

Finally, there are nationality and professional pressure groups. Italian organizations, for example, complained that too many gangsters in the Prohibition era series, "The Untouchables," were Italian. The number of Italian villains was sharply curtailed and a bigger part was given to an Italian who played the assistant to the hero. "We try to spread it around now," said Allen Armour, executive producer of the series. "A Polish heavy one week, a German heavy another, and so on. After all, you want colorful names for heavies. Smith and Jones are pretty dull. The colorful names are usually foreign."

Many professional groups complain about shows. One top television executive said it was almost impossible to do a script showing a member of any profession in an unfavorable light without getting a complaint from that profession's organization.

As in movies—and even more so—the main cause of censorship in television is fear. There is some reason to explain TV's fear of the government. For the government, as custodian of the channels for the public, has the theoretical right to revoke or refuse to renew a license. Yet the networks show more determination in defending themselves against the government than they do against sponsors, advertising agencies and pressure groups.

The trouble is that to keep advertisers, television feels it must strive for the largest possible audience and guard against the loss of even a fraction of the audience lest it lose a sponsor. With an audience so much larger than movies it is a bigger target for censors. But more important, it is too deeply involved in the advertising business to assert the independence of either a newspaper or a movie company. To win respect, television must insist on the same control over dramatic shows that it has over news programs. It then can deal with criticism from strength instead of weakness. One producer of many series and anthologies summed up what is probably the prevailing attitude of creative men toward censors. "I don't mind censors who differ sincerely with me on matters of taste," he said. "The ones I loathe are those who censor because of cowardice. They are our enemies."

8 | what next?

Money is Hollywood's guiding light in living with censorship. Regardless of court decisions, stature, pressure groups, the American movie industry tries to tailor its attitude to censorship to fit the box office. Film executives know that present conditions require a minimum of censorship to meet the creative freedom of foreign movie-makers. They also know that the surest way to artistic liberty is through the adoption of voluntary classification—a system of labeling movies to show which are not for children. However, classification may mean less revenue. So Hollywood wants it both ways—no censorship and no classification. Every important religious and civic organization in the nation favors voluntary classification. The leading creative men in Hollywood are for it. Every civilized country in the world, except the United States, has some form of classification. Eventually the film industry will have to make major concessions to this trend.

In television the future is very uncertain. What, for example, will be the effect of educational stations on the networks? How will the spread of ultra-high-frequency stations influence commercial programming? What will Telstar do to international censorship? It is clear that, for the ·time being, commercial television would rather placate advertisers than its creative men and women. It seems willing to risk governmental interference.

1. *The Battle for Classification*

Today one of the hottest controversies in the field of movie censorship is classification. It is being carried into the courts. It echoes in legislatures, from town hall to Congress. It is on the agenda of discussion groups in churches and parent-teachers' meetings. The outcome of the argument about classification will seriously affect the American movie industry and every American moviegoer. It may raise movie-making from a complex craft to a fine art and transform Hollywood from an aesthetic joke into a great center of American culture. Classification has already split the industry into camps and has pitted most of the top directors against the top executives of the industry. The entire field of movie censorship may be drastically changed by the outcome of the debate about classification—the most significant development since the movie industry adopted its code of self-censorship.

By classification is meant the labeling of a movie so that the public will know whether it is suitable for youngsters or not. Classification can be done either by the government or by the movie industry. There is virtually no desire for governmental classification. However, the nation's most important religious, educational and civic groups favor classification by the movie industry, preferably by the men who apply the censorship code.

Among the organizations that favor voluntary classification are: The Catholic Legion of Decency, the Protestant Broadcasting and Film Commission of the National Council of Churches, the American Jewish Committee, the General Federation of Women's Clubs, the National Congress of Parents and Teachers, the American Library Association. It is difficult to find any important religious, civic or educational group opposed to voluntary classification.

Strongly opposed to any kind of classification are the heads of major movie companies and studios and their primary lobbies, the

Motion Picture Association of America and the Motion Picture Producers of America.

What are the arguments for voluntary classification? First, it would protect children from exposure to unsuitable films. Second, it would head off a campaign for governmental classification. Third, it would raise the artistic standards of American movies.

The arguments against voluntary classification are several. First, it is a form of censorship and, as such, dangerous. Second, it may lead to governmental classification. Third, it usurps the authority of parents. Fourth, there are already sufficient methods of informing parents if a movie is not for children.

Among the ablest comments made for voluntary classification are the following:

Msgr. Thomas F. Little, executive secretary of the National Legion of Decency: "Such classification would serve several purposes. (1) It would be an information service for the parents. (2) It could be a guarantee that morally wholesome adult films would be produced for the public. (3) It would forestall undesirable action by the states."

S. Franklin Mack, executive director of the Broadcasting and Film Commission of the National Council of Churches: "The Broadcasting and Film Commission of the National Council of Churches has gone on record as strongly preferring industry self-regulation to such external controls as government regulation, boycott or censorship. In so doing it has recognized, however, that unless the motion picture producers and exhibitors give impressive evidence that they recognize the need for more effective self-regulation and are prepared to do something about it, the imposition of external restraints is only a matter of time. If and when producers and exhibitors do take positive steps to remedy the present unhappy situation it will be incumbent on church and civic groups to meet them halfway by improving review services, encouraging the public to take a more intelligent and mature attitude toward films and by building box office for films of special merit."

Prominent directors who favor voluntary classification include: Wilder, Brooks, Preminger, Kazan and William Wyler. It should be noted that Kazan has no affection for the Legion of Decency, having fought that organization bitterly, as we have seen, over *A*

Streetcar Named Desire. However, he believes that *A Streetcar Named Desire* should have been classified "for adults only."

The directors who favor voluntary classification make two important points. First, they are not ashamed of their films and they try to make them for mature persons. Second, rather than be forced to undermine films because children might be exposed to them, they would prefer to see them labeled "adult" by the industry.

In a symposium on classification in 1961 in the *Journal of the Screen Producers Guild* the late Charles Schnee, then president of the Writers Guild of America, wrote: "Self-classification of our own movies by our own movie-makers—may be coming too late to help. If it comes. But it should be tried . . . Self-classification should start before a movie is shot. It should start before the movie is written. If a movie is aimed ab initio at a limited adult audience, the writer will work hard on his script to keep costs of the finished movie down to a point where the limited audience can still provide a healthy profit. . . ."

In the same issue of the magazine (September 1961) Albert M. Pickus, then president of the Theatre Owners of America, said: "I, personally, in my own theatre, practice voluntarily rating the pictures. I believe we will always be subject to censorship and classification problems until the day comes when theatres play only pictures with a Production Code Seal and the men who make the picture advise whether they consider every such picture suitable for a child or an adult audience."

In view of this formidable force for voluntary classification it is understandable why individual top executives of the movie industry are chary of becoming involved in disputes on this subject. But through their official spokesman Eric Johnston, until his death in August 1963, they argued against any kind of classification.

At a hearing held by a Congressional subcommittee, Johnston delivered a speech that he said represented the thinking of the nine leading American producers and distributors of movies. Unfortunately, nowhere in the speech did he discuss *voluntary* classification. He confined himself to an attack on the straw man of governmental classification. However, subsequently—after he was taken to task by advocates of voluntary classification, he considered the possibility of classification by the industry. Then he said: "Basically, classification is one of those things that has never been fully defined. There are many kinds of classification, ranging from advisory to statutory . . . We only get on solid ground when we consider the effects of classification—any form of it. For here we see it for what it is: censorship, nothing more, nothing less. Who can dispute that classification is essentially a surrender of parental authority . . . And no system of classification could ever be devised to reflect accurately the quality of a motion picture. Doesn't classification say two things to a parent? Someone else's idea of suitability is what counts. Quality, individual tastes, intellectual value don't matter."

One of the most prominent of the producer-directors opposed to voluntary classification is Kramer. He said in an interview printed in the *Film Bulletin:* "Classification means somebody classifies and that is censorship . . . I think that any shackle on what I hold films to be, that is, an art form, is ridiculous. Some people suggest that the producer himself ought to classify his films. But I am not sure that even my censorship would be objective."

In its fight against self-classification, the American movie industry, with its extraordinary history of chicanery, is trying to perpetrate a hoax on the American public that would be hilarious if it were not so serious. It has tried to create the impression that it is fighting censorship. Actually, it is perverting freedom of the cinema art in its lust for cash. For the first law of Hollywood is that money is thicker than blood. Money dictates Hollywood's present position on self-classification, just as it has governed its attitude toward the code.

But so successful are the movie industry's lofty and hypocritical platitudes, so efficient its legislative lobbies, that it has bamboozled officials as high as the President. It has seduced the support of some of the best newspapers beyond anything that could have been bought with paid ads. One of the weirdest aspects of these adroit maneuvers is that reputable and sincere organizations with many millions of members are being cast as villains, while Hollywood adorns itself with halo and wings—a truly diabolical case of miscasting.

The industry has decided that classification would cost it dollars. That its evidence may not be trustworthy, or only part of the story, is beside the point. Consider the foreign market, which supplies American movie companies with half their revenue.

In European countries, where classification is invariable, American movie companies have spotted a disturbing condition. Many theaters abroad refuse to book pictures on week ends that are not for youngsters. Since in the United States movie business has become a week-end business, a film that cannot get a week-end booking will have trouble showing a profit. The movie industry has received proof that American theater owners may follow the example of Europe in week-end bookings if classification is introduced.

Concrete evidence came when *Fanny*, which is among the milder of recent "adult" films, went into the better neighborhood theaters. Some theater owners who had booked this picture for week ends refused to show it for the Saturday early shows attended mainly by children. Instead, they ran films they considered more suitable for youngsters. Warner Brothers, which owned *Fanny*, objected strenuously. Not as a matter of pride, but because the theater owners refused to pay Warners for the performances at which *Fanny* was not shown. Warners insisted that the film had been booked for the week end and that the theater owners had to pay for an entire week end, whether they showed the film or not. The theater owners were adamant and Warners gave up.

This case set an important precedent. Every major movie company now knows theater owners have won the right to refuse to show a movie before an audience containing many children, even after signing a booking agreement. This Saturday matinee practice could easily be extended to the Easter or Christmas seasons. But equally important, those parents who make a family affair of a trip to the movies are almost certain to bypass a film that has been dropped from the early Saturday programs.

Less dramatic has been another development that has stimulated the movie industry's terror of the financial cost of classification. Hundreds of theater owners in the United States are, by their own volition, classifying movies. They are refusing, whenever they think the movie too adult, to sell tickets to youngsters unless accompanied by adults. And this does not happen in just the neighborhood theaters. For instance, Grauman's Chinese, the Hollywood tourist spot with its famed footprints of stars in the forecourt, refused to admit anyone under sixteen to *The World of Suzie Wong* unless accompanied by an adult. Theaters all over the country have taken similar steps on such movies as *Butterfield 8* and *The Dark at the Top of the Stairs.*

Two films yielded conflicting evidence of the box office effect of classification. The first was *Elmer Gantry*, which United Artists said might not be considered proper for children. This movie received good notices. Its star, Burt Lancaster, won an Oscar. So did Shirley Jones, for best supporting actress. Richard Brooks, who wrote and directed the movie version of the Sinclair Lewis novel, won an Oscar for the script and was nominated for best direction. But the box office did not reflect the critical acclaim and the number of Oscars. Robert Blumofe, vice president of United Artists, who is in charge of United Artists' West Coast operations, says the advice to parents that the movie was not recommended for children unquestionably hurt the film's profits.

On the other hand, there was *Lolita*, the film about a middle-aged man desperately in love with a fourteen-year-old girl. The movie adhered closely to the plot and comic flavor of the book by Vladimir Nabokov when it was produced by Seven Arts Productions. This picture was classified by its makers for persons over eighteen. So far as the company's executives are concerned its profit was not curtailed by the limitation.

Though the box-office results were different, the cause of the classification by the producers was the same. It was really not voluntary. It was a matter of either classify or receive a "Condemned" rating from the Legion of Decency.

Hollywood ignores the fact that art houses are not hurt by self-classification. For example, an art house in Hollywood that did wonderful business with *Room at the Top* and *Never on Sunday* invariably refused to admit children without adults. And even when parents were with the youngsters the manager took them aside to make certain they knew what the movies were about. But Hollywood executives point out that the volume of business done by these theaters is not large enough to be important when the cost of a film is in excess of two million dollars. Thus, *Never on Sunday* grossed about $2,000,000 in the United States. Since its original cost was under $150,000 this is magnificent. But if it had cost $2,000,000—a fairly commonplace figure in Hollywood these days—it would have required a gross of about $4,000,000 to break even. The film earned about $4,000,000 abroad, where it was forbidden to youngsters.

It is deduced then by movie moguls that classification can cut business. It is all very well to try to woo adults away from television sets with mature films if there is no greater movie loss among the adolescents and children. Classification confronts Hollywood with a difficulty. It can concentrate on "family" pictures and risk driving mature audiences to night baseball, books, magazines or even television. Or it can make low-cost adult movies that earn a profit with a small audience. Except that Hollywood has still not yet learned to cut costs that far. It does not really want to learn. So the alternative is to fight voluntary classification as well as censorship.

The problem is: how to fight voluntary classification and not admit the fight is strictly a matter of money. Film executives do not contend that the movie industry's own censorship code is a deprivation of its constitutional rights. It is not argued by Hollywood that the industry's self-censoring board violates the Constitution when it withholds a seal of approval from a movie that does not fulfill the requirements of the censorship code. On the contrary, whenever Hollywood's self-censoring board refuses to grant a seal of approval it is, in effect, exercising a form of classification. Movies, the industry now says, are no different from the legitimate theater or books. This is a flat reversal of Hollywood's traditional position. Over and over again, the studios used to point out that the influence of films on young minds is far greater than is the impact of a play or a book.

If the movie industry claims it is no different from the auto or detergent businesses, then it risks its claim to the constitutional rights enjoyed by newspapers, magazines or books—rights of press and speech granted in *The Miracle* case. Instead, film heads now claim that movies have become adult and need artistic freedom to mature as an art form. This, they say, is why films must not be chained to outworn customs by classification. They ignore, as has been pointed out, that the countries that have classification have the highest artistic movie standards.

Should Hollywood accept voluntary classification no pressure group can blame the industry for making movies that are too adult for youngsters. The movie-makers will be limited only by pornography in choosing subjects and in treating themes. The artistic argument for voluntary classification was stated clearly by Lord Morrison of Lambeth, president of the British Board of Film Censors, which is a nongovernmental classifying body. "Classification," he says, "has enabled us to avoid the American censorship dilemma about what to do about movies that are artistic and interesting to adults but not suitable for children. Classification has enabled us to approve movies we might otherwise have been forced to reject."

Sometimes Hollywood creates the most absurd straw men in its effort to avoid the responsibilities that are accepted by all other media guaranteed freedom of expression. It speaks with horror at the thought of special legislation covering children. Even assuming this happened, it is by no means unprecedented. There are laws preventing minors from visiting bars, driving cars, working. Public libraries have long had children's sections and special cards for youngsters.

Every argument offered by the movie industry against voluntary classification is camouflage for its historic primary motive—money. The day the movie industry decides it is more expensive to fight classification than to live with it, arguments against voluntary classification will be abandoned. And if, for any reason, Hollywood should decide it can make more money with voluntary classification than without it, the industry's position will change overnight. For there is only one argument that really carries weight in Hollywood—the box office.

2. *Yesterday and Tomorrow*

Censorship in the United States has lost much of its power in the movie industry. All evidence is that state and municipal censors may, like the horse-drawn carriage, become a casualty of the twentieth century. Public morality, movie profits, artistic inclinations and court decisions are all arrayed against the political censor —the censor whose authority stems from state and local laws.

It is likely that some greedy and shortsighted movie-makers will continue, from time to time, to offend public morality and thus give political censors an excuse for prolonging their existence. Pressure groups of all sorts will, as they do in other mass media, continue to try to influence film-makers. Their success will vary with the courage of the producer and studio executive. Government agencies will, as they do in other mass media, try to impose, through threats, cajolery or promises, their own ideas on movie content. But barring a political revolution—or a moral one—the tide of American opinion is running strongly against movie censorship.

This trend has already been reflected in changes in the movie industry's voluntary censorship code. Taboos against homosexuality and the use of narcotics in movies, for example, have been tossed out. At the same time, the administrators of this code, the Hollywood censors, have become more liberal in their interpretation of movie behavior, speech and costume. Over-all good taste has become more important to the Hollywood censors than a bit of dialogue or a shot in a scene. In short, the movie industry's own censors are now abiding by Supreme Court interpretations and prevalent moral attitudes.

Decisions by the Supreme Court, though they too lagged behind the times, have stripped political censors of most of their power. The court has made a habit of overriding these censors in recent years. Obscenity is now the only valid ground for censorship of movies. And even this cause has been narrowed down by a series of decisions until the burden of proof now rests on the censor to prove that a movie is obscene, rather than on the producer to show that it is not. Sex and obscenity can no longer be adjudged synonymous. Censors can no longer ban a movie because it may "incite" the audience or because it is "sacrilegious."

Lawyers who have led the fight against censorship are by no means agreed on how to define obscenity. Professor Zechariah Chafee in his book, *Government and Mass Communications*, contends that obscenity is not capable of legal definition. Morris L. Ernst argues that even the movie industry's voluntary censorship code is a restraint of trade. Professor Melville B. Nimmer has suggested a criterion for judging obscenity. He believes nothing should be censored in a movie that would not, in real life, be considered indecent exposure. This he calls an irreducible minimum, rather than a yardstick. Ephraim London contends that only the courts, not political censors, are capable of judging obscenity. Felix J. Bilgrey wonders how a censor, since he judges a film before it is shown to the public, can tell whether it will arouse the prurient interest of the public. There often seem to be as many definitions of obscenity as there are lawyers.

The only other remaining constitutional question involving movie censorship is the right of prior restraint. Why, it is asked, does a movie censor have the right to judge a picture before it has been shown to the public? He does not have the right to judge the contents of a newspaper, magazine or book before they are placed on sale. Supreme Court minority opinions have already attacked the entire concept of prior restraint by movie censors. Ernst speaks for many legal authorities when he says: "The Supreme Court is moving very fast toward declaring all pre-censorship unconstitutional." He suspects that the movie industry "prefers the aroma of pre-censorship to the danger of local vigilantism proceeding against movies after they have been shown."

It is significant, however, that Hollywood as a whole is now showing signs of being willing to fight for constitutional rights instead of leaving it to independent producers of limited means. This development has been forced by economics more than by the desire for artistic freedom. The American movie industry has been in a slump since television became a national habit. It needed material not available on video. Foreign movies, with their growing audience here, showed the way. Sex and realism seemed the answers. The appeal of the better foreign movies demonstrated what many critics had long argued—that public education had raised the average American above many movie executives both intellectually and artistically. As Hollywood tried to copy foreign films it was forced, out of economic desperation, to fight censorship.

Since only those producers and directors with taste, talent and integrity are capable of making such movies, their value began to rise. They were drawn into alliance with stars who felt the same way. It became necessary to seek out the best of the movie writers —even if it meant delving into the fearsome blacklist for a Dalton Trumbo or a Nedrick Young. Unfortunately, Hollywood has been mired for so many years in mediocrity, compromise and fear that it is fumbling and stumbling in its attempt to establish its claims as an art medium. Increasing freedom from censors will tend to raise the quality of Hollywood movies.

But American producers must have a large foreign sale to show a profit on their high-budget movies. The more expensive the picture the greater the audience needed—and the greater the number of censors to be placated. Shall the kiss be eliminated to please Asian censors; the fist fight lose its impact to suit Scandinavian regulations? American movies can become quite dull that way. The foreign movie-maker has learned by necessity to make low-budget movies that can recoup the investment in his own country. He need not worry about outside censors. Anything he makes outside his own borders, particularly in the United States, is gravy. For the American market he can sex up the movie. He does not care if he never gets a seal of approval from the Hollywood censor. He is happy to have a long run in a few American art houses. Not so the American. To him an art house is just a showcase. Hollywood sacrificed its artistic standards by catering to what it considered the "average" American public. It may do itself even greater damage by grappling for the "average" world public.

However, film-makers run the greatest risk in their fight for freedom in their attitude toward voluntary classification. By opposing this device of voluntarily labeling movies not intended for children, the movie industry has irritated huge religious and civic organizations that represent the vast majority of the American public. These organizations are, for the most part, opposed to censorship. They are willing to give Hollywood the freedom of European directors. But they insist that Hollywood, in return for this artistic liberty, accept the responsibilities of foreign movie-makers. All civilized countries in the world, except the United States, have some kind of classification. Since classification by political censors would be idiotic as well as unconstitutional, these organizations want some kind of voluntary classification by the industry. In a showdown fight Hollywood will probably revert to cowardice and the "family" picture. The American movie industry will thus trap itself between Europe's quality films and the mass mediocrity of television.

If, on the other hand, Hollywood works out a plan for voluntary classification—and it could operate quite simply through its own censors—it will then be in a strong position to destroy the most powerful weapon of political censors, prior restraint.

The major transformation in movie censorship has already been made. The political censor is now the villain in the public's eye, not the movie-maker. For state and local censors it will become increasingly difficult to justify their work, even if they waive salaries. It is only a matter of time, perhaps less than a decade, before state censors of movies vanish entirely and local censors become rarities to be laughed out of existence.

In television the censorship situation is much more complex. Though eventually it will probably follow the same trend as the movie industry, it is certain to lag considerably. And it may be the cause of the most critical censorship explosion in world history.

Since commercial television needs sponsors, the executives and producers are, necessarily, more subject to the whims of even small pressure groups than the movies. The speed with which television shows are ground out works against artistic integrity and independence. Too many noncreative persons have the right to change scripts at almost any moment. Writers have little authority and directors not much more. The television industry's voluntary code of censorship is undermined by the private censorship phobias of all sorts of executives and their wives. In television, pre-censorship is one of the most serious menaces to artistic freedom.

There are some who think that increasing competition from noncommercial television will force the major networks to raise their standards. This may be the long-run effect of the so-called educational network. But its short-range impact may be the opposite. Commercial networks may feel less obligated to meet the desires of the better-educated sections of society. They can argue that the intellectuals can watch noncommercial television.

Two other factors make television's censorship plight much more complicated and serious than that of the movie industry. First, since the channels belong to the public, and stations are licensed by the government, the government has the power to influence programming. The Federal Communications Commission may cause infinite problems in censorship. Thus, as foreign nations censor.

Then there is Telstar. The potentialities of this means of transmitting television shows to all parts of the world simultaneously may cause infinite problems in censorship. Thus, as foreign nations continue to increase their own television output, this country may find itself in the position of trying to cope with shows that are acceptable in the country of origin but offensive to many in the United States. What a foreign nation may consider an artistic documentary, television drama or movie, could easily be considered anti-American propaganda in the United States.

Censorship of movies and television may thus become more important than ever. It may become a part of international diplomacy, a world problem, not a discussion of aesthetics in the United States. Whether movies and television become forces for world pleasure and enlightenment, or stimuli to hatred and annihilation may, in part, be decided by how the world deals with the new specter of international censorship.

APPENDICES

Appendix I

CURIOUS EXAMPLES OF FOREIGN CENSORSHIP

Social and political scientists have studied many facets of national life to understand the forces and fears that dominate different countries. Someone could do a doctoral thesis on the uncertainties, prejudices, religious and ethical standards of a country merely by studying the movie censorship regulations of that nation. They reflect the diplomatic attitude; its feelings about democracy, militarism, racial equality. They show sensitivity about violence and maturity about sex. In a study of a nation's movie censorship rules can be discerned that country's feelings about artistic freedom.

If one sees a sign on a train saying spitting is forbidden, two things can be deduced. First, some passengers do spit on the floor. Second, spitting is considered either unpleasant or unhealthy, or both. So it is with censorship regulations. They show what movies contain and also what the nation finds most objectionable in movies. Incidentally, these regulations also demonstrate how the power of movies is feared and respected.

It is therefore of interest not just to students of censorship but to those who are curious about behavior patterns throughout the world, to see examples of varying censorship regulations. The brief excerpts that follow are based on reports gathered from all over the world by movie companies and their agents. Most of this information is arranged and revised by the Motion Picture Association of America. Some regulations may have been eased or altered by the time this is published.

AUSTRALIA—Censor may refuse entry of any film deemed blasphemous, indecent or obscene; likely to be injurious to morality, or to encourage crime; likely to be offensive to the people of any friendly nation; likely to be offensive to the people of the British Commonwealth.

AUSTRIA—The Federal Minister of Trade and Reconstruction claims that his ministry receives frequent complaints from the provincial governments and the municipality of Vienna requesting measures to prevent the showing of films based on gangster, Wild West or other plots that would "prejudice the moral and ethical welfare of juveniles."

BELGIUM—Films likely to disturb the public order are subject to rejection.

BURMA—Main grounds for censorship include misrepresentation of the conditions in Burma or offense to friendly foreign country; glorification of crime; suggestive scenes.

CZECHOSLOVAKIA—Subjects that are construed as conflicting with Communist ideology are taboo.

DENMARK—Most censorship is on grounds of violence or brutality.

EGYPT—Pictures may be rejected for excessive nudity, subversive political ideas, "denigration of the honor and prestige of the Arabic peoples." In his decision not to admit Marilyn Monroe films in 1959, the censor wrote: "This decision has been taken for the general security of the country." This was Egypt's way of saying that Miss Monroe had adopted the Jewish faith upon her marriage to Arthur Miller.

FRANCE—Severe on brutality.

GERMANY (West)—Against themes that promote national socialistic, militaristic, imperialistic or nationalistic tendencies or race hatred; that endanger relations of Germany with other states; that depreciate constitutional and legal foundations of the republic; falsify historic facts by showing persons or events in a propagandistic manner.

GUATEMALA—This country is almost unique in that it says a film can be banned "for lack of artistic merit."

HONG KONG—Bars films if strongly anti-Communist or if they deal with the Korean War; if likely to frighten children.

INDIA—Tough on kissing scenes. Not to be exhibited if involve defamation or contempt of court or if likely to incite the commission of any offense against the state. India is also wary of anything that may irritate a friendly state. One factor in making India tough on sex—apart from its own moral standards—is the complaint by Indian producers that Indian censors are more tolerant of sex in foreign films than in Indian pictures.

INDONESIA—Demands cuts on almost every imaginable ground.

IRAQ—Censors severe on anything considered pro-Israeli, pro-Communist, derogatory of Moslems or Arabs.

ISRAEL—Its movie censorship regulations run counter to all traditions of artistic freedom among Jews. Its code provides for ban on pictures that belittle law enforcement, officials or judges; infringe on religious susceptibilities or tradition; attack ethics, truth or justice; depict murder, theft, cursing or disgusting habits; show persons killed; create mass fears; show use or sale of opium; depict prostitution, sexual perversion or white slavery; show births; insult foreign states; contain propaganda.

ITALY—Weird situation here is that though the Supreme Court has ruled movie censorship unconstitutional, the censorship committee of the Ministry of Tourism, Entertainment and Sport has become increasingly severe.

JAPAN—Basically, this code is built around that of the United States. But the exception is interesting. It holds that films "must not justify violence or militarism, nor advocate the solution of problems by means of force and violence; must not advocate antidemocratic ideals nor justify feudal ideals."

LEBANON—Bans all pictures that "have any connection with Zionism." This has been stretched to forbid films with Danny Kaye and Elizabeth Taylor because of their "Zionist activities."

MALAYA—Like most countries in Asia, it is wary of sex, violence, religion. In addition it is severe on interracial references.

NETHERLANDS—Has strong aversion to gangster scenes.

PAKISTAN—Opposed to any film that may stir hatred among

sects or communities; portray mixed social activity among the sexes that may be interpreted as moral laxity.

PHILIPPINES—Against films that suggest overthrow of a government by force; depict ruthlessness by government officials.

SPAIN—Very strict on films that suggest anything novel in the form of a political ideology; that question morality or religious dogma.

SWEDEN—Tends to ban films that have a "horrifying character"; offend friendly state.

SYRIA—Censorship largely based on teachings of the Koran. In addition, the usual Arabic ban against pro-Zionist material.

THAILAND—Severe on films that in any way tend to disparage royalty.

TURKEY—Will almost certainly ban a movie that shows the military in an unfavorable light.

UNION OF SOUTH AFRICA—Will ban anything that smacks of miscegenation, of social equality of Negroes and whites; of scenes that may be construed as fomenting racial frictions.

Appendix II

HOW SOME FOREIGN COUNTRIES
CLASSIFY FILMS

ARGENTINA—No picture may be banned or cut before it is released. However, some films can be forbidden for anyone under 18.

AUSTRALIA—Films classified into the following main categories: general exhibition; not suitable for children, but with decision left to parents; suitable only for adults, with no exception; suitable only for those over 15. All horror films are rejected.

AUSTRIA—Films classified as follows: adults; limited to those over 16; limited to those over 14; authorization for all ages.

BELGIUM—Children under 16 are not permitted to attend a movie house unless the censorship board says the film is suitable.

BRAZIL—Censors may pass films entirely or prohibit entirely. They may limit them to audiences over 10, 14 or 18. Minority of movies are on unrestricted list.

CHILE—Make-up of censorship committee, which is part of Ministry of Education, is interesting. Its chairman is the Director General of the National Libraries and Public Museums. Other members include two teachers, a psychiatrist, two representatives of the president. Pictures can be authorized for all ages, or over 14, 18, 21.

COLOMBIA—Here the National Board of Censorship includes

four appointees by the archbishop, two by the National Association of Writers and Artists. Classification similar to that of Chile.

Costa Rica—Special classification of pictures that may not be shown before six in the evening. Other classifications are for all ages and those prohibited to anyone under 21.

Ecuador—Special classification here provides that some movies have to be shown separately for men and women. Other classifications include: available for all; banned for minors; absolute ban.

El Salvador—Apart from classification by age groups, general approval and flat ban, some movies can be shown only at certain hours in the evening.

Finland—Has total ban, complete authorization, adults only, anyone over 12.

France—Film control board, with representatives from government and the movie industry, can give complete approval, absolute rejection, forbid for those under 16.

Germany (West)—Voluntary classification by movie industry, with agreement to abide by all producers, distributors and theater owners. The courts have held that the police cannot ban a film approved by this procedure. Classification includes general authorization; ban to those under 16, to those under 10 and flat ban. Censorship group specifies films particularly suitable for religious holidays.

Greece—Censorship board, under Minister of Interior, includes representatives of police, church and interior ministry. Classifications are: authorized for all; for those over 14; complete ban. Indicative of attitude for this board is that in 1959 it found 87 U.S. films suitable for minors and 176 not suitable for minors.

Guatemala—Censorship is by the Department of Fine Arts. This is the country in which a movie may be banned for lack of artistic value. Its classifications are: general authorization and banned to those under 16. If there is a public protest after exhibition, a film can be reclassified.

Iceland—This country has, in addition to censorship by the Censorship Board of the Ministry of Education, a Child Protection Committee that ascertains whether films are suitable for children below the ages of 12, 14, 16.

Italy—The Censorship Committee of the Ministry of Tourism,

Entertainment and Sport can permit universal showing, limit to those over 16 or forbid entirely.

MALI—The censorship setups of new nations are particularly interesting. Movie censorship in Mali is under the Director of National Security, with previous approval of films required by a committee composed of the Director of Public Security, a representative of the Ministry of Education; an appointee from the Department of Social Affairs; another from the Department of Information; two from women's organizations; two from labor unions; two from theater owners. May ban a film, limit it to those over 16 or show it generally.

MEXICO—Censorship is by the National Cinematographic Commission, under the Ministry of Interior. Classification can be universal; over 18 or 14.

NEW ZEALAND—Most categories are advisory. They are general; general, but suitable for adults only; general, but suitable for those over 13. Some classified as "recommended for family entertainment." Others listed as "not recommended for young and nervous children or nervous women." Then there is a mandatory or "R" category. Pictures in this category can be limited to age group; to audiences in which sexes are not mixed; to specialized groups such as doctors or medical students.

NORWAY—Classifications for general, over 16, 14.

PARAGUAY—Though this country has no official censorship board, the government or a police chief may ban films considered immoral or offensive. And in Ascunción, a Municipal Morality Committee publishes, each Sunday, pictures deemed suitable for children.

PERU—Censorship Board of the Ministry of Public Instruction classifies general, over 15, 18. It recommends films for special merit and singles out films it calls not suitable for women.

SPAIN—An interesting feature of Spanish classification is that the Catholic Church representative on the government censorship committee has veto power if a movie raises any question of morals or religious dogma. Classification is general and adults only.

SWEDEN—This country has a special Government Cinema Bureau. It classifies for general showing; adults only; over 11. To be acceptable for children no picture must show suicide, rape, or contain information on how to commit crime. It must not have anything construed as encouraging brutality or crime.

SWITZERLAND—Censorship according to cantons. Classification varies. They have general, but some have category for over 18, others for over 16.

UNITED KINGDOM—Censorship not by government. Local authorities, while they have authority to censor, seldom exercise it. They accept the ruling of the British Board of Film Censors, a nongovernmental agency. This board was set up in 1912 by the cinema industry to overcome the handicap of 700 different censorship authorities and to maintain proper standards in screen entertainment. The classification follows: universal; suitable for adults and for persons under 16 if accompanied by parent or guardian; not suitable for persons under 16 even if accompanied by adult. The power of the British system is that every theater has, in its license, a provision forbidding violations of rulings by the British Board of Film Censors. A violation can cost a theater its license.

URUGUAY—Censorship here is handled by the Department of Child Welfare. Classification is: general; suitable for minors; not suitable for minors; not suitable for minors under 18; not suitable for women and girls.

UNION OF SOVIET SOCIALIST REPUBLICS—All movies made in the Soviet Union must be submitted to the Ministry of Culture or to regional boards for censorship. Movies are classified as universal or for sixteen years old and up. All imported films are subject to strict censorship with particular attention to their "propaganda" contents.

Appendix III

THE MOTION PICTURE PRODUCTION CODE

Motion Picture Association of America, Inc.
December, 1956

FOREWORD

Motion picture producers recognize the high trust and confidence which have been placed in them by the people of the world and which have made motion pictures a universal form of entertainment.

They recognize their responsibility to the public because of this trust and because entertainment and art are important influences in the life of a nation.

Hence, though regarding motion pictures primarily as entertainment without any explicit purpose of teaching or propaganda, they know that the motion picture within its own field of entertainment may be directly responsible for spiritual or moral progress, for higher types of social life, and for much correct thinking.

On their part, they ask from the public and from public leaders a sympathetic understanding of the problems inherent in motion picture production and a spirit of cooperation that will allow the opportunity necessary to bring the motion picture to a still higher level of wholesome entertainment for all concerned.

The Production Code

GENERAL PRINCIPLES:

1. No picture shall be produced which will lower the moral standards of those who see it. Hence the sympathy of the audience shall never be thrown to the side of crime, wrong-doing, evil or sin.

2. Correct standards of life, subject only to the requirements of drama and entertainment, shall be presented.

3. Law—divine, natural or human—shall not be ridiculed, nor shall sympathy be created for its violation.

PARTICULAR APPLICATIONS:

1. CRIME:

1. Crime shall never be presented in such a way as to throw sympathy with the crime as against law and justice, or to inspire others with a desire for imitation.

2. Methods of crime shall not be explicitly presented or detailed in a manner calculated to glamorize crime or inspire imitation.

3. Action showing the taking of human life is to be held to the minimum. Its frequent presentation tends to lessen regard for the sacredness of life.

4. Suicide, as a solution of problems occurring in the development of screen drama, is to be discouraged unless absolutely necessary for the development of the plot, and shall never be justified, or glorified, or used specifically to defeat the ends of justice.

5. Excessive flaunting of weapons by criminals shall not be permitted.

6. There shall be no scenes of law-enforcing officers dying at the hands of criminals, unless such scenes are absolutely necessary to the plot.

7. Pictures dealing with criminal activities in which minors par-

ticipate, or to which minors are related, shall not be approved if they tend to incite demoralizing imitation on the part of youth.

8. Murder:

   (a) The technique of murder must not be presented in a way that will inspire imitation.

   (b) Brutal killings are not to be presented in detail.

   (c) Revenge in modern times shall not be justified.

   (d) Mercy killing shall never be made to seem right or permissible.

9. Drug addiction or the illicit traffic in addiction-producing drugs shall not be shown if the portrayal:

   (a) Tends in any manner to encourage, stimulate or justify the use of such drugs; or

   (b) Stresses, visually or by dialogue, their temporarily attractive effects; or

   (c) Suggests that the drug habit may be quickly or easily broken; or

   (d) Shows details of drug procurement or of the taking of drugs in any manner; or

   (e) Emphasizes the profits of the drug traffic; or

   (f) Involves children who are shown knowingly to use or traffic in drugs.

10. Stories on the kidnapping or illegal abduction of children are acceptable under the Code only (1) when the subject is handled with restraint and discretion and avoids details, gruesomeness and undue horror, and (2) the child is returned unharmed.

2. BRUTALITY:

Excessive and inhuman acts of cruelty and brutality shall not be presented. This includes all detailed and protracted presentation of physical violence, torture and abuse.

3. SEX:

The sanctity of the institution of marriage and the home shall be upheld. No film shall infer that casual or promiscuous sex relationships are the accepted or common thing.

1. Adultery and illicit sex, sometimes necessary plot material, shall not be explicitly treated, nor shall they be justified or made to seem right and permissible.

2. Scenes of passion:
   (a) These should not be introduced except where they are definitely essential to the plot.
   (b) Lustful and open-mouth kissing, lustful embraces, suggestive posture and gestures are not to be shown.
   (c) In general, passion should be treated in such manner as not to stimulate the baser emotions.

3. Seduction or rape:
   (a) These should never be more than suggested, and then only when essential to the plot. They should never be shown explicitly.
   (b) They are never acceptable subject matter for comedy.
   (c) They should never be made to seem right and permissible.

4. The subject of abortion shall be discouraged, shall never be more than suggested, and when referred to shall be condemned. It must never be treated lightly or made the subject of comedy. Abortion shall never be shown explicitly or by inference, and a story must not indicate that an abortion has been performed. The word "abortion" shall not be used.

5. The methods and techniques of prostitution and white slavery shall never be presented in detail, nor shall the subjects be presented unless shown in contrast to right standards of behavior. Brothels in any clear identification as such may not be shown.

6. Sex perversion or any inference of it is forbidden.*

7. Sex hygiene and venereal diseases are not acceptable subject matter for theatrical motion pictures.

8. Children's sex organs are never to be exposed. This provision shall not apply to infants.

---

* On Oct. 3, 1961 this was amended by the board of governors of the Motion Picture Association of America to permit "sex aberration" when treated with "care, discretion and restraint."

4. VULGARITY:

Vulgar expressions and double meanings having the same effect are forbidden. This shall include but not be limited to such words and expressions as chippie, fairy, goose, nuts, pansy, S.O.B., son-of-a. The treatment of low, disgusting, unpleasant though not necessarily evil subjects should be guided always by the dictates of good taste and a proper regard for the sensibilities of the audience.

5. OBSCENITY:

1. Dances suggesting or representing sexual actions or emphasizing indecent movements are to be regarded as obscene.

2. Obscenity in words, gesture, reference, song, joke or by suggestion, even when likely to be understood by only part of the audience, is forbidden.

6. BLASPHEMY AND PROFANITY:

1. Blasphemy is forbidden. Reference to the Deity, God, Lord, Jesus, Christ, shall not be irreverent.

2. Profanity is forbidden. The words "hell" and "damn," while sometimes dramatically valid, will if used without moderation be considered offensive by many members of the audience. Their use shall be governed by the discretion and prudent advice of the Code Administration.

7. COSTUMES:

1. Complete nudity, in fact or in silhouette, is never permitted, nor shall there be any licentious notice by characters in the film of suggested nudity.

2. Indecent or undue exposure is forbidden.

   (a) The foregoing shall not be interpreted to exclude actual scenes photographed in a foreign land of the natives of that land, showing native life, provided:

      (1) Such scenes are included in a documentary film or travelogue depicting exclusively such land, its customs and civilization; and

(2) Such scenes are not in themselves intrinsically objectionable.

8. RELIGION:

1. No film or episode shall throw ridicule on any religious faith.

2. Ministers of religion, or persons posing as such, shall not be portrayed as comic characters or as villains so as to cast disrespect on religion.

3. Ceremonies of any definite religion shall be carefully and respectfully handled.

9. SPECIAL SUBJECTS:

The following subjects must be treated with discretion and restraint and within the careful limits of good taste:

1. Bedroom scenes.

2. Hangings and electrocutions.

3. Liquor and drinking.

4. Surgical operations and childbirth.

5. Third degree methods.

10. NATIONAL FEELINGS:

1. The use of the flag shall be consistently respectful.

2. The history, institutions, prominent people and citizenry of all nations shall be represented fairly.

3. No picture shall be produced that tends to incite bigotry or hatred among peoples of differing races, religions or national origins. The use of such offensive words as Chink, Dago, Frog, Greaser, Hunkie, Kike, Nigger, Spig, Wop, Yid, should be avoided.

11. TITLES:

The following titles shall not be used:

1. Titles which are salacious, indecent, obscene, profane or vulgar.

2. Titles which violate any other clause of this Code.

12. CRUELTY TO ANIMALS:

In the production of motion pictures involving animals the producer shall consult with the authorized representative of the American Humane Association, and invite him to be present during the staging of such animal action. There shall be no use of any contrivance or apparatus for tripping or otherwise treating animals in any unacceptably harsh manner.

REASONS SUPPORTING THE CODE

I. Theatrical motion pictures, that is, pictures intended for the theatre as distinct from pictures intended for churches, schools, lecture halls, educational movements, social reform movements, etc., are primarily to be regarded as entertainment.

Mankind has always recognized the importance of entertainment and its value in rebuilding the bodies and souls of human beings.

But it has always recognized that entertainment can be of a character either helpful or harmful to the human race, and in consequence has clearly distinguished between:

  a. Entertainment which tends to improve the race, or at least to re-create and rebuild human beings exhausted with the realities of life; and

  b. Entertainment which tends to degrade human beings, or to lower their standards of life and living.

Hence the moral importance of entertainment is something which has been universally recognized. It enters intimately into the lives of men and women and affects them closely; it occupies their minds and affections during leisure hours; and ultimately touches the whole of their lives. A man may be judged by his standard of entertainment as easily as by the standard of his work.

So correct entertainment raises the whole standard of a nation.

Wrong entertainment lowers the whole living conditions and moral ideals of a race.

Note, for example, the healthy reactions to healthful sports, like baseball, golf; the unhealthy reactions to sports like cockfighting, bullfighting, bear baiting, etc.

Note, too, the effect on ancient nations of gladiatorial combats, the obscene plays of Roman times, etc.

II. Motion pictures are very important as art.

Though a new art, possibly a combination art, it has the same object as the other arts, the presentation of human thought, emotion and experience, in terms of an appeal to the soul through the senses.

Here, as in entertainment,

Art enters intimately into the lives of human beings.

Art can be morally good, lifting men to higher levels. This has been done through good music, great painting, authentic fiction, poetry, drama. Art can be morally evil in its effects. This is the case clearly enough with unclean art, indecent books, suggestive drama. The effect on the lives of men and women is obvious.

Note: It has often been argued that art in itself is unmoral, neither good nor bad. This is perhaps true of the thing which is music, painting, poetry, etc. But the thing is the product of some person's mind, and the intention of that mind was either good or bad morally when it produced the thing. Besides, the thing has its effect upon those who come into contact with it. In both these ways, that is, as a product of a mind and as the cause of definite effects, it has a deep moral significance and an unmistakable moral quality.

Hence: The motion pictures, which are the most popular of modern arts for the masses, have their moral quality from the intention of the minds which produce them and from their effects on the moral lives and reactions of their audiences. This gives them a most important morality.

1. They reproduce the morality of the men who use the pictures as a medium for the expression of their ideas and ideals.

2. They affect the moral standards of those who, through the screen, take in these ideas and ideals.

In the case of the motion picture, this effect may be particularly emphasized because no art has so quick and so widespread an appeal to the masses. It has become in an incredibly short period the art of the multitudes.

III. The motion picture, because of its importance as entertainment and because of the trust placed in it by the peoples of the world, has special moral obligations.

A. Most arts appeal to the mature. This art appeals at once to every class, mature, immature, developed, undeveloped, law abiding, criminal. Music has its grades for different classes; so have literature and drama. This art of the motion picture, combining as it does the two fundamental appeals of looking at a picture and listening to a story, at once reaches every class of society.

B. By reason of the mobility of a film and the ease of picture distribution, and because of the possibility of duplicating positives in large quantities, this art reaches places unpenetrated by other forms of art.

C. Because of these two facts, it is difficult to produce films intended for only certain classes of people. The exhibitors' theatres are built for the masses, for the cultivated and the rude, the mature and the immature, the self-respecting and the criminal. Films, unlike books and music, can with difficulty be confined to certain selected groups.

D. The latitude given to film material cannot, in consequence, be as wide as the latitude given to book material. In addition:

    a. A book describes, a film vividly presents. One presents on a cold page; the other by apparently living people.

    b. A book reaches the mind through words merely; a film reaches the eyes and ears through the reproduction of actual events.

    c. The reaction of a reader to a book depends largely on the keenness of the reader's imagination; the reaction to a film depends on the vividness of presentation.

    Hence many things which might be described or suggested in a book could not possibly be presented in a film.

E. This is also true when comparing the film with the newspaper.

    a. Newspapers present by description, films by actual presentation.

    b. Newspapers are after the fact and present things as having taken place; the film gives the events in the process of enactment and with the apparent reality of life.

F. Everything possible in a play is not possible in a film:

    a. Because of the larger audience of the film, and its consequential mixed character. Psychologically, the larger the audience, the lower the moral mass resistance to suggestion.

    b. Because through light, enlargement of character, presentation, scenic emphasis, etc., the screen story is brought closer to the audience than the play.

    c. The enthusiasm for and interest in the film actors and actresses, developed beyond anything of the sort in history, makes the audience largely sympathetic toward the characters they portray and the stories in which they figure. Hence the audience is more ready to confuse actor and actress and the characters they portray, and it is most receptive of the emotions and ideals presented by its favorite stars.

G. Small communities, remote from sophistication and from the hardening process which often takes place in the ethical and moral standards of groups in large cities, are easily and readily reached by any sort of film.

H. The grandeur of mass settings, large action, spectacular features, etc., affects and arouses more intensely the emotional side of the audience.

In general, the mobility, popularity, accessibility, emotional appeal, vividness, straight-forward presentation of fact in the film make for more intimate contact with a larger audience and for greater emotional appeal.

Hence the larger moral responsibilities of the motion pictures.

REASONS UNDERLYING THE GENERAL PRINCIPLES

I. No picture shall be produced which will lower the moral standards of those who see it. Hence the sympathy of the audience should never be thrown to the side of crime, wrong-doing, evil or sin.

This is done:

1. When evil is made to appear attractive or alluring, and good is made to appear unattractive.

2. When the sympathy of the audience is thrown on the side of crime, wrong-doing, evil, sin. The same thing is true of a film that would throw sympathy against goodness, honor, innocence, purity or honesty.

Note: Sympathy with a person who sins is not the same as sympathy with the sin or crime of which he is guilty. We may feel sorry for the plight of the murderer or even understand the circumstances which led him to his crime. We may not feel sympathy with the wrong which he has done.

The presentation of evil is often essential for art or fiction or drama.

This in itself is not wrong provided:

a. That evil is not presented alluringly. Even if later in the film the evil is condemned or punished, it must not be allowed to appear so attractive that the audience's emotions are drawn to desire or approve so strongly that later the condemnation is forgotten and only the apparent joy of the sin remembered.

b. That throughout, the audience feels sure that evil is wrong and good is right.

II. Correct standards of life shall, as far as possible, be presented.

A wide knowledge of life and of living is made possible through the film. When right standards are consistently presented, the motion picture exercises the most powerful influences. It builds character, develops right ideals, inculcates correct principles, and all this in attractive story form. If motion pictures consistently hold up for admiration high types of characters and present stories that will affect lives for the better, they can become the most powerful natural force for the improvement of mankind.

III. Law—divine, natural or human—shall not be ridiculed, nor shall sympathy be created for its violation.

By natural law is understood the law which is written in the hearts of all mankind, the great underlying principles of right and justice dictated by conscience.

By human law is understood the law written by civilized nations.

1. The presentation of crimes against the law is often necessary for the carrying out of the plot. But the presentation must not throw sympathy with the crime as against the law nor with the criminal as against those who punish him.

2. The courts of the land should not be presented as unjust. This does not mean that a single court may not be represented as unjust, much less that a single court official must not be presented this way. But the court system of the country must not suffer as a result of this presentation.

REASONS UNDERLYING PARTICULAR APPLICATIONS

I. Sin and evil enter into the story of human beings and hence in themselves are valid dramatic material.

II. In the use of this material, it must be distinguished between sins which repel by their very nature, and sins which often attract.

    a. In the first class come murder, most theft, many legal crimes, lying, hypocrisy, cruelty, etc.

    b. In the second class come sex sins, sins and crimes of apparent heroism, such as banditry, daring thefts, leadership in evil, organized crime, revenge, etc.

The first class needs less care in treatment, as sins and crimes of this class are naturally unattractive. The audience instinctively condemns all such and is repelled.

Hence the important objective must be to avoid the hardening of the audience, especially of those who are young and impressionable, to the thought and fact of crime. People can become accustomed even to murder, cruelty, brutality, and repellent crimes, if these are too frequently repeated.

The second class needs great care in handling, as the response of human nature to their appeal is obvious. This is treated more fully below.

III. A careful distinction can be made between films intended for general distribution, and films intended for use in theatres restricted to a limited audience. Themes and plots quite appropriate for the latter would be altogether out of place and dangerous in the former.

Note: The practice of using a general theatre and limiting its patronage during the showing of a certain film to "Adults Only" is not completely satisfactory and is only partially effective.

However, maturer minds may easily understand and accept without harm subject matter in plots which do younger people positive harm.

Hence: If there should be created a special type of theatre, catering exclusively to an adult audience, for plays of this character (plays with problem themes, difficult discussions and maturer treatment) it would seem to afford an outlet, which does not now exist, for pictures unsuitable for general distribution but permissible for exhibitions to a restricted audience.

I. CRIMES AGAINST THE LAW

The treatment of crimes against the law must not:

1. Teach methods of crime.

2. Inspire potential criminals with a desire for imitation.

3. Make criminals seem heroic and justified.

Revenge in modern times shall not be justified. In lands and ages of less developed civilization and moral principles, revenge may sometimes be presented. This would be the case especially in places where no law exists to cover the crime because of which revenge is committed.

Because of its evil consequences, the drug traffic should not be presented except under careful limitations.

II. BRUTALITY

Excessive and inhumane acts of cruelty and brutality have no proper place on the screen.

III. SEX

Out of regard for the sanctity of marriage and the home, the triangle, that is, the love of a third party for one already married, needs careful handling. The treatment should not throw sympathy against marriage as an institution.

Scenes of passion must be treated with an honest acknowledgment of human nature and its normal reactions. Many scenes cannot be presented without arousing dangerous emotions on the part of the immature, the young or the criminal classes.

Even within the limits of pure love, certain facts have been universally regarded by lawmakers as outside the limits of safe presentation.

In the case of impure love, the love which society has always regarded as wrong and which has been banned by divine law, the following are important:

1. Impure love must not be presented as attractive and beautiful.

2. It must not be the subject of comedy or farce, or treated as material for laughter.

3. It must not be presented in such a way as to arouse passion or morbid curiosity on the part of the audience.

4. It must not be made to seem right and permissible.

5. In general, it must not be detailed in method and manner.

6. Certain places are so closely and thoroughly associated with sexual life or with sexual sin that their use must be carefully limited.

IV. VULGARITY

This section is intended to prevent not only obviously vulgar expressions but also double meanings that have the same effect.

V. OBSCENITY

Dances which suggest or represent sexual actions, whether performed solo or with two or more; dances intended to excite the emotional reaction of an audience; dances with movement of the breasts, excessive body movements while the feet are stationary, violate decency and are wrong.

This section likewise applies to obscene words, gestures, references, songs, jokes and gags.

VI. BLASPHEMY AND PROFANITY

It is clear that neither blasphemy nor profanity should be permitted on the screen.

VII. COSTUMES

General principles:

1. The effect of nudity or semi-nudity upon the normal man or woman, and much more upon the young and upon immature persons, has been honestly recognized by all lawmakers and moralists.

2. Hence the fact that the nude or semi-nude body may be beautiful does not make its use in the films moral. For, in addition to its beauty, the effect of the nude or semi-nude body on the normal individual must be taken into consideration.

3. Nudity or semi-nudity used simply to put a "punch" into a picture comes under the head of immoral actions. It is immoral in its effect on the average audience.

4. Nudity can never be permitted as being necessary for the plot. Semi-nudity must not result in undue or indecent exposures.

5. Transparent or translucent materials and silhouette are frequently more suggestive than actual exposure.

VIII. RELIGION

The reason why ministers of religion may not be portrayed as comic characters or as villains so as to cast disrespect on religion is simply because the attitude taken toward them may easily become the attitude taken toward religion in general. Religion is lowered in the minds of the audience because of the lowering of the audience's respect for a minister.

IX. SPECIAL SUBJECTS

Such subjects are occasionally necessary for the plot. Their treatment must never offend good taste nor injure the sensibilities of an audience.

The use of liquor should never be excessively presented. In scenes from American life, the necessities of plot and proper characterization alone justify its use. And in this case, it should be shown with moderation.

X. NATIONAL FEELINGS

The just rights, history, and feelings of peoples and nations are entitled to most careful consideration and respectful treatment.

XI. TITLES

As the title of a picture is the brand on that particular type of goods, it must conform to the ethical practices of all such honest business.

XII. CRUELTY TO ANIMALS

The purpose of this provision is to prevent the treatment of animals in films in any unacceptably harsh manner.

INDEX